UNDRAFTED

UNDRAFTED

HOCKEY, FAMILY, AND WHAT IT TAKES TO BE A PRO

NICK KYPREOS

with PERRY LEFKO

Published by Simon & Schuster

NEW YORK LONDON TORONTO SYDNEY NEW DELHI

SIMON &
SCHUSTER
CANADA

Simon & Schuster Canada
A Division of Simon & Schuster, Inc.
166 King Street East, Suite 300
Toronto, Ontario M5A 1J3

This Simon & Schuster Canada edition October 2020

SIMON & SCHUSTER CANADA and colophon are trademarks
of Simon & Schuster, Inc.

For information about special discounts for bulk purchases,
please contact Simon & Schuster Special Sales at 1-800-268-3216
or CustomerService@simonandschuster.ca.

Manufactured in the United States of America

1   3   5   7   9   10   8   6   4   2

Library and Archives Canada Cataloguing in Publication
Title: Undrafted : hockey, family, and what it takes to be a pro /
Nick Kypreos with Perry Lefko.
Names: Kypreos, Nick, 1966- author. | Lefko, Perry, author.
Description: Simon & Schuster Canada edition
Identifiers: Canadiana (print) 20200203339 | Canadiana (ebook) 20200203347 |
ISBN 9781982146825
(hardcover) | ISBN 9781982146887 (ebook)
Subjects: LCSH: Kypreos, Nick, 1966- | LCSH: Hockey players—
Canada—Biography. | LCSH: Sportscasters—
Canada—Biography. | LCGFT: Autobiographies.
Classification: LCC GV848.5.K97 A3 2020 | DDC 796.962092—dc23

ISBN 978-1-9821-4682-5
ISBN 978-1-9821-4688-7 (ebook)

To my wife, Anne-Marie,
and my children, Zachary, Theo, and Anastasia

—Nick Kypreos

For my father-in-law, Don Lloyd

—Perry Lefko

CONTENTS

CONTENTS

FOREWORD

By Doug MacLean

It may be hard to believe for anyone who watched Nick Kypreos and I verbally battle together over the years at Sportsnet, but he's one of my best friends. I don't know if I've met a better person than Nick and, in fact, I owe my broadcasting career to him. He was the driving voice behind Sportsnet hiring me in 2008. But I think the story of how we first met, and how our relationship evolved, will tell you all you need to know about him.

I first met Nick when we were part of the Capitals organization, but I really got to know him when I was appointed head coach of the Baltimore Skipjacks of the American Hockey League, midway into the 1989–90 season. I'll never forget Nick coming into my office, wondering whether he was going to make it full-time in the NHL after being sent down by the Washington Capitals. I remember clear as day the heart-to-heart talk I had with him. "Kid, you're still young, you're going to play a long time." Of course, they never believe that when you're coaching them.

Our journeys went in different directions after that, but our paths crossed at major NHL events, such as the NHL draft, the All-Star Game, or the NHL awards. But we were always working in different franchises and it was never more than a nod to each other.

We reconnected in 1998, when he began at Sportsnet and I was starting out in Columbus as president and GM. He had become an insider and would phone me for scoops all the time. When I'd see his name pop up, I'd think to myself, "What does he want now?"

That all changed when I was fired by Columbus in 2008 and Sportsnet hired me—upon Nick's recommendation. I was surprised when he called asking if I would be interested in working at Sportsnet. At the time, he was almost by himself, grinding away in the rivalry against TSN. He thought we'd be a pair to challenge them. It was a battle to match their team and we had a blast putting a dent in TSN's machine.

Nick was helpful to me. He had a great feel for the players' side of the business and encouraged me to work the management/ownership side of the sport. I began doing a two-hour general sports show in the afternoon with Jack Armstrong and worked on the hockey TV broadcasts at night with a panel that included Nick. A couple of years later, I began working with Nick and Daren Millard on a radio show called *Hockey Central at Noon*. We would talk about hockey for two hours, and as always, the most enjoyable aspect of working with Nick was the laughs. As hard as we fought about league issues, it always came back to what was best for the team and Sportsnet.

With the 2013 NHL lockout, Nick and I battled as much as anybody on player/management topics. The shows were informative. We'd both been in the trenches, he as a player and me as a president, GM, and coach. The listeners knew they were getting what was really going on. We knew the dressing rooms to the boardrooms in the NHL and appreciated each other's expertise. But man, did those disagreements become heated, us screaming at each other during the shows. We'd laugh after and Nick would say, "Now that was great TV." We had a unique relationship that way and it was never personal between us.

Nick and I had different opinions and fans enjoyed the confrontations. Maybe half would take my side and half would take Nick's. I'd meet people in the street and they'd say, "How do you stand Kypreos? You guys must hate each other." It's really kind of funny to work with somebody for ten years and with that much confrontation, and yet we maintained a great relationship. It sort of made the show. The more we could get into it, the more fun we had.

I used to love when we'd go into the playoffs and players would tell us, "We watch you guys every day in our dressing room." We were always fair to the players; we weren't ripping them. It was a real perspective. I would hear from GMs and coaches, too, who said they listened to us each day in their offices. After coaching and managing for some twenty-six years in the NHL, and Nick playing for eight seasons, we were able to read the situations, and tell it like it was. Players appreciated it and so did management.

I was shocked how many people watched our show. I would go to Chicago to visit my son and every time I was around the rinks I'd have people come up to me and talk about *Hockey Central at Noon*. It was bizarre how popular that little show was. I'd be out for dinner and CEOs of major corporations would say, "I watch you guys at every lunch hour on my computer." We had every sort of group—hockey fans, management people, business types. We had a wide base. I don't know if Sportsnet ever got that. They looked at ratings, but people watching on the computer don't show on their ratings. It was a widespread base, I'll tell you that.

Nick has an infectious personality, cares about people, and has a great feel for the game. I learned a lot from him. His advice gave me a chance to become a TV person. He would often say, "Mac, we've lived it, let's give the fans the goods." And we did.

I had more fun with him than you could imagine. Nick likes to say I was his greatest hire at Sportsnet. That's nice of him, but I'd like to think I also made his career.

Just joking.

Doug MacLean
May 2020

PROLOGUE

With one year left on my contract with the Toronto Maple Leafs, there was no question I had to fight to keep my job, literally. I had over 400 career games and 1,200 penalty minutes, yet it meant absolutely nothing. With Cliff Fletcher out as general manager, and Ken Dryden taking over as president, and Mike Smith as associate GM, I would have to prove myself all over again, just like back when I was a rookie at training camp with the Flyers twelve years earlier. That night, we had a preseason game in New York and I knew I was going to have to fight. It was September 15, 1997.

They like to tell you the slate is clean for every player starting training camp, but that couldn't have been further from the truth for me. Leafs management put the bug in Tie Domi's ear that they wanted to see more toughness out of me. Tie gave me the heads-up just before we embarked on the preseason games. GMs have a tendency to forget your contributions in the past and, more importantly, they don't really give a damn. "What have you done for me lately?" is really all that matters to them. That part of the game will never change.

The major off-season roster changes that brought the Leafs Derek King and Kris King (no relation) made that abundantly clear. Kris and I had similar tough player reputations. I knew at this training camp I wasn't just fighting for my job with the Leafs: I was fighting to prove to the rest of the league that I could still get the job done, that I still had value as a role-player.

This training camp could play out in a number of ways. The season before I had played only 35 games. I missed half the season with a spiral fracture I suffered in a fight with the Buffalo Sabres' Matthew Barnaby, which set me back in the eyes of management. So this preseason game would set the tone for my hockey future. Would I make the season-opening roster? Could I be traded, waived, or demoted to the minors? It wasn't only about surviving training camp; it was about saving my career.

Like so many other nights that I fought—over a hundred—I tried not to overthink. Get the job done. It became a mantra of sorts. *Don't overthink. Get the job done. Don't overthink.* Wash. Rinse. Repeat.

Some enforcers in the NHL had so much anxiety that they couldn't sleep the night before a game. The anticipation was intense and some resorted to alcohol or sleeping pills. For me it was the opposite. I had to be in control of my mind. That's why I never did drugs. I was quite comfortable with my ability to control alcohol generally, but with drugs I was never willing to take that chance.

When I broke into the league, I had never seen players throwing up before a game. If there's anything that can deflate a dressing room full of testosterone, it's the sound of a guy puking in the garbage can. In this way, tough guy Neil Sheehy is one of the players I remember most. When I played with him in Washington, Neil fought some big boys. I watched him on some occasions and his way of dealing with nerves was through his stomach. Maybe it had something to do with his Battle of Alberta rivalry against Wayne Gretzky and the Oilers in the eighties. Facing Dave Semenko, Marty McSorley, and Kevin Mc-Clelland would be enough to make anyone sick. Believe it or not, for some players getting sick before a fight became so commonplace that it was actually routine. There is no denying the brain-gut connection. Tough guys did whatever it took to help alleviate their nerves. Who am I to ever question that? But I could never comprehend being that affected before competition. Maybe it was my saving grace. Maybe it was my demise.

My routine that night before the exhibition game was the same as usual. I'm not overly superstitious, but my pregame routine was similar from one game to the next. I arrived at the rink at the same time, around 4:45 p.m. I taped my sticks, and then put my equipment on in the same order, all prior to warm-up. I wanted to let my instincts take over from there. *Get the job done. Don't overthink.* I'd keep telling myself this before heading onto the ice for the first period.

I always knew I could lose a fight, end up with a black eye, maybe stitches. Or a long shot: maybe a broken bone. But never could I have imagined that just a few short minutes into the game, my career would end.

CHAPTER 1

Growing Up Greek

I remember going to see my first hockey game like it was yesterday. It was 1975 and my father, George, had saved up enough money to take me. When I think back to my childhood, it's the one memory I have that is so deeply etched that I can remember everything about that night. The smell of burnt roasted chestnuts and the crowds pressing towards the gates. I was eight years old and I held on tightly to my father's hand. Maple Leaf Gardens looked enormous to me. I had never seen anything like it. It's funny how things seem so much larger to a little kid.

We walked into the building and I can still remember how vibrant the colours were. The seats were gold, red, green, grey, and blue. For home games, white was the predominant colour back then for the Maple Leafs, with blue trimming against the white ice. I didn't know that because I had only watched games in black and white. I remember asking my father why the play-by-play man wasn't explaining what was going on. That's what I was used to from watching the games on television. I didn't realize there wasn't a play-by-play announcer for the fans at the game.

Going to my first Leaf game at Maple Leaf Gardens was magical. I sat for three periods fixated on the passion of the fans and the drive of the players. My mouth must have been wide open the entire time. That night the Leafs beat the Kansas City Scouts 4–2.

Hockey wasn't just my favourite game. It was also a big part of how my family came to feel more Canadian. My father knew nothing about hockey when he came to Canada from Greece, but he fell in love with the speed and grace of the game from the first time he saw it on television. He quickly learned the names of the stars: Bob Pulford, Red Kelly, Eddie Shack. On his way to work he would take a detour just to see Maple Leaf Gardens. He told me that on game nights the hair on the back of his neck stood up because of the crowds and the energy. From outside on the street, he could hear the roar of the fans inside the arena. Just like today, the Leafs were a big deal then—maybe even bigger. In 1962 they started their consecutive three-year Stanley Cup run. On rare occasions my dad would buy a two-dollar standing-room-only ticket. You'd have to arrive pretty early to get a good place in line. My dad would wait for hours outside in the cold for a chance to see the Leafs, broken English and all.

I couldn't fully appreciate the impact of that first game, sitting there with my dad, watching the Leafs play. But when we left the building, I felt like a real Canadian for maybe the first time. I didn't know it then, but the trajectory of my life had changed forever.

I got lucky right off the bat and I know that. My parents are two of the nicest people you could ever meet. I always like to say that they speak with their hands and laugh with their eyes. The Greek culture is a strong one, with everything centred on family. The movie *My Big Fat Greek Wedding* captured the true nature of growing up Greek, without exaggeration. In case you never saw the movie, it's about a Greek family that is larger than life. It actually ticked me off that I didn't come up with the idea first. I could have written that movie in fifteen minutes if I actually thought for one second people would want to watch my family. We might be even bigger and fatter, but we're most definitely louder than the one in the movie.

We grew up in a traditional Greek Orthodox home. We had crosses all over the house and an icon of Jesus in the corner at the top of the stairs. My mother, Dorothy, would light a candle in oil and leave it burning—I guess so maybe God could find us if the lights went out. From lambadas to baptisms, moussaka and my thea Dimitra's baklava, we always had reasons to be together. Being from an immigrant family was tough, but with cousins, aunts and uncles, friends who we called family, nounas and nounos (godparents)—it was never lonely.

We celebrated Easter later than everyone else, which was based on the Orthodox calendar. Greek Easter was more important to us than Christmas. We always hunted for eggs weeks after all the other kids. Not exactly a hit on the playground. But by then chocolate Easter bunnies were half price for my parents, which was a bonus. They put a lamb on a spit at the side of the house where the whole neighbourhood could see, and the aunts and uncles would dance in a circle, waving their worry beads around, talking about the old country.

No matter who hosted Easter and how small the house was, we'd manage to sit around one big fat Greek table: forty people with twenty different conversations going on at the same time. Among the first cousins there are four Nicks, three of whom are named Nick Kypreos. We went by Big Nick, Medium Nick, and Little Nick. I am Big Nick. There also are five Stellas, five Georges, and three Anastasias—with no middle names, I might add. What is with Greeks and their refusal to add a middle name to a birth certificate?

Having the same exact name did, however, come in handy at times. In the summer of '86 when Medium Nick found out he needed one more credit to graduate from Bethune high school, he convinced the front office that my grade-twelve English credit was actually his and they had made a mistake. I had already graduated. At this point I was only too happy to help him earn his diploma.

Being Greek is both amazing and embarrassing. For so many years

I always felt different from the other kids. What immigrant student doesn't cringe on the first day of school when the teacher mispronounces their last name on three or four different attempts? Being from a strong Greek family was inclusive, yet at times it was also isolating. Other kids didn't necessarily understand our values and traditions.

Most Greek first names are based on religious saints and name day celebrations are given more value than even a birthday. For example, everyone named Nicholas in the Greek tradition celebrates December 6 as their name day.

Greeks also have a tendency to be superstitious. If you have a high fever or if something isn't going right in your life, the Greeks believe you could have caught the "evil eye." We'd call my thea Tula and have her bless holy water mixed with oil while she said our names over the bowl with a special cross. It was called the *Mati*, the Greek word for eye. She would say a blessing and we did the sign of the cross three times for the Father, the Son, and the Holy Spirit. Then we were sprinkled with the holy water my mom always had on hand. Ironically, most of the time we instantly felt better or the fever would break.

Now, one of the more questionable traditions of all is "spitting" on things to keep evil away. Okay, not real spit but pretty close. If there was a baby being baptized, the aunts and uncles would pretend to spit on them, three times of course. If you bought a new house or a new car, you'd again spit three times. Again, not real spit, just a subtle reminder to Satan that we got this one covered. These were the sorts of things my non-Greek friends never understood.

I was anything but an easy child. When I was three, if you picked me up, I bit you. If you tried to hold my hand, I bit you. If you even looked like you wanted to hold me back in any way, I bit you. Other than my parents, people were afraid of me. Babysitters worked for us once, then quit. My poor mother nearly pulled her hair out trying to control me. There are plenty of labels for kids like me today, but back then I was just *feared*.

My mother finally convinced my father to pay for building a fence around our house so she could keep her overly active three-year-old contained. They dug into their pockets and had a six-foot fence installed with a locked gate. My mother could finally breathe easy. She could go about her business in the house while I was kept out of harm's way in a safe area. Two days after the fence was installed she went upstairs to vacuum in peace, but when she looked outside the front window, there I was across the street in Thea Maria's front yard. I had to cross a very busy street to get there. I was able to easily wedge the tip of my toes into the spaces in the chain links. That fence could have been fifteen feet high, but I was still going up and over. My mother ran across the street, grabbed me, then sat down on the curb and cried.

I don't know if it was because we lived in a predominantly immigrant neighbourhood where people tended to watch out for each other, but in those days, kids could walk home from school on their own. In kindergarten my favourite television show was *Batman* and Adam West was my hero. I remember racing home to watch the conclusion to a two-part episode. It was a cliffhanger. Batman and Robin were in big trouble. When I got home I found the side door locked. When no one answered I took two steps back, dropped my shoulder, and broke the door wide open. The lock splintered away from the frame. My mom had just been at a neighbour's house. When she came home her first thought was that we had been burglarized. Then she found me sitting on the floor two feet from the TV and she had to explain to my father why we needed to replace the door. I'm pretty sure she sat down on the curb and cried again.

Like so many other immigrant families, mine got into the restaurant business. When I wasn't playing hockey, I would sometimes hang out there. At thirteen I worked as a busboy and dishwasher at the Mercury, a diner on Bay and Front. My uncles Peter, Jim, Tom, and George owned it along with my father. I helped at the counter and with takeout orders. It was a real family atmosphere. My father explained that all glasses have an imaginary half-full mark. If the water ever went below that line, I wasn't taking good enough care of the customers. I took that seriously. Customers would jokingly suggest I was trying to drown them. "No," I'd say, "I'm just trying to keep my boss happy." It was then that I saw first-hand how great my dad was with people.

In those early years working at the Mercury, he'd get up at 4:30 a.m., drive to pick up waiters or busboys who had no other way to get to work, and then he'd work well into the night. I think introducing me to the restaurant business was pretty calculated on his part. He did what he had to do to run a successful business, and having me work there helped to teach me a work ethic.

Years later my dad and his brothers purchased Peter's Steakhouse in Markham. If customers missed the bowl of Jelly Belly candy on their way out, my father was the type of guy who'd walk outside with the bowl in his hand. If there were one hundred customers, he couldn't be happy until every one of them was well taken care of.

My mother is cut from the same cloth as my dad. She is a giver, too. She's happiest when she's cooking and feeding people. Whenever my team would be in Toronto on a road trip, if there was time my parents would have my teammates over to the house for dinner. Pastitsio, dolmades, spanakopita, roasted lamb, souvlaki, moussaka—we ate like kings. Years later, when I was traded to the Toronto Maple Leafs, I'd invite many of the guys, like Mats Sundin, Tie Domi, Todd Warriner, and Freddy Modin, to my place and let my mom cook up a feast. Tie said he never felt so stuffed in his life as he was that night. When my mom tried to load his plate up with more food yet again, he was in absolute disbelief. He asked her, "Are you crazy?" We all broke out laughing.

Both of my parents grew up in small farming villages in Sparta in the southern part of Greece. My father lost his father, Nicholas Kypreos, when he was fifteen years old. My grandfather died during the civil war, in the middle of a field during tensions between the village and rebels, but not from any violence. It was heart failure. During a lull in gunfire my father went to the field to help him. He tried to revive him by pressing on his heart for what must have been two hours. The other villagers finally made him stop. I can't think of anything more heartbreaking than a child doing everything to save their parent, not knowing it was already too late. As the oldest son of five children, he became the "father" of the family as a teenager.

He came over from Greece at the age of seventeen. When he embarked on a ship heading to Halifax with a final destination of Oshawa, he was alone and given the gargantuan task of working to earn enough money to bring his entire family from Sparta, away from the civil war. He worked as an upholsterer and then as a restaurant busboy. He did anything he could to make enough money to bring his siblings over, one by one. In those days you didn't question things, you just did them. If you ask my dad he will never complain. He'll tell you Canada is the greatest country in the world; it gave his family a new chance at life.

Although they had similar backgrounds, my parents didn't know one another until they met in Canada. It was through the restaurant business that my father met my mother. In 1957, at the age of sixteen, she followed two sisters and three brothers who had moved to Toronto. Her brothers wanted her to go to school, but she was too embarrassed because she'd have to start off with elementary classes. She moved in with her siblings, who owned a home, and cleaned and cooked for them while they saved money to buy a restaurant called Steffi's.

At the time my father worked at a restaurant called Ciro's, in Toronto's west end at Bloor Street and Lansdowne Avenue. One of his regular customers, my mother's brother, came in to ask him to be the nouno of his firstborn child. Being asked to be a godparent is a true honour in the Greek culture. Both my uncle and my father came from Sparta, and even though the two men didn't know each other well, this is how it was done. Two weeks later, my father went to Steffi's to talk about the ceremony, saw my mother, and fell in love. They married in 1961. One year later they celebrated the birth of their first child, Anastasia, then came my other sister, Stelle, in 1964, and me in 1966.

Growing up, our best friends were our first cousins, thirteen on my father's side and seventeen on my mother's. We'd get together at every Christmas, New Year's, and Easter. When I was old enough to appreciate the NHL, Easter became a bit of an issue. Orthodox Easter is later in the year than other religions and always coincides with the first round of the Stanley Cup playoffs. I remember one Sunday during the playoffs when the Leafs were playing Boston. I was beside myself. I said, "Ma, I'm dying here. The Leafs are playing. I'm not going to church!" She popped me on the side of the head. "No, the only one dying is Jesus on the cross! Get in the car!" She was sweet until you messed with Jesus.

Otherwise, we would all get together as a family and watch the Leafs games. No matter if we were at a cousin's house or our house, we would squeeze in all together on the floor. We were glued to the television on Saturdays, for *Hockey Night in Canada* on CBC. I never imagined I'd sit on the panel of that show forty years later.

Although High Park is now a very trendy Toronto area, at the time its residents were working-class families. Many of our neighbours were factory workers, meat-packers, upholsterers, and restaurant workers. We lived next to families from Poland, Malta, and Greece. My next-door neighbour Joey Grech taught me how to play road hockey. We bought a plastic blade from Canadian Tire and attached it to a broken wooden stick. Joey showed me how to curve a blade by heating it over the burner on the stove until we got it just right. He played house-league hockey, and when his parents invited me to watch him play, my face was pressed against the glass as I tried to get as close as I could to the ice. I was hooked.

A few months later, my parents had saved enough money to buy a bigger home away from downtown Toronto, in the north end of the city.

It was a largely undeveloped area at the time. I was traumatized, to say the least. Joey had been my role model, but my father promised that if we moved I could play real ice hockey, just like Joey. The next season, at the age of seven, I started playing.

I was naturally fairly athletic. I played baseball, football, soccer, and hockey, but it was really soccer and hockey that I loved. I was so crazy for hockey that I begged my sister Stelle to be my goalie at home. She was the brother I never had. We took the hockey net from the garage, brought it into the basement, rolled back the carpet, and set it up for practice shots. We took cushions off my mother's good couch and duct-taped them to Stelle's legs. She could barely stand. I proceeded to pummel slap shots at her for hours while my parents worked at the restaurant. Then we'd put the carpet back to hide the scratches on the floor and rearrange a few photos on the wall to hide some dings. No one was the wiser.

I should note that Stelle wanted to play women's hockey. Two houses down from us there was a girl about her age, playing girls' hockey, but my parents wanted no part of their daughter playing the game. At the time it wasn't like it is now, with various women's leagues and women's hockey in the Olympics. It just wasn't fashionable at the time for girls to play hockey. Years later my dad was watching the Olympics and felt bad. He said he should have let her play.

I was also very close to my older sister, Tess, but in a different way. When I was five years old I convinced my mom to let me walk to the corner variety store to buy a jug of milk. Alone. It took me less than thirty seconds to see Tess following, hiding behind trees and bushes, trying to keep an eye on me. While I could get Stelle to wrap a towel around her neck to play Robin to my Batman, Tess took over the role of my mother when Mom was at the restaurant. Now, that wasn't necessarily a bad thing, especially when my school would call home on occasion. Tess would take calls about late assignments, or when my friends and I were caught putting thumbtacks on the other students' chairs, or getting kicked out of typing class with future Vancouver Canucks legend Kirk McLean—we went to junior high together. I could get Tess to call my school pretending to be our mom. She was incredibly believable. She would always end the call "Thank you for letting me know. Nick will never do that again."

When I was eight years old, I played hockey in the winter and soccer in the summer up until September. There was no real overlap in those days. You could specialize in two sports. In fact, the cross-training probably helped make me stronger and more competitive. In summer there was no hockey pulling you away for off-season training, which has become the case now for elite players focusing on one sport. It's as if parents feel at the age of ten if you haven't chosen one sport to focus on, the train will leave the station. Which is really a huge shame and so untrue. But today athletes don't seem to get the same chance to really enjoy two sports without one affecting the other. Spring and summer hockey leagues, off-ice skill training, tournament leagues—I'm not convinced it does anything to help kids long-term and potentially you will burn them out. I'm so thankful that my soccer and hockey coaches never made me feel I needed to choose.

Soccer appealed to me because of my competitive nature. I could score goals if the coach put me on forward, but I ended up being a full-back and became the last line of defence. I was the Rod Langway type for the North York Spartans. There was added pride playing for the Spartans when both my parents grew up in the town of Sparta. I would defend anything hard—slide tackles, shoulder-to-shoulder markings. It's weird because I was a forward in hockey and became a good goal scorer, but in soccer my job was to play defence and protect my goalie, and I loved that responsibility.

I began soccer with one of my cousins. George (yes, another George) and I played up until we were seventeen. We started out in house league at eight years of age and moved up into a competitive National Soccer

League team in our teens until I quit to focus on hockey. If I were playing today, it probably would have been much harder deciding what sport
to pursue full-time. For me, growing up in Canada, soccer just wasn't
as popular back then as hockey. There was no first-tier Pro League in
North America with international draw. Of course, there was European
soccer, but I didn't have any access to that. I didn't follow any teams like,
perhaps, another die-hard soccer fan might have: Manchester United,
Chelsea, Liverpool. I knew of big-name players like Paolo Rossi and
Franz Beckenbauer, but I didn't envision myself becoming the next
Giorgio Canali.

Instead, I wanted to be the next Darryl Sittler, who was the captain
of the Leafs in 1975. I had posters of him plastered all over my room. I
cut out articles about the Leafs from the *Toronto Star* and *Toronto Sun*
and pinned them on the walls in my bedroom just like my older cousin
Olga did. She loved the Leafs as much as I did. I collected hockey cards,
and like a typical kid at the time, I took the lesser-known players and attached them to the spokes on my bike's wheels to make noise.

At the age of six I knew every player on the Leafs team: Brian Glen-
nie, Gord McRae, Garry Monahan, Denis Dupéré. Players that most
people wouldn't know anything about, but I gravitated to them. I knew
every stat. At Christmas the Leafs opened up Maple Leaf Gardens to
allow kids to watch the practice for free. A grocery chain called Domin-
ion sponsored the practice and there were sixteen thousand kids screaming while watching the players they idolized. Harold Ballard owned the
team, and his sidekick, King Clancy, entertained all the young fans by
broadcasting the action over the sound system. I remember attending
one of those practices in 1976. I worked my way down from the third-
level green seats to the gold seats by the glass. Jack Valiquette, one of
the Leafs' centres, was balancing his stick on his nose when he turned
around, saw me, and then lifted his stick over the glass, handing it to me.
Twenty hands grabbed at that stick, but Jack tapped on the glass and

pointed to me. I was the one he wanted to give that stick to. It's funny how such a small gesture can stay with a kid. I had that stick in my room for about eight years. Years later, when I ran into Jack at a Leaf alumni event, I told him what he did and how much it meant.

Even as a pro, I collected some signed sticks over the years. I'd come home at the end of the season and see half my collection of valuable sticks being used to stake tomatoes in the backyard. "Dad, what are you doing?" I would scream. "That's Mario Lemieux's stick!"

When we moved to North York, my family didn't know any hockey people in the area yet, and without my friend Joey, I was on my own to find a hockey team. I didn't have any problem finding a good road hockey game, though. Jeff Guilbert, Casey Boynton, John Bozanis, Jeff Hayes, Dave Penny, Neil Mason, Chris Manos. We would have epic games. I was pretty good back then; sometimes it was me versus three or four of them and I'd still find a way to win.

The worst thing was when my mom called me in for dinner right in the middle of a game. I hated quitting to come in for dinner. I never crossed her, but sometimes I would eat with my hockey gloves on in protest. Have you ever tried holding a fork with a hockey glove? My mom didn't care as long as I ate.

Because skates cost a lot, Dad bought a pair two sizes too big. He wanted them to last. But I could barely skate my first year. My teammate Jim Mandala noticed one time I was having trouble standing up. His father, Conrad, who played minor pro hockey, asked my father if he'd had my skates sharpened. Dad didn't know you had to actually sharpen the blades. From that point on Jim's father took my dad under his wing.

Skating was still tough, though. I'd like to blame my problems on the skates, but that wouldn't be the truth. I found it nearly impossible to glide on those skinny metal edges, but I was determined. Skating was a bit of a weak link compared to my stick handling, so I had to really work on it. I couldn't get from point A to point B as fast as the other kids, but

I could read the play really well and "think the game," even at a young age. I had a good shot and always felt very comfortable with the puck. I could maneuver around players and manage to protect the puck despite my skating. I loved every second of it. I gradually improved and did well enough that I was recruited to the Don Valley Villagers, which was like a collection of all-star players.

Moving up from house league to playing rep hockey meant having two different-coloured jerseys, one for home games and another for away games. It felt like it was a step towards being a professional. We had a good team with the Villagers. Jimmy Mandala played on the team. Another teammate was Brian Wilks, who in later years would become a teammate of mine in the Ontario Hockey League with the Kitchener Rangers.

I began the season with the Villagers on defence, but that didn't last long. In one game I ended up with a penalty shot and buried the puck right under the bar. No one except me knew where that shot had come from. After that goal my days of defence were over. The coach realized I could shoot the puck and moved me to centre—unfortunately, it's the position that requires the most skating.

We travelled to North Bay that season for the Challenge Cup Tournament. Going on a bus with teammates was the biggest thrill of all. We were travelling for four hours, singing songs and telling jokes. There were no movie screens or VCRs on buses back then to keep everybody quiet for hours. We belted songs by the Bay City Rollers. We must have sung "Saturday Night" at the top of our lungs about a hundred times. I can't tell you if we won or lost the tournament, but I can still remember every word to that song.

We played so well that season that we made it all the way to the championship final and played the favoured team, the Hillcrest Summits. We had never managed to beat them all season long. From the moment the puck dropped, we were in complete control. I don't remember what the score was, but we might have won by four or five goals. We absolutely buried the number-one team. To say we weren't expected to win would be an understatement. The organizers couldn't give the big trophy to us because they had already engraved "Hillcrest Summits" on the front.

The following year our coach, Ian McPherson, took us into Don Valley A of the Metro Toronto Hockey League. At the time there were two classifications for competitive minor hockey: AA and A. When I was asked what jersey number I wanted, I had no idea. But my father said to ask for number 9 because he knew that was the number of NHL stars Gordie Howe and Bobby Hull. I was given the captaincy. That year I must have scored more than 60 goals. My parents didn't keep track, but my father remembers me scoring and another parent telling him it was almost 60. I still have the trophy that the team presented to me with the actual puck from my 50th goal. It is the only trophy I ever kept from minor hockey.

Because the goals came fairly easily to me, I copped a little bit of an attitude. I wasn't that interested in practices and only wanted to play in the games. At age eleven, I thought I was wise beyond my years. My mother asked me why I didn't try harder. I told her I was trying hard, but the other kids were trying just as hard—and if I tried harder then they'd have to try harder, and it was just going to be pretty exhausting for all of us. Early success had already gone to my head.

When my dad wanted me to try power skating, I was reluctant. I just thought I'd keep outsmarting the goalies. It didn't dawn on me that power skating would actually help in the long run, that I'd score even more goals. Ironically, the only regret I have now is that I never worked hard enough on my skating at an early age. On skates there are Thoroughbreds and there are Clydesdales. At times I was the latter.

My parents didn't really know anything about being hockey parents. They were learning along the way. They never yelled at me on the ice.

And they certainly never screamed at the refs. Who are they to question a ref? They didn't usually comment about my efforts on the way home in the car either. We'd often go for a hamburger after the game. My father might say a little sarcastically, "Boy, getting beaten like that you must have built up an appetite." But that was about as far as it went with criticism. Ex-Leaf John Anderson had a burger place near our house. I'd sit with a burger and fries and stare at his framed jersey, dreaming that one day I might wear one.

Sometimes I'd get a ride with other parents. I'd sit in the backseat while they berated their sons on the drive home. It must have been humiliating. But if you ask my dad today, he'd joke around and say that if he ever knew I had a chance to play in the NHL there would have been fewer trips to John Anderson Hamburgers and more where he really gave me his opinion. My mom and dad truly had no expectations. They didn't sacrifice money and time for me to play in hopes that they'd get something in return.

Because my dad worked seven days a week, he often couldn't take me to practice, so my uncles would drive me. When they say it takes a village, we lived it. I remember watching my older cousin George Dizes, who played hockey in Newmarket. He spent most of his time in the penalty box. He was a force to be reckoned with. It became an ongoing joke that we'd drive forty-five minutes just to watch him bang his stick against the boards on his way to the penalty box. Off the ice he was one of the sweetest guys I've ever known. In our family you were either a Leafs fan or a Canadiens fan, but George worshipped the New York Rangers. When I won the Stanley Cup with the Rangers in 1994, I felt his spirit on the ice with me. I gave a tribute to him right after Game 7 on *Hockey Night in Canada*. Tragically, George had been killed by a drunk driver in 1986, but almost ten years later I felt like he was watching from high above, cheering me and his beloved Rangers to a Stanley Cup.

If there was ever a turning point in minor hockey for me, it happened in 1978. I joined a team called Toronto Wexford when I was twelve. Up until that point I had always been one of the better players. But on Wexford my skills started to wane. Remember, I wasn't the biggest fan of practices and never truly put that much stock in honing skills outside of a game. Maybe I needed the adrenaline of competition, but this is the year it caught up to me. This was around the time my dad was working long hours at the restaurant. As I said, he never critiqued my game like other dads, but he asked me to start working in the restaurant more. I think my lack of passion for hockey practice around this time must have concerned him a little, as he thought I was getting lazy. He made sure I understood what real work meant by dragging me into the restaurant at 5 a.m. on weekends.

Wexford had entered the biggest international minor hockey tournament in the world, the Carnaval de Quebec in Quebec City. It was the most prestigious tournament I had ever played in, with ten thousand fans watching the games. As twelve-year-old players, we signed autographs. There was media coverage, with reporters hovering ready to interview the better players. It was a showcase for some of the young hockey talent from around the world. Eric Lindros, Guy Lafleur, Sylvain Côté, Mario Lemieux, Wayne Gretzky, Patrick Roy—they all played in this event. But what should have been an amazing experience was anything but for me.

I remember getting sick with a flu that kept me out of the lineup for one game. When I was good enough to play, I couldn't score or keep up with the pace of the other players. When you get shoved to the end of a bench all season, you have a lot of time to think. For the first time I realized how much hockey meant to me and how close I was to losing it. The lack of "homework" and passion to find an edge had led me to this humiliating place. It wasn't about getting sick—my lack of work ethic kept me from being able to hold my head up high at one of the greatest minor hockey tournaments in the world.

From this moment everything about me changed. It's strange how these sorts of things can either cut you off at the knees or build you up. For me, being benched much of the year gave me time to reflect. Having to look the other kids in the eyes and either see their ridicule or pity gave me the sort of inspiration I had never had before. I was cut from the team at the end of the year, but I had gained something far better from the experience. After being cut from Wexford, I was ready to go down a level in hockey. But at the last minute another AA team asked me to join—the North York Flames. A young coach, Andy Thornley, gave me the chance to redeem myself.

During the season a lot of my buddies signed up to try out for Don Valley Junior High School basketball. They tried to get me to join but I took a pass. I was a pretty decent athlete but I never played a real game of basketball. I wasn't even sure what the rules were. Hockey had surrounded everything I did. After they pushed hard to have me try out, I reluctantly signed up. I didn't want to do it in fear of embarrassing myself again. I had just gotten cut by a hockey team for the first time in my life, and didn't need to relive that feeling. After three hard tryouts I remember walking up to the gym doors to check the list, assuming I probably didn't make the team. To my surprise I did.

I later asked Coach McCarthy how I managed to make the team. He said, "For three days straight no one ran harder than you up and down the court, and no one fought harder for basketballs under the rim. You were my hardest working guy on the court and no one was even a close second. I had to keep you."

Wow. I was speechless. It wasn't just the coach who felt this way either. The best and most talented player on the team was our point guard, Howard Campbell. He nicknamed me "The Bull" after tryouts.

That was amazing for me. That experience taught me something about myself that seven years of hockey hadn't. I had so much more to give when I really focused. I was able to channel my fear of failing into a different goal. It was a really fun year playing on the school basketball team.

Over the next two hockey seasons I was able to create a true work ethic playing Minor Midget for the North York Flames. The Flames were selected by the Greater Toronto Hockey League to be the Canadian representative in a tournament in Landshut, West Germany. Allan Green, whose son Tim was on our team, played a pivotal role in making this happen. Allan worked hard at putting together a plan for fundraising and acquiring sponsors. In the summer we stood outside malls wearing our team jackets selling raffle tickets for a Chrysler Cordoba that a few of the players' fathers bought off a dealer. Through money raised from the tickets and sponsors, we had the financial means to pay for the flights, hotel, and other expenses. It not only brought the team closer together but the family members, too. My parents and Stelle went to the tournament, which was played over the Christmas/New Year's holiday season.

The tournament consisted of eight teams. Two were from Germany and some others comprised the best players pulled from their respective clubs. In the case of the Russian and Czechoslovakian players, they were their country's Under-16 National team. And there were future NHLers Michal Pivonka and Petr Svoboda for the Czechs. In comparison the North York Flames was a good team, but we had no idea the quality of players we'd be facing.

The teams that had travelled to the tournament from outside Germany were housed in a three-floor dormitory, two to a floor. There were three players to a room, housed by position, and I remember Tim Green was in my room because we both played left wing.

The Russians were on our floor. For Tim and me, the entire experience was pure innocence and brilliance—a bunch of young kids who had zero in common culturally and with no ability to communicate. But we had a blast together. The Russians had two sets of clothes: beat-up track pants and T-shirts, and jackets that looked like they were handed down from their fathers and grandfathers. From what we understood, for some part of their journey the Russians had to travel by boat and it was clear they had very little as far as possessions.

We traded clothing because they were desperate for clothes from the West. "Blue jeans" were the only English words they seemed to know. We played sports in the dormitory basement and without speaking the same language made up competitions between us—proof that no matter what, sports can bring the best out in all of us.

Before our first game, we watched the Russians play the Czechs and it became political right from the start. Both teams hated each other and that was my first introduction to vicious hockey. We're talking two-handed slashing with baseball swings. I'd never seen anything like it in my life, but that's the way it was. It wasn't two hockey teams playing each other; it was two political rivals trying to prove a point. This was another level of dirty hockey. Somehow when we played those teams it was not nearly as vicious as it was when they played each other. Being down 3–0 in the first five minutes may have had something to do with that. We did manage to finish fourth overall.

A year later, during the Christmas/New Year's holiday season, I played in the annual Mac's AAA World Invitational Tournament for the top sixteen-year-old players in Canada. It takes place in Calgary, Alberta. The big games usually had three thousand spectators and the final, played at the Saddledome, drew ten thousand. Unlike the tournament in Quebec a few years before, I had done the homework and my determination was starting to show. I turned it around and became a top scorer again. Tim Green, my former teammate, was at the tournament, but was playing for the Young Nationals. That's where he stepped back and saw me as a competitor and realized I had finally broken away from the pack.

All the players that made it to the NHL were hard workers in the off-season, and that's what I was now doing. I finally knew what I wanted and the price I was willing to pay. It was paying off.

According to Tim, it was fun to watch me finally break through. In Calgary I was voted best left-winger and selected for the first All-Star Team. That was a very big deal for me. Scouts for Junior teams were there and noticed. I felt ready for the next level.

CHAPTER 2

Junior Hockey

A handful of American colleges and universities sent letters to my home. Some wanted me to visit their campuses and sports facilities to talk about potential scholarships. Princeton stood out among them. My parents thought that would be a good option because at least I would get an excellent education. My father would always say, "In hockey your first game could end up being your last game."

But the truth was my heart was set on playing Junior Hockey. At the time, American colleges didn't have a great track record for producing NHL players. It certainly wasn't like today. Now the NCAA skill level of the top players is on par with top Junior players. But back then, playing Junior Hockey was the best route to a pro career. Even so, making up my mind which way to go was a huge decision. Some players had agents or advisers who would help them make that type of decision, but at the time I didn't have one. As supportive as they were, my parents weren't able to give me any guidance. The thought of going to the U.S. weighed on me, but at the time I never seriously considered playing college hockey. I loved my Junior experience in the Canadian Hockey League (CHL), but if I had the same option today, it would be hard to turn down an Ivy League opportunity.

The Ontario Hockey League (OHL) draft took place at North York Centennial Arena, where I had played many times before in minor hockey. Overall there were twenty-two rounds and fifteen players selected per round. It was like a herd of cattle that day—hundreds of kids piled into the arena with hopeful looks on their faces. Their parents stood next to them wondering if all the hard work would pay off.

As a local boy, I was hoping to be selected by the Toronto Marlies so I could stay in Toronto, but it really didn't matter because all I wanted was to play Junior Hockey. My parents had already received calls from teams outside the Toronto area wondering if I would consider moving. At that stage I would have gone just about anywhere, but my mom had reservations about me being so far away.

My parents were there with me at the draft and we had heard I might be selected somewhere in the third or fourth round. After the Kitchener Rangers selected David Latta in the first round and Shawn Burr in the second round, they took me with their third pick, fifty-sixth overall, in the fourth round.

The Rangers, coached by Tom Barrett, were one of the premier organizations in the OHL and one of the best-run franchises in all of Canadian Junior Hockey. Founded in 1963, they had won the OHL championships in 1981 and 1982, and won the Canadian Major Junior Hockey League championship—the Memorial Cup—in '82. The Rangers had so much history developing future NHL stars such as Bill Barber and Larry Robinson. And around the time I was coming up, they produced NHLers Al MacInnis, Jeff Larmer, Brian Bellows, and Scott Stevens. I remember looking at my mom and telling her Kitchener was only an hour away from home. It was destined to be a great team for me, or so I thought.

The Rangers had been chosen to host the 1984 Memorial Cup that season and had a stacked lineup that included forwards Wayne Presley, John Tucker, Greg Puhalski, David Bruce, and Shawn Burr. My former Minor Atom teammate Brian Wilks was one of their centres. The defence had stars Jim Quinn, David Shaw, and Kent Paynter. American

Ray LeBlanc was Kitchener's top goalie. He represented the USA in the 1992 Olympics, where for two weeks he was arguably the greatest goaltender in the world. He took an otherwise unknown U.S. hockey team to medal contention. Overall, I was drafted to a team that had fifteen NHL draft picks, eleven of whom were selected in the first three rounds.

To me, the Rangers were like the New York Yankees of the OHL. Everything about them was big league. The Oshawa Generals were rich in tradition, having been established in the 1930s, but at the time they didn't have the big arena like Kitchener had, filled with eight thousand fans each game.

A few weeks into training camp my skates had gotten a little beaten up, so the organization bought me a new pair. It seems like a small thing now, but I couldn't believe it. Knowing I was finally at a level where a team would pay for my skates was an incredible feeling. The Kitchener Rangers were run like a business and annually turned good profits on their operations, so buying new skates was not a second thought to them. But to me it was a great sign that they intended for me to make the team.

Al MacInnis, future Hall of Famer and former Kitchener Ranger, was still in town prior to leaving for the Calgary Flames training camp. I didn't know him personally, but he was the one to introduce me to my billet in Kitchener. He had billeted across the street from my new "adopted" family. Junior Hockey billets are fantastic because they often become your new families. They play a vital role for young players spending time away from home.

My billets were Monty and Gerta Lovegrove and their two young children. Peter Bakovic, a young forward from Thunder Bay trying out for the team, was also billeting with the Lovegroves. He was a really good guy that would go on to play briefly for the Vancouver Canucks.

The next step for me was registering for the local high school, Kitchener Collegiate Institute (KCI). That school was huge but felt much smaller when you walked through the hallways with your Kitchener Ranger teammates.

I remember wanting to show the team that I was strong. Unlike Midget Hockey, there were no cages attached to the helmets. It was another sign that I was that much closer to the NHL. Without a cage, fighting was allowed; in minor hockey you would get kicked out for dropping the gloves. Because I wanted to make an impression, I was eager to try to fight. Although Darryl Sittler was my childhood hero, Tiger Williams was also one of my favourite players. I liked how he stood up for his teammates and had such a physical passion for the game. Nothing intimidated him, especially when he played in those drawn-out playoff series against the Broad Street Bullies of Philadelphia.

I ended up squaring off with David Bruce during our first intrasquad game. David was a player who could score, check, and fight. The year before he scored 36 goals in 67 games and totaled 199 penalty minutes. I thought I was strong enough to handle myself, but as the fight progressed I was doing the swim move, head down and arms flailing. Bruce calmly put his hand on my back and landed two uppercuts, cutting me above the eye. I ended up bleeding pretty badly. It was not a good moment. After the game, David was sitting in a hot tub and gave me some advice.

"You need better balance," he said. "That will naturally help you keep your head up more. Once you put your head down, you're done. You can't see where the punches are coming from."

His words stuck with me from that point forward. When I emerged from the dressing room, I was humbled and wiser. I wasn't discouraged by a less-than-memorable initial fight. In my first preseason game against the Toronto Marlies, I picked another fight. This one was against Steve Thomas, who went on to have a lengthy career in the NHL. He was strong and stocky, and appropriately nicknamed "Stumpy," but he could score and fight. I had just turned seventeen and he was twenty (an overage Junior). It was a tough game and I was trying to give my team an edge. He fed me my lunch. Again, two punches and I dropped. This balance thing was not coming easy. Stumpy and I have been friends for over thirty years now and we still laugh about him beating me up.

My parents were, of course, getting discouraged. In fact, my mother wanted to take me home and forget about hockey. She didn't want me fighting all the time and made it very clear to me that I could call it quits anytime.

In the later part of training camp, it seemed like I wasn't getting the same feedback other draft picks were. I wasn't playing in as many exhibition games as I would have liked and was feeling uneasy. My parents and I were still green when it came to Junior A.

We didn't know anything about the business. I managed to play the very last exhibition game and then immediately afterwards the head coach cut me from the team. It broke my heart. Tom Barrett told me that the team really liked me, but didn't have a spot for me on the roster. I was the last cut. They told me they wanted me to play for the Dixie Beehives, their Ontario Junior Hockey League affiliate, where I would get a lot of ice time and continue to develop. I was crushed. This didn't sit well with my parents either. The Dixie Beehives were just outside Toronto, close enough that I could live at home, but it felt far from Major Junior A hockey. My mom and I scrambled to register me back in my old high school, where I was well over a month behind in classes.

Larry Stern was the Beehives' coach and he gave me lots of playing time, as I was promised. I started off strong, scoring goals and feeling good. I was also enjoying being back in school even though I had some catching up to do. Everything seemed to be fine, but a few weeks after I scored 3 goals and 7 assists in 10 games, the Rangers decided to call me up. My parents and I had not been informed that this was even an option. The Rangers told me it was for one game only, but I didn't really care. For my parents it didn't make much sense, but all I cared about was playing my first OHL game. In my head I'm saying, *I got called up. I got called up!* I remember trying to stay focused in warm-up while looking around and thinking, *This is the big leagues. I'm finally here!*

In the dressing room before the game, some of the veterans did their best to calm my nerves. Brian Wilks was in his second season with the team and he was great. He told me to just go out and have fun and enjoy myself.

Even though I was only supposed to be called up for one game, I ended up playing three more over a week and a half. I didn't register any points in the first game, but in my next one against Oshawa I scored two goals, including the opening one, in a 10–2 victory. I scored the first on a forehand and the second on a backhand underneath the bar. I won't ever forget that. It was such an unbelievable feeling, not only to be playing, but to score my first two goals in the OHL. I felt like a pro.

The whole Kitchener organization is a lot like being in the NHL. It's a big-league feel for Major Junior Hockey. As a kid, I'd go to Maple Leaf Gardens to see the Marlies play and maybe there would only be a thousand people in the stands, but it was still the Toronto Marlies. Playing for Dixie was one level below the OHL and there might be seventy-five people watching the game, most of them family and friends. With the Kitchener Rangers, it's in front of eight thousand fans and the same league that Wayne Gretzky had played in. I felt if I worked hard I had a chance because there would be NHL scouts at every game. But I wasn't nearly as close as I thought.

I played four games in about two weeks, commuting from home with my parents. Even though I didn't register any more points, I still felt good about things. But all that changed when I received a call from North Bay's GM and coach, Bert Templeton, saying he had acquired me in a trade. The call-up now made total sense to me. The Rangers had been showcasing me the whole time for Bert and North Bay. The Rangers acquired a veteran, Carmine Vani, who was a second-round draft pick of the Detroit Red Wings in 1982.

North Bay acquired me along with Rob Nichols, who had scored 17 goals and 26 assists in 54 games the year before for Kitchener. North Bay also got a third-round pick, who wound up being future NHL defenceman Bill Houlder.

The Rangers wanted reinforcements for their drive to the Memorial Cup, but it didn't happen. They lost to the Ottawa 67s in the final. Carmine Vani only scored 15 goals the rest of his Junior career for Kitchener, while Rob Nichols, Bill Houlder, and I would go on to score 270 for North Bay. Tom Barrett not only lost his Memorial Cup that year, he may have made one of the worst Junior trades in history.

The trade was my wake-up call to the business of hockey. What I found out after the trade was that North Bay had been interested in two of us from the Beehives—it had been between me and another player, Bert Weir. Bert Templeton picked me because I was considered an unpolished jewel—at least that's what he told my father. I also found out Templeton had wanted to draft me that summer, but Kitchener had beat him to it.

When Templeton called, I told him my parents weren't going to let me go. To put it bluntly, my mom was sick of the whole thing. The yo-yo effect of Junior Hockey had not impressed her in the least. North Bay was a four-hour drive from home. But mostly my parents had serious reservations about me going to my third team and third high school in five weeks. When I told Templeton my mom had had enough, he asked to speak to her.

He said, "Mrs. Kypreos, you have nothing to worry about. Nick is coming up here to play for the Centennials and go to school. I'm not going to trade him. He's not going to come up here only to move again. He will be on my team and it is only school and hockey." He gave her his word.

I turned to my father and said, "Dad, you've got to let me go. I'll make you proud one day." My dad thought if he didn't let me go, I would hold it against him forever. So he gave me his blessing. The last thing he said to me before I left was, "If it doesn't work out again, you don't have to worry about coming back home with your tail between your legs; this will always be home for you." I can't begin to put into words what this meant to me, hoping to have a second try at making Junior Hockey.

I drove up with Rob Nichols, whom I barely knew, to North Bay. He had an old car with a broken heater and I could just feel the temperature dropping as we got farther north. It was only late fall. We froze. All I could think was, *Where the hell are we going?*

I had played in North Bay in a tournament when I was seven, but that was just for a weekend. I was too young at the time to really know or care about the temperature in North Bay, but this was ten years later and it was going to be my new home. Nichols was two years older but a natural leader already. He had style and tremendous confidence. I was a rookie and as green as you could get.

Hazing rookies was a big thing in the 1980s. It could be shoving six rookies in the small bathroom on a team bus or shaving them from head to toe. Teams would tape half-naked young players in a chair and slide it out to centre ice after practice. Believe it or not, I watched one guy torpedoed to the middle of the ice during a public skate in only his underwear. It was a real thing in those days to put rookies in their place. Things that veteran players deemed fun could be traumatic for younger guys. I sat in that freezing car for four hours and worried about what my new team might do to me.

When we arrived in North Bay, none of the other rookies had been "initiated." After a few weeks, like clockwork, the veterans came after me along with all the other young players. It was time for my reckoning and I was shitting my pants. But then something unexpected happened. Rob Nichols stepped up and said, "Kyper is not to be touched. The Rangers already initiated him back in Kitchener. Leave him alone." So Rob, as a senior player in the room, got other vets to back off. He never even mentioned to me that he was going to lie to get me out of a hazing situation. It could have been the nicest thing anyone had ever done for me up to that point. I hated hazing back then and to this day have never really understood the point of trying to humiliate your teammates. Today hazing is unacceptable. Maybe the rookies are forced to buy team dinners, but that's about as crazy as it gets. Rightfully so. There is zero tolerance now in the OHL.

Even back then Bert Templeton was a legendary coach in Ontario Junior Hockey. He still holds the record for the second-most wins, behind Brian Kilrea of the Ottawa 67s. He also did a pretty nice job of selling my parents on his organization. When I walked into his office and sat down the very first time, he had a serious look on his face. He said, "I want you to know I treat all my players the same." He paused and then added, "Like shit!"

I didn't know whether to laugh or cry. The season had already been such a roller coaster. This is the same guy that was all sweet to my mom. But that's the type of guy he was. He was probably laughing on the inside, thinking to himself, *I've got this kid where I want him.*

It was really simple as far as he was concerned: go to school, play hard, and we'd all get along just fine. Bert could be intimidating. Because many of his previous teams had a *Slap Shot* "Hanson Brothers" vibe to them, he had a reputation for being the fiercest coach in Junior Hockey, and for good reason. He *was*. His teams were feared. Thus the nickname "Dirty Bert." His early coaching years were legendary. In the early seventies he had a team so dirty an opposing team forfeited. The label, however, was unwarranted in his later years in North Bay. He was still tough and had tough teams, though. I knew when I was traded I had to show him that I was a Bert Templeton type of player.

It was rough in North Bay. They had begun operations the year before and were owned by a businessman whose principal income came from owning a Canadian Tire store. A franchise at the time could have been purchased for $200,000, but the Rangers had considerably more value. The Centennials' organization was completely different from the Rangers'. We were not allowed shin pad tape for practices, just games. We practiced with semibroken sticks that we had to tape over and over. We had to beg for a new hockey stick for games. It was just different.

I ended up with three different billets during my stay in North Bay. The first two years Peter Abric and I stayed with Eva Leslie. I stayed with the Haskins family the third year. My best friend on the team was Tom Warden, who later ended up being the athletic director at Lakehead University in Thunder Bay. I spent most of my time going between his billets, the Lloydses', and my billet. They became my unofficial second home I was there so often. The last year in North Bay the Daigles family billeted me. I am friends with the Daigles, Haskins, and Lloyds families today.

Every Sunday night my parents drove up to watch me play, which was always comforting. They would bring tons of food from home. On the nights they came all my teammates wondered, "Hey Kyper, what did your parents bring us to eat this week?" On weekends when there were whiteouts from heavy snowfall, they would still make the drive up north, on single-lane roads, with no cell phone or GPS, which no one had then. I always felt a great sense of relief when I saw them enter the arena. Road trips in general were hazardous during bad weather. Then I'd worry about them heading back home. A four-hour drive could take them up to seven hours on some nights. It wasn't any easier for my two sisters at home waiting for them. Neither Tess nor Stelle could sleep until they knew Mom and Dad were safe. The moment they heard the sound of the garage door opening, even at 3 a.m., they could relax enough to fall asleep.

Many of us were devastated by the news of the Swift Current Broncos, a western Junior team that hit black ice on their way to a game in Regina, in 1986. Four members of the team had died when the bus slid off an overpass, hitting an embankment. The four players killed were veterans who always sat in the back of the bus. I never felt comfortable sitting in the back of the bus again. When you are out on the road with terrible conditions, it's hard to not think of those sorts of things. Many of those nights were tough along Highway 400 up to the Bay. Single lanes in whiteouts travelling 40 km per hour were not easy. Some guys had no problem sleeping through it. I'd be up front talking to the bus driver. Thirty-two years after the Swift Current accident the hockey community had to live through an even more devastating bus tragedy with the Humboldt Broncos in Saskatchewan. This one shockingly cost sixteen lives. It had nothing to do with icy conditions, but as an ex-player you can't help but feel devastated for the deceased and their families all over again.

North Bay, Ontario, is the quintessential small-town Canadian hockey community. Hockey is a big focus. People recognized us on the street and would stop to chat, and as players, we felt like celebrities signing autographs. It really gave us an idea of what being a professional hockey player might be like, and to have people look up to you. I've been back many times, and even though the franchise has changed ownership and is now known as the Battalion, I'm still treated with warmth and kindness because I am a part of the hockey history there.

It took me a while to adapt to the cold. I remember going ice fishing with Rob Nichols, Rob DeGagné, and Kevin Vescio, and it blew my mind that we could be out on a lake and dig a hole in it. Hey, I was a big-city guy. The whole concept of being on Lake Nipissing, sitting in a hut and digging a hole in the ice, and warming up a bowl of chili was pretty different. I didn't mind it, but it was bloody cold.

The arena, Memorial Gardens, was a typical old barn with a capacity of about 4,300. We had some sellouts, but nothing like in Kitchener. I ended up playing with two other rookies and we struggled many nights. The joke was, instead of being called the Kid Line, a few of the veterans called us the You've Got to Be Kidding Line.

On November 13, in my first game with the Centennials, I had 2 assists in a 7–2 win at home against Guelph. Four days later I scored the game-winning goal on the road in a 5–3 win over Brantford. The next day I registered a goal in a 4–2 win in Guelph. Overall, I was beginning to feel like I belonged. When I'd first met Bert Templeton, I stressed how much I wanted to be a good hard-nosed player for him, yet all he did the first month was encourage me to score goals.

I liked to be one of the last players to the leave the dressing room after games, but it drove my parents nuts. It didn't happen all the time, especially when I knew the weather was bad and they needed to get on the road. But the dressing room was always kind of a nice place to take your time and hang out with the guys and the trainer, and talk about the game a little bit. I was never in a hurry. I wanted to take it all in and learn from what happened in the games. Plus, trainers were always good for an ice pack and some time to sit back and talk.

While I grew up watching Junior Hockey in southern Ontario, I gained a new appreciation for northern hockey. The loop between North Bay, Sudbury, and Sault Ste. Marie was known for passionate hockey fans. Sudbury had that crazy stuffed wolf attached to a clothesline that they'd run down every time they scored. We did everything we could not to see it. I also witnessed firsthand one of the greatest accomplishments in Junior Hockey history when the Soo Greyhounds went 33–0 on home ice during the 1984–1985 season. It was late February and we had a really good chance to be the only road team to beat them. After twenty-eight straight home wins we were the only team to push them to overtime. Then five minutes into OT, Greyhounds defenceman Chris Felix takes a pass from Derek King off the face-off circle and throws a seeing-eye-dog wrist shot through six pairs of legs. I can still picture that goal. We had the best chance to go into their barn and break that streak and couldn't do it. It still bothers me today.

I remember the first time I played for the Centennials in Kitchener.

When a team trades you or waives you, regardless of whether it's in Junior Hockey or the professional level, you always feel like they made a mistake. Kitchener beat us soundly that night, but I was glad I was able to come back to the arena and show them I was now a solid player in this league.

I finished my rookie season with 10 goals and 11 assists in 47 games and was moved up to the third line to start the playoffs. Even though my offensive numbers didn't show it, Bert had a good feeling that I could improve playing with older veterans on the team, like Rob DeGagné. We finished fifth in the Emms Division, 57 points behind the team that traded me away—they finished first overall in the standings. The Rangers Wayne Presley finished second in league scoring with 139 points, including 63 goals.

We played the London Knights in the playoffs. They had finished fourth in the Emms, 16 points ahead of us. The opening round was a best three-out-of-five series. The Knights won it in four games. However, Bert's hunch to move me up in the lineup paid off, as I had a good series, scoring three goals and two assists. This series gave me momentum going into the next season. But what it really did was catapult me into the scorer I was soon to become in Junior.

I was eligible for the NHL draft, but I had no expectations that any team would select me. I had a feeling I didn't accomplish enough in my rookie season to warrant being drafted. And not hearing from any team pretty well sealed my fate. I still had no agent. The draft took place in Montreal and it was a big one. This was the year that Quebec Hockey League scoring star Mario Lemieux was going to be selected first overall. That was a given. I was following the proceedings on TV, but the coverage was limited. It certainly wasn't like it is now, with the whole draft televised live throughout the weekend. Historically, most of the players who expect to be drafted attend with their parents. Not only did we not go, we didn't even discuss it.

Many guys eligible for the draft make the decision to go despite no assurance that they will be chosen. While cameras catch the sheer jubilation of realizing a lifelong dream, it's quite a sad sight seeing so many young athletes leave the arena disappointed that their names were never called out. The cameras don't show that. Back then there was no Internet to follow the draft, just a very long list in the paper the next day. When I picked up the paper the day after, I was still disappointed at not getting drafted, but even more so when I read some of the players that were chosen. It turned out to be one of the deepest drafts in NHL history. *I'm better than him*, I thought, *and better than that guy, too. That guy can't play.*

All this gave me real motivation to play a great second season in North Bay. What I found out a short time later, though, was that I didn't need to wait for the next season to start. One phone call changed my life.

CHAPTER 3

The Call

I remember that it was a hot day, and a week after the draft. I was sitting around the patio table with my sister Stelle and my dad on his rare day off from work. We were sitting by the pool eating watermelon when the phone rang. My sister ran inside to answer it and yelled out to me that "some guy that says he's Bob Clarke from the Philadelphia Flyers" was calling.

"That's a mean trick to play on me after not being drafted," I said.

"I'm serious," she replied. So of course I grabbed the phone.

"Is this really Bobby Clarke of the Flyers?" I asked.

"Yep," he replied.

It took me a few minutes to convince myself it wasn't someone playing a prank on me. He called to invite me to training camp in September and had to call me directly because I didn't have an agent.

I turned to my Dad and said, "He's invited me to training camp."

And, no word of a lie, my dad said, "You know the name Philadelphia derives from the Greek word *philos*, which is brotherly love. 'Philanthropy' is from *hilos*. 'Delphia' comes from the city Delphi, where Apollo lived."

I said, "Dad, I don't need a Greek history lesson right now—what should I tell him?"

He looked straight at me and calmly said, "Go."

Bob Clarke had just ended his fifteen-year Hall of Fame career with the Flyers and transitioned into the team's GM. He hadn't watched any Junior A hockey, but one of the team's scouts, Dennis Patterson, recommended me. He scouted the OHL and told Clarke that even though I wasn't drafted, I still had a chance to play for the Flyers because I was a rugged player who could body check and throw my weight around. The Flyers liked that. So, off I went to my first NHL training camp, barely a legal adult.

While I tried my best to fit in and look the pro part, it was intimidating. There was hotel check-in and the guys I watched play the game on *Hockey Night in Canada* were rolling into the hotel one by one: Tim Kerr, who had nearly 60 goals the year before, looked more like a linebacker for the Philadelphia Eagles than a winger for the Flyers; defenceman Mark Howe, a future Hall of Famer; and, preeminent goalie Pelle Lindbergh. I felt I was in over my head, to say the least. As intimidating as it was, it paled in comparison to meeting my childhood hero Darryl Sittler, who was traded from the Leafs to the Flyers a couple years prior. The mere thought of being on the same ice with my hero was incomprehensible. Darryl was not participating in training camp because of back issues. Word had gotten to him that a Toronto kid who was a big fan of his was attending camp. When team trainer Dave "Sudsy" Settlemyre told me after my first scrimmage Darryl was outside waiting for me to say hi, I completely froze. Darryl, class act that he is, tried his best to welcome me and put me at ease. Unfortunately, it didn't work. I don't remember stringing one coherent sentence together because I was so nervous.

Like your first NHL goal, you don't forget your first NHL training camp. You get a booklet that has your daily routine mapped out for you. Bus pickup, departure, and arrival times are written in there. Medicals with doctors and physical testing with the trainers is mapped out. Scrimmage times and off-ice conditioning with trainer Pat Croce were scheduled in along with team meals. This booklet was our bible.

Lose that thing and lose your life for the next two weeks. Training camp would break into four competing teams all vying for the "Clarke Cup," the training camp championship. We were all assigned to either Team Orange, Team Blue, Team Black, or Team Red.

Every team had a certain number of pros and amateurs with both junior and college players. And it was so much fun. My first year I had Dave Poulin, Rick Tocchet, and Mark Howe on my team. "Howie" was the most natural hockey player I ever witnessed in my life. The kind of guy that takes a pair of skates out of a box for the first time and skates as if he was born with them.

As a first-time guy, I couldn't get enough of being around those players. I was like a sponge soaking everything up. I remember competing with them, but it's the more intimate settings, like sitting beside them on the bus, or going for lunch in a Philly diner, that I remember the most. Roughly ten days after I arrived, I was asked to go see Bob Clarke in his office for what I thought was a token "thanks for coming" and here's your one-way ticket back to your Junior team in North Bay.

Clarkie says to me. "Nick, I invited fifteen free agents to training camp with the thought of offering a contract to one. Guess who I want to offer it to?"

"John Kemp?" I guessed.

"No, you," he said.

"Really?" I could barely believe it. He asked me if I had anyone I wanted to call for advice like an agent and I had to admit I didn't have one.

"Do you know of any agents you can call?" he asked.

"No, do you?" I asked back.

He laughed, and with that he reached behind his desk and pulled out his Rolodex. He rolled it a few times before settling in on Bill Watters from Branada Sports Management. Clarkie called him: "Wilber, I've got a Toronto boy who could use some help." Bill had worked for the agency that represented Clarke during his career. The contract was fairly straightforward: I would receive $90,000 to play in the NHL, $25,000 in the American Hockey League, and a $10,000 signing bonus in two installments. It was the most money I had ever seen. I remember leaving his office thinking it was so awesome. I could buy a new ten-speed bike and a new stereo.

I returned to North Bay and played 64 games, scoring 41 goals and 36 assists. I also totaled 71 penalty minutes, almost double the number from my rookie year. This season was special for another reason: I had former Flyer and Hall of Fame member Bill Barber calling my billet house asking for me. Bill is a big deal up in northern Ontario. He grew up next door in Callander, and because he was working in the organization, I'd get a call once a month from him.

The Flyers brought me back the next year for training camp. I felt a little bit stronger physically, but I was really immature mentally. For an undrafted player, the expectations weren't to make it into the NHL so seamlessly, so they sent me back to Junior again after camp.

I returned to the Flyers training camp for a third time and I felt that I was getting closer, but still not ready. At the time, no one cracked the Flyers roster as a nineteen-year-old, not even first-round picks.

I ended up scoring 62 goals in 64 games and had 35 assists in North Bay. I had the third-highest goal total in the league and was voted a first-team All-Star. I had the best plus-minus in all of Canadian Junior Hockey with a plus-52. I also totaled 112 penalty minutes. But the season came to a disappointing end. In the last regular-season game versus the Hamilton Steelhawks, Angelo Catenaro caught me with my head down after I scored my 62nd goal and I missed the playoffs with a separated shoulder.

I had to have a pin surgically implanted in my shoulder, a type of surgery that seldom happens today. Now they let the shoulder heal with rest and physio. The doctors drilled a two-inch screw into my collarbone which had to be removed years later for fear of long-term risks, including arthritis.

It was around that time that I changed agents, deciding to part with Bill Watters and Rick Curran of Branada Sports Management and go with a lesser-known agent named Harry Francis. I switched to him because one of his clients was Chris Kontos, a first-generation Greek Canadian who had been selected fifteenth overall in the 1982 NHL draft by the New York Rangers. Chris suggested that even though Harry didn't have a list of star players, he'd show me the attention I felt I was missing. He was much more accessible than agents who had higher-rated clients.

Chris took me under his wing that summer while my shoulder healed and I skated with pros in the off-season. To get invited to a Toronto pro summer skate was another achievement. It was organized by the late Jack Ridgeway, who was a coach and also a player representative who counselled young players with pro aspirations. It's not often that so many talented pros come together outside of a team environment. It included NHL players Börje Salming, Gary Nylund, Vince Damphousse, Rick Tocchet, Gary Leeman, Peter Zezel, Pat Flatley, Steve Thomas, and Glenn Healy—another guy that in later years helped mentor me. It cost ten dollars for each player getting invited to this skate. In one game, I remember being up against Pat Flatley, who later became the captain of the New York Islanders, and I tried to lift his stick. It was like trying to lift steel. I'm thinking, *Oh my God, this is what the NHL is really like?* I knew then I had a lot of work still ahead of me.

After that summer I drove down to the Flyers training camp for a fourth time. But that summer had changed me. Most nineteen-year-olds under NHL contract find a place to play pro hockey if they don't make the parent hockey club. I knew if I didn't stick with the Flyers out of training camp, I would in all probability be sent to their American Hockey League affiliate, the Hershey Bears, but I was also eligible to finish off my Junior career as a twenty-year-old overager. Back then Junior Hockey teams were allowed to carry two twenty-year-old players each season. That was something I didn't want. It would mean the Flyers didn't feel I was good enough to turn pro. But that summer I went from training camp to the AHL and I was thrilled thinking Junior Hockey was in my rearview mirror.

Just as I thought, Bob Clarke assigned me to Hershey in the AHL and it was quite an experience, on and off the ice. Hershey is one of the most historic franchises in the AHL. If the Kitchener Rangers were the New York Yankees of the OHL, the Hershey Bears were the Yankees of the AHL. They began in 1938 and are still the longest continually running franchise in the same city in the league. The organization was a powerhouse, with sixteen conference championships won (as of this writing, it's twenty-three) and six league championships (now eleven). The team played in the Hersheypark Arena, which was the place to be, selling out to capacity every Saturday night. Winning was important to that franchise. I was a green twenty-year-old. The team was loaded with veterans such as Tim Tookey, Al Hill, Don Nachbaur, Kevin McCarthy, Kevin Maxwell, Ross Fitzpatrick, Mitch Lamoureux, Mark Lofthouse, Mike Stothers, and Steve Smith. They were guys with years of pro experience already under their belts.

Similar to my first year in Junior, I was there to just play hockey and keep my mouth shut. There was something still missing from my game and it was more mental than anything. I was finally getting paid a salary of $25,000 a year, and that was an amazing feeling. Being paid to play the game you love is like a cherry on top of a sundae. I didn't have to spend too much on housing. I roomed with two other rookies, Jeff Chychrun, a defenceman who was drafted in the second round in 1984, and Mike Murray, a centre who was drafted by the New York Islanders but later traded. We each paid $250 a month for a pretty nice house. Perfect.

Still, I was nervous. In many ways, team veterans first look upon young rookies as a job threat more than anything else. Guards are up until they see how rosters turn out. This is especially true in the AHL, where it's common for veterans to get waived, traded, or otherwise sent somewhere else. It's a pro league where many players carve out wonderful careers that don't include the NHL or million-dollar contracts. That meant many of the players were married with kids. Their livelihoods depended on their performance.

As a newcomer, I kept my head down and tried to take it all in. What I soon learned, though, is that some of the most talented veterans in the AHL had deficiencies that kept them from the big show. Those weaknesses could range from subpar skating to alcohol abuse. For many lifetime AHL players, it was clear to see that something had always been missing that kept them from the NHL.

My official pro debut started in the 1986–1987 season with the Hershey Bears. Damn if that whole town didn't smell like chocolate every day. Even the streetlamps are shaped like little Hershey's Kisses. I felt like Charlie with Willy Wonka's golden ticket. I had finally found a way to work hard and get noticed.

A two-week road trip led me to the first place my father had ever stepped foot in Canada: Halifax. He had landed in that town from Sparta and started a new life in Canada. My new pro hockey life was beginning there, too. It seemed almost poetic.

The effect didn't last. That night in Halifax an errant stick from Mike Ware cut my bottom lip wide open. I was taken to a hospital where I waited two hours for someone to locate a plastic surgeon. It was a young doctor who looked my age, and boy, was he excited. My status as a hockey player disappeared and my lip became exhibit A. This guy was young, but he was good. One hour after he began, he closed my lip up with microsurgery. "How many stitches, Doc?" I asked him. He told me he was too busy to count.

I wish the story ended there, but I also had five broken teeth. So like any small-town hospital, the nurse started looking through the Yellow Pages for a dentist to help me. To her credit she got a response from someone who could see me that night.

I met him in front of his office at about 1 a.m. In an effort to lighten the mood I asked him how much he'd had to drink that night. He said, "Clearly not enough." I was in too much pain to laugh, but I did find that funny. The five broken teeth were not my concern at this point. It was the exposed nerves dangling from them—the most excruciating pain I've ever dealt with in my life. The dentist said patients need two to three visits for one root canal. But after he did the first root canal, I asked him to do another. Then the third, and fourth. We proceeded to do all five that night. I sat in his chair until well after the sun came up. I returned to a waiting team bus with a lip ten times its original size.

Now, if that didn't make me want to quit hockey, nothing ever would. Hockey culture has always been tough: play hard, do your job, be a man. An injury like the one I suffered can always test your resolve. I was young and naive in so many ways, but I was smart enough to know many around me would judge me on my ability to downplay this traumatic experience. So I didn't make it a big deal. I had no choice but to suck it up and not complain. I was far from my comfortable home, with a lamb on the spit at the side of my house, and all my Greek uncles and aunts. I was almost two thousand kilometres away and there was no one to reach out to for sympathy.

Two days later, because I was no longer in unbearable pain, Hershey coach John Paddock decided to throw a full shield on my face and put me back on the ice. My face was still very swollen, but the only concern he seemed to have was whether he could shove my swollen fat lower lip into a full visor. I swear, these days that would constitute some form of abuse. I probably should have missed some games, but I didn't. The culture didn't allow me that choice, and my coach needed to know what kind of player I was.

Paddock didn't play me regularly, choosing to go with his veterans. Minor-league coaches have a difficult mandate. On one hand, they are expected to develop young talent for the franchise, and on the other, they are trying to win championships. Back then, it felt to me there was a lot less emphasis on development compared to today. Paddock's top priority was to win every night in hopes of advancing his coaching career, no different from any player. But that doesn't mean he didn't care about us, and a coach's attitude can make a big difference.

While there are plenty of coaches in the league who are remembered as being heartless, John Paddock may be remembered by his players as one of the nicest. He genuinely felt bad every time he told me I wasn't dressing. It actually helped me to know the guy had a heart. He was a gentleman who could also win championships.

I didn't do well in the 10 games I played for Hershey. I had only 1 assist. It's not a good stat when you have more root canals than points. I had to make a tough choice. I could go to the Kalamazoo Wings of the East Coast Hockey League or back to North Bay, where I still had eligibility for my overage year. Yes, personal development was a top priority, and in the East Coast I would be playing against some of the most physical players in pro. The biggest reason to return to my old Junior team came down to this: I would be coming back to the strongest North Bay team yet. It was a real opportunity to win a national championship: the Memorial Cup.

I chose North Bay. But the choice came with a price: instead of making $1,700 every two weeks in the AHL, I was back to making $30 a week. It was hard at first not to feel like I failed at my chance to turn pro. Would I be remembered as one of those players who was great in Junior but simply couldn't make the leap?

When I got back to North Bay, I had another short but poignant meeting in Bert Templeton's office. "Don't come back here with your lip dragging, feeling sorry for yourself," he warned me. "I need you to help me get to the Memorial Cup."

Even though I returned to North Bay feeling down on myself, in time I found that the experience with the Flyers organization had helped enough to boost my confidence in Juniors. I felt like more of a leader than ever. Wayne MacPhee was the other overage player and our captain. He was all heart. They pinned an *A* on my sweater in hope that I could help him lead. The team response was great. It was a strong group, but I definitely gave them another layer.

It didn't take me long to get going. I don't think I scored in my first game back, but then the barn doors broke open. I averaged over a goal a game and we easily won the Emms Division by 13 points over Hamilton. I scored 49 goals and totaled 90 points in just 46 games. I was also voted to the second All-Star Team. At that rate, if I had played the whole season, I might have scored 75 goals. But it wasn't about my totals. That year was about so much more. Did I feel more responsibility to help lead, besides only scoring goals? Was I even stronger, tougher, and more resilient than the year prior? Was I more well rounded as a player? The answer was yes to all those questions.

It was a unique year in the OHL because our first-place finish in our division had us playing the Oshawa Generals, who had finished first in the Leyden Division, in what was called the Super Series. Usually people would expect to see us in a final, but the league office still needed to determine a host team for the Memorial Cup and the winner of this Super Series would gain automatic host entry. It had never worked this way in the past. They tried that format one more time in 1993 with Peterborough and Sault Ste. Marie. After that it was never repeated. We lost the series in seven games, which may have saved the town some grief as a major air-force convention had booked up all the rooms the same week the Memorial Cup was scheduled. Would have been fun watching the mayor explain that one. Our Super Series loss also turned out to be a prelude to the championship. We went at each other again like cats and dogs. It was the kind of fast, hard hockey that longtime Junior executive Sherwood "Sherry" Bassin describes as some of the best he'd ever been a part of. We fought hard but limped into Oshawa for Game 7. We lost many key players, including Rangers draft pick Darren Turcotte, hard-nosed Blues pick Darin Smith, and Devils prospect and toughest guy in the league Troy Crowder. It was that kind of series. It just didn't seem meant to be. Again, it took seven games to decide the series. And again, the Generals got the better of us, and my season came to a disappointing end.

From a team perspective, losing two series to Oshawa was heartbreaking, but as a player, I really felt I continued to develop, minus a Memorial Cup win. And I had shown enough to be worthy of another opportunity to attend training camp with the Flyers organization. They told me they didn't stop believing I could play pro hockey and I didn't stop believing in them. Even though I had the reputation for scoring goals in Junior, I also carved out a reputation for handling myself with my gloves off. Perhaps it was the 78 penalty minutes during the playoffs they noticed the most. If there was one thing I needed to do better, it was to control my temper. I didn't score at nearly the rate I had during the regular season, and being in the penalty box was the biggest reason. The only saving grace was that I was now far less intimidated about fighting.

In the 1970s, the Flyers' Broad Street Bullies style had dominated the NHL. Ten years later the culture of intimidating play had carried over to the Hershey Bears. The Flyers blueprint was simple: they perfected the culture of tough hockey that could win championships. Philly wanted to win and they needed all their players to be tough. I'd started to make it a part of my game. After my overage Junior season, I had a new chance to prove I could play pro hockey. I was stronger and more mature. I was now a twenty-one-year-old player, no longer eligible to play Junior. I went back to Philly's training camp trying to get noticed again, and for the first time without that Junior Hockey safety net.

During an NHL preseason game one year against the Buffalo Sabres, I decided I was not going to back down from anybody. My former Junior teammate Mike Hartman was with the Sabres organization, and we spoke during the warm-up. He told me to stay away from Andy Ristau. He was six-foot-five and weighed 250 pounds. He was like Jaws from the James Bond movies. We lined up for a face-off and he tried to muscle me off the face-off line. I whacked him twice really hard to send a message back that I wouldn't be intimidated. Ristau actually laughed in my face, like I had made the stupidest decision of my life. So we both dropped our gloves. A few short seasons earlier I would have been hurt badly by him, but now I was able to cut him. I remember the Flyers brass were really impressed. This fight showed Bob Clarke that I still wanted to be taken seriously. The fight earned me praise from preseason teammates Rick Tocchet and Tim Kerr.

I found ways to update my mom and dad with collect calls back home but failed to mention the fighting part. They were always supportive of my decisions, but I knew that having to prove myself like that would worry them. It was hard to explain to them that getting noticed didn't always come in the way of goals. I was doing everything I could to show the organization that I wasn't the player I had been the year before. If I wasn't on the Flyers roster after that training camp, I was determined to be on the opening night roster for the Hershey Bears.

True to that promise to myself, I made the Hershey team and felt much more comfortable. Physically, mentally, and emotionally, it was night and day from the year before. I believe the level of compete I showed against Oshawa had a lot to do with it. I started to earn the respect of the veterans and carried myself differently. I also trained harder than I had ever trained before. I came to camp built like a brick house. I had been in an amazing summer training program at the Fitness Institute in Toronto that I followed religiously. Peter and John Renzetti were strength and conditioning coaches who would later join the Detroit Red Wings training staff. Our group included the late Peter Zezel, Kris Draper, Rob DiMaio, Craig Woodcroft, and Greg Walters; a tight-knit group who constantly pushed each other.

I showed up to the Flyers training camp winning the Outstanding Conditioning Award and received a cheque for $1,500. I managed to bench my weight of 205 pounds twenty-three times. Only Tim Kerr pushed the bench press further than me in training camp. Kerr would bench-press 225 pounds like it was a little bag of feathers. After twenty-five reps, the Flyers staff would beg him to stop in fear of the pin in his shoulder breaking. It later came back to me that some thought I was doing steroids that summer. Not a chance. My strength came from hard training and my mom's fasolada—Greek bean soup. When I came back from that summer I felt different.

Don Nachbaur was a fourteen-year pro who had done stints in Hartford, Philly, and Edmonton. He made sure the rookies knew their place, never letting us forget what the pecking order was in the dressing room, on the team bus, and during team meals. He scared the crap out of us with hazing stories, too. He never did follow through with anything, but loved rattling us with the threat. He was a tough but honest player. He later found great success as a hockey coach. Nachbaur also showed a great appreciation for my Greek culture.

Although everyone called me Kyper, my mother still called me Nicky. Nachbaur, who everyone on the team called "Snackbar," would watch how my doting mother acted around me and would mimic her. He wouldn't do it in a mean-spirited or disrespectful manner—he thought my mother was sweet. Snackbar greeted me most mornings with "Neeky, Neeky, my boy, Neeky!" in a big Greek accent. He'd pinch my face. "You're a good boy, Neeky . . . Are you eating enough?" It sounds annoying, but then he would often tell me how much he and his wife, Kim, loved my parents. His teasing was fun for me, too, and it helped that a respected veteran had warmed up to me. Earning his respect wasn't easy, but once you had it, you had a friend for life.

This season in Hershey went well for us. We had what appeared a perfect blend of veteran leadership and a young group of kids, like me, ready to contribute. John Paddock didn't let my last-season failure cloud his judgement twelve months later. I was ready for him to give me more responsibility, and he did. My first full season of pro hockey, I ended up scoring 24 goals, 7 of them game winners, which led the team, and added 20 assists in 71 games. I also totaled 101 penalty minutes. We had a strong record of 50 wins, 25 losses, and 5 ties in 80 games, and finished first in the South Division with 105 points, the most in the league. It was a historic season for the franchise and I played a big part in it.

In the playoffs we swept the Binghamton Whalers in four games and then repeated that against the Adirondack Red Wings. This brought us to the Calder Cup final, where we played the Fredericton Express. This was the Quebec Nordiques' farm team, and a younger team than us. At age twenty-seven, Claude Julien may have been their oldest player, while we had three over thirty. We swept them, too. My first full year in the pros and we finished with an unprecedented 12–0 run to win it all, setting an AHL record in the process for the most consecutive games won in the playoffs. This victory, in 1988, marked the Hershey Bears seventh Calder Cup championship.

Despite scoring only two points in the playoffs, I played in all 12 games, bringing a heavy forecheck. I was discovering how successful I could be in finding ways to contribute without scoring goals. Many top goal scorers coming out of Junior are never able to find different ways to add value to a pro team. In this playoff run I finally proved I could. It was a special time for our whole team. Kevin Maxwell, Steve Smith, Ross

Fitzpatrick, Mitch Lamoureux, and Don Nachbaur were great character guys who had waited many years to win that championship. And the young guys, like me, Gord Murphy, Glen Seabrooke, Don Biggs, Brian Dobbin, Mike Murray, and Jeff Chychrun had a chance to experience a championship early in our pro careers.

Hockey people see you differently when you are part of a championship team. It's weird, but other teams longing for a championship look at you as if you have the secret sauce to winning. It's a huge benefit for your career—all things being equal, the prevailing wisdom is to pick the guy who knows how to win. This was also my first championship at such a high level of hockey. Winning my last game of the season was also new to me. While losing in the playoffs makes you reflect on what went wrong, winning has the opposite effect—you reflect on everything that went right. To win a championship, so many moving parts have to line up. That's what this cup taught me.

When I look at this season, I'm reminded of a thirty-two-year-old Al Hill. He had left a lot of good hockey behind him, but still had enough to show us what one last opportunity would mean. Winning teaches you how to take advantage of a small opportunity and make the most of it. It also helped to remind me that it takes a village to win a championship. Our training staff was such a huge part of it, too—Dan "Beaker" Stuck, Brian Bucciarelli, and Harry Bricker, who started out filling water bottles for us and then went on to join the training staff of the Philadelphia Flyers for twenty seasons. Everyone who was a part of that team played a role. And that could have been my biggest takeaway from winning that year.

A month into that summer I got a call from Bob Clarke asking if I was interested in going to Switzerland for a few weeks with Brian Dobbin and Murray Craven to train with a Swiss pro team. Andy Murray, who coached there before coming to the Flyers coaching staff, set the whole thing up. I believe at the time the Flyers may have been grooming us for a potential line. However, plans changed at the last minute and Murray Craven went to train with a different Swiss team while Brian Dobbin and I stayed in Rapperswil, training with a Division II team.

We were told we'd be staying in a nice apartment with access to a car. Not quite the case. When we arrived we were picked up at the airport by head coach Alex Andjelic—a huge figure in European hockey—and dropped off in what felt like the middle of nowhere. We spent the first two nights in a thirty-year-old mobile home in mid-August during a heat wave with no air-conditioning. Perfect! You would never have met two more miserable human beings in your life. We were clearly North American spoiled. Sadly, at first we didn't fully appreciate the great opportunity it was to be there. We were too stupefied by the fact that there was no ice served in the soft drinks and we could only find a four-day-old *USA Today* newspaper. Once we started to actually train on and off the ice, many of those petty inconveniences didn't seem to matter as much. By the end of our trip we'd had five fantastic days of altitude training at a mountain resort in Arosa, in the Alps, which gave us an edge at training camp.

When I returned, I was finally ready to challenge for a spot on Philadelphia's roster. During that training camp I developed a friendship with Tim Kerr. Like me he was an undrafted player, but had signed as an unrestricted free agent four years before I came along. Kerr's previous season had been a spectacular one, with 58 goals. In fact, with that 1986–1987 season, he had just achieved four consecutive years with 50-plus goals. He missed the playoffs when a shoulder injury kept him off the ice. He was still in physio at the camp and became another mentor. He'd walk by and tap his pocket as if to say, "Your spot on the team is in the pocket."

The Flyers had a preseason game against the New Jersey Devils in Richmond, Virginia. Jamie Huscroft and I got into a fight halfway through the game and I ended up with a torn ligament in my right knee.

I knew right away it was really bad. I felt it pop and it just started swelling up. That injury notwithstanding, it was a good fight and I think I did okay. I was taken to the emergency room of the nearest hospital, still in my equipment. A short time later Jamie shows up. Turns out I wasn't the only one to come away hurting from that fight. Huscroft was a pretty good fighter, but he had broken his hand. We had just beaten the crap out of each other and here we were sitting in the waiting room, having a conversation in our uniforms.

"How's your hand?" I asked.

"Good. Hope your knee's okay."

"Yeah, thanks."

The knee was worse than I thought, though. I called my parents from the hospital, and unlike the preseason game in Rochester, when I didn't mention my fight with Andy Ristau, this call I couldn't avoid mentioning what had happened. One of the Richmond doctors ended up talking to my dad and mentioned to him that the injury could be career ending—without mentioning a word to me. My dad spared me that detail until well after Dr. John Gregg, the Flyers chief orthopedic surgeon, had reevaluated my knee back in Philadelphia.

They drove down first thing in the morning from Toronto and met me at the hospital. My father had been working all night and only had a couple hours' rest, but he arrived just after I had surgery. Funny, I don't ever remember having an in-depth talk about the options. I was in the hands of the Philadelphia Flyers with a complete rupture of my ACL, a torn meniscus, and a strained MCL. Dr. Gregg said, "Trust me, you'll be good as new in a few hours," and I guess I did trust him. He had a reputation for being a little different in the medical field. This doctor had a strut to him that I'd never seen before. He was not lacking confidence. He was also a lieutenant commander in the Naval Reserve, which may have had something to do with it. He decided to try a fairly new procedure on me. A young man had sadly just died from a motorcycle accident, and as I was lying on a gurney, ready to go under, the doctor picked up with tongs a thick piece of muscle.

"Take a look at your new knee," he said.

I got queasy, to say the least. That's the last thing I remember before I went out. With this new type of surgery, the doctor was able to rebuild my knee with the strongest tendon in the body, the Achilles. Even so, my biggest concern after the operation was that for the rest of my career, I would have to wear a bulky knee brace, like so many other players who had similar injuries. I asked the doctor about wearing a brace.

"Well, do you want to wear a brace?" he asked.

"No," I said.

"Then don't wear one," he told me.

For a lot of players who'd had bad injuries, he believed that the knee braces became more of a mental thing than a physical one. He later assured me that my leg would be as good as new, that I'd be able to run the New York City Marathon when I was fifty. He was right: I actually ran the New York City Marathon when I was forty-seven.

It wasn't an easy recovery, though. The pain was excruciating. I was released from the hospital within a couple of days and told my rehab would fall between six and eight months. The Flyers flew me home for a week with a removable cast.

Seven days of Greek cooking left me ready for a vigorous rehabilitation upon my return. I worked with Philly trainer and physical conditioning coach Pat Croce. Pat started his career as a physical therapist and ran a very successful sports medicine clinic at the time. He was able to parlay the sales of that clinic into an empire that included ownership of the NBA Philadelphia 76ers. He also had a black belt in Tae Kwon Do, so we all knew he could kick the shit out of anyone of us if push came to shove. We rarely gave him any lip. Days after my return, he put me on a rowing machine, which shocked me. I figured I'd be looking at a few leg lifts and massages for the first two weeks. It couldn't have been further from the truth with Pat. My good knee was doing the work on the rower while my hurt knee was strapped to the empty rowing seat of another machine next to me. With every forward-and-back movement, my hurt knee was there gliding alongside. Croce had me doing a hard twenty minutes of one-legged rows to start, and we increased that quickly. Then it was off to the VersaClimber for another painful twelve minutes. It was an aggressive approach that I never saw coming. Pat's belief was my good leg was "talking" to my bad knee. He believed in neurological health and that my injured knee would reap benefits from signals coming from my healthy leg. Who was I to argue? In fact, to this day my reconstructed knee is the stronger and tighter one. Because of Pat's rehab methods, I was able to resume my career in a little over five months.

I also got to rehab with team superstar Tim Kerr, who was yet again dealing with a bad shoulder. I cannot express what having Tim Kerr beside me during this difficult time meant to me, how he helped shape my attitude. Tim was one of the greatest goal scorers in our game, but unfortunately injuries plagued him from reaching historic numbers. Tim had a soft spot for me that I'll never forget. He made a point of telling me that he and I shared a similar story. Both OHL grads who went undrafted and both slow starters to the pro game. What a gift Tim gave me by sharing his story. We would leave physio together and kids would come up to him asking for his autograph. He would sign his name and then, at some point, he started passing the paper to me, asking me to sign, too. The first time he did, I wasn't sure what to do. "They don't want my signature, they want yours," I said.

"No, no, no, you're going to be a Philadelphia Flyer, so you need to sign it," he assured me. So I signed it and he looked at my signature in pure disgust.

"What the hell is that?" he asked.

"I don't know. My autograph?" I said.

"That's not an autograph, that is chicken scratch. The kids have to be able to read it or it's useless," he replied. "Go home tonight and work on a new one."

Not wanting to disappoint, I went back to the hotel and worked on a brand-new signature. For hours I dotted the *i* and made sure the *K* was legible. I was so petrified by what Tim had said that I totally revamped my autograph—that's the influence those type of veterans had on me.

As expected, the Flyers sent me back to Hershey in February. I played the last twenty-eight games on my rebuilt knee, finishing with 12 goals, 15 assists, and 19 penalty minutes. We finished second in our division and beat the third-place Utica Devils in five games. Then we played the Adirondack Red Wings, who finished 10 points ahead of us. The Wings' coach was Bill Dineen, who I had great respect for. After we won the first three games, he didn't dress his two top scorers, Murray Eaves and Joe Murphy, because he didn't like the way they were playing in the series. Benching their top players gave us a pretty comfortable feeling going into the fourth game. Only a few pro hockey teams had ever come back from a 3–0 deficit. We knew of the 1975 Islanders as the latest, but none of us knew it had happened before in the AHL, with the Rochester Americans coming back against Cleveland. Ironically, Bill Dineen was on the losing side of that series. We clearly got way ahead of ourselves losing 6–3 in Game 4. Then they won the next two games. Now we were facing elimination for the first time, with the series tied, and we're playing in Adirondack. We just couldn't seal it up and the game went to overtime. The deciding goal came from Wings forward Adam Graves. (I didn't know it at the time, of course, but he and I would one day play some big playoff games again, though on the same team.) Seven games in this series, and six of them decided by just one goal. No one remembers that. Everyone just knows we blew a 3–0 playoff series lead. I ended up with 4 goals and 5 assists in the series, which didn't feel like much of an accomplishment.

After the loss in Adirondack, the Flyers kept Glen Seabrooke, Brian

Dobbin, Shaun Sabol, and me back in Glens Falls, New York, because our parent club was in the conference finals against the Canadiens and they wanted us to meet up. They hired a stretch limo for the four-hour drive to Montreal. We walked into the hotel where the Flyers were staying and went into team meetings with Captain Dave Poulin, Tim Kerr, and Rick Tocchet, among others. Ilkka Sinisalo had suffered an injury and there were some whispers to the effect that if he couldn't play one of their call-ups could be summoned for action. I had a tough time falling asleep that night. All of a sudden I'm facing the chance to play in my first NHL game—a playoff game in the Montreal Forum. Selfishly speaking, it was unfortunate for me that Ilkka Sinisalo, with his shoulder issues, felt strong enough to play the remainder of the series. Despite the six-game series loss to Montreal, it was a great experience. Watching for the first time the intensity of a Stanley Cup playoff series from the inside is something I'll never forget. Ron Hextall put the cherry on top when he attacked Montreal's Chris Chelios in the dying minutes of the series.

I trained all summer and was now heading into my fifth Flyers training camp. At the end of camp everyone told me I was going to make the lineup. but at the hotel in Philly I received a call from Bob Clarke, who told me I was going to the Washington Capitals.

"I didn't even know I was on waivers," I said to Bob.

There were still things about the business of hockey that I had to learn, and one of them was this: if a player has three years pro experience, he has to be either protected or exposed in a waiver. Because one season I had played 10 games for the AHL Hershey Bears before I was sent to Juniors in North Bay, it counted for one pro season. Clarke said he knew the rules, but didn't expect anyone to claim me on waivers. Maybe that's why he didn't make me aware of the waiver situation, to draw less attention. Washington GM David Poile put in the claim, and just like that, I became a member of the Washington Capitals. Clarke was pissed off because they had invested so much time and energy developing me. He felt I wasn't quite ready to play at the NHL level, but knew it was going to happen at some point. In the end he was happy for me, though. He felt the Flyers didn't have any right to keep me in the minor leagues if some other NHL team wanted me. As for me, I had some very mixed feelings. I truly wanted to become a Philadelphia Flyer. After five hard years of building something for that team, it was over in a matter of minutes. I was sad for that but was now guaranteed to start my season in the NHL.

CHAPTER 4

Washington

On October 6, 1989, two nights after Washington GM David Poile claimed me, I played my first NHL game at the Capital Center. If I wasn't already nervous enough, the team we were playing was the Flyers. But before that, I met with Poile and his director of player personnel, the late Jack Button. Jack was the man behind me getting claimed on waivers. Not much was said but I remember Jack telling me, "You're the next Bert Olmstead." "Who?" I asked. Jack went on to say, "A little before your time, but that's a very good compliment about a very honest hockey player." I said, "Great, Mr. Button, but how about someone more current, like John Tonelli?" He laughed.

I remember going into the practice facility and finding my practice jersey in my stall. It had "Kypreos" with the number 9 printed on it. I didn't think too much of it until I saw the same number on my new helmet and garment bag. That was my official number, which had been randomly assigned. It was the same number my father had insisted I get when I first started playing. Gordie Howe. Bobby Hull. Maurice Richard. I might have been a little out of my league.

I didn't know anybody on the Capitals except former North Bay Centennials teammate Kevin Hatcher. His last game in North Bay, I'd asked him for his game stick as a memento. He signed it "See you one day in the NHL." And here we were. I loved being a Washington Capital and appreciated the opportunity they gave me, but it wasn't an easy transition. Trying so hard to be a Flyer for so many years still felt fresh. But that is the business part of hockey.

In that first game, against the Flyers, the hardest part was that my ex-teammates were chirping and having fun with me in the warm-up. I had just spent a month with all of those guys. It might have been easier if they were assholes, but they had all been encouraging when I was with them. Now, as their opponent, they started ribbing me. Still, they weren't all bad. "Take it easy, Kypreos," Tocchet kept saying. Mike Bullard noticed my nervousness, too, and reminded me to "settle down." Tim Kerr gave me a wink during warm-up as if to say, "You've arrived." How was I supposed to play hard against those guys?

I joined a strong team in Washington. The Capitals finished first in their division the year before and had a good combination of forwards with offensive skill, led by Dino Ciccarelli and Mike Ridley. The Caps had one of the best blue lines in the league, too, including future Hockey Hall of Famers Rod Langway and Scott Stevens. My job was to establish myself as an everyday player; I needed to show the right mix of scoring and toughness. That was the challenge.

I didn't get much in terms of individual instruction from head coach Bryan Murray. He did mention I'd start on a line with Michal Pivonka and 1980 U.S. gold medalist Dave Christian and then we'd figure it out as we went along. I managed to get my one good scoring opportunity, but my former Flyer training camp roommate Ken Wregget made a good glove save. More chirping, this time from Wreggs—"Nice try, but I got your number." We were down 3–2 halfway through and my ice time diminished. We won 5–3 and although I didn't play very much it was a memorable game nonetheless. Because I'd become a Capital and arrived in Washington so fast, my parents didn't have a chance to come to my first NHL game. There was no way they were going to miss watching it, though. They drove all over Toronto that night trying to find a restaurant with a satellite dish willing to show them the game. The Hickory House restaurant had a dish and they found it very strange that my parents wanted to watch a Flyers-Capitals game. The Toronto Blue Jays were in the MLB playoffs and everyone there was piled into one room watching that game while my parents were watching our game in another. Steve Dryden, who was the editor of the *Hockey News*, happened to be there watching the Jays game. When he saw my parents along with my aunts and uncles being very emotional and loud, watching a hockey game in another room, it piqued his curiosity. The Blue Jays were in the ALCS series vs. Oakland, down 2–0 in the series, with reliable Jimmy Key on the mound. "Why are you the only people not cheering on the Jays?" Steve asked my dad. He replied, "It's my son's first NHL game." My father was clearly proud. Steve was so moved by my parents that he decided to write an article about them in the *Hockey News*. He described my mother as a black-eyed beauty, something we teased her endlessly about for years. Clearly, she made an impression on Steve.

My next two games were also at home, which helped me settle in and get my bearings. By that point all of the single guys on the team had roommates, so I found an apartment for myself. I had gone from making $25,000 a year to $110,000, and even though that was a huge hike in pay I couldn't exactly go crazy with my money. It had been a bouncy ride to the NHL that came with no guarantees, so I saved every dime I could.

That first road trip with the Capitals was surreal, like an out-of-body experience. I'd seen all the famous arenas on television my entire life, and now I was playing in them. The Forum in Montreal was one of the most historic in the NHL. When we played there, I felt like I could still hear the voice of the legendary Danny Gallivan. I'd been there once to support the Flyers in the playoffs, but I didn't get the chance to actually play. For a kid who grew up loving hockey, it was mind-blowing to play in the same buildings as my heroes.

Five days after playing in Montreal, I played for the first time in Toronto. That was a huge thrill. I remember coming up to Maple Leaf Gardens before the game and it was one of those pivotal moments—an actual dream come true. I remember thinking about the night I went with my dad to my first Leaf game, and going to the Leafs' open practice and receiving that stick from Jack Valiquette. It all came back to me.

I didn't get much sleep the night before and couldn't wait to go for the morning skate. From the stands I had watched Darryl Sittler, Mike Palmateer, Lanny McDonald—guys I idolized growing up—and now I was about to play against the Leafs in Maple Leaf Gardens. I don't know what the final count was in terms of cousins, aunts, uncles, and friends who showed up for the game; it felt like a hundred.

I only wish the game itself had been a cause for celebration. We lost 8–4, blowing a 4–1 lead. We practiced the next day in Toronto before departing for Calgary. I remember our coach, Bryan Murray, telling us Leaf forward and ex-Capital Lou Franceschetti brazenly asked him why his team didn't hit anymore. That enraged Brian and in the dressing room he couldn't wait to tell us what had happened, how weak we appeared to Lou. My euphoria about playing in Maple Leaf Gardens quickly subsided and the harsh reality of needing to perform to keep my job settled in. I made some quick calls to say goodbye and jumped onto a very quiet bus. Just like that, we were off to the airport for the next game.

It wasn't too long before I experienced my next NHL first—a fight ten days later in Washington against Robert Dirk. Our top scorer, Dino, went into the corner with the six-four Dirk and looked like a little kid. Dino tried to bump him back to gain a step, but Dirk stayed on him and fed him a cross-check, a slash, and a high stick. When Dirk drove Dino's head into the glass from behind, I went right at him. Dirk easily had twenty pounds on me, but at that point it was too late to matter. I didn't get off to a great start, but I landed three or four lefts that pushed Dirk back and cut him open above his right eye. Like your first NHL goal, you never forget your first NHL fight. Even though that fight would be the first of many in my career, I wasn't the type of player who would look back at tapes and study how I could have done better. I truly didn't want fighting to define my career, nor did I consider myself a true heavyweight. I was more of a middleweight who once in a while would be dumb enough to take on a heavyweight.

When I first got traded to Washington, my father thought it would be a good idea to contact a fellow Greek. He asked me to call Peter Anas, the son of a man my father had met when he first arrived in Canada. I was never one to call people I'd never met out of the blue, but I had such a strong trust for my dad as a good judge of character that I never questioned calling Peter. Being new to Washington as I was, Peter and his wife, Deme, were so helpful in getting me acclimated to life around the area. They even gave me a key to their home to use until I found a place of my own. I knew if I ever needed anything they'd help me out in an instant. Nine years later, when I was working the Stanley Cup Final as a sideline broadcaster in the 1998 playoffs in Washington, Peter and his five-year-old son, Sam, came to visit me during the Capitals morning skate. I introduced him to Don Cherry, who was there as part of *Hockey Night in Canada*'s broadcast. In true Grapes fashion, he made sure that Sam got a signed goalie stick from Olaf Kölzig. Ollie signed the stick "To Sam, your friend." From that moment, Sam fell in love with the game. He later went on to earn first-team All-American honours, leading his Quinnipiac Bobcats to an ECAC Championship in 2016. He then signed his first pro contract with the Minnesota Wild organization. He had that stick in his room and was inspired by it years after Ollie took the time to sign it.

It's funny how Greeks seem to find each other. I met another Greek family in my first year in D.C.: Chris and Debbie Zourdos, who remain one of the longest-reigning season-ticket holders for the Washington Capitals. Chris owned one of the most successful Chrysler dealerships in Maryland. He had rented a suite at one of the Capitals games and invited some kids from a church youth group to join him. He put in a request for me to come up to the suite to visit the kids after the game. Much like Peter and Deme, Chris and Debbie opened their home to me. They had two young and impressionable boys who liked having a Washington Capital playing ministicks in the basement with them. It was always important to me to have strong families around after being away from my own.

In a very short time I felt grounded in Washington, and that had everything to do with the Anas and Zourdos families. They opened their homes to me and I got to know their children; it was as if I had become an extension of their families. I never took that lightly. Both Chris and Debbie Zourdos were koumbaros at my wedding, which is similar to a best man. As a couple, they became godparents to my first child, Zachary.

I was adjusting to life in the National Hockey League, but I was having difficulty scoring goals like I could in Junior or the American League. I don't know whether it was the reconstructed knee, but I lost a little bit of my ability to pivot. The knee was still strong and sturdy, but it was sore—I just didn't feel quite as comfortable as I did before the surgery.

I was in and out of the lineup for about the first six weeks and didn't register a point. It took 13 games before I did. I assisted on the final goal of a game, scored by Dale Hunter on the power play, in a 7–4 loss to Pittsburgh. I also had a ten-minute misconduct in the game for some rough stuff with Phil Bourque in the first period. It was good to finally get that first point behind me, but it's hard to feel good about a game like this one.

We played the Penguins again the next night, this time in Pittsburgh. I was finishing my checks and trying to wreak a little havoc on the ice. Mario Lemieux, who was owning the league back then with Wayne Gretzky, chirped me. His Penguins down 4–0, and feeling a little frustrated, Mario tells me, "Hey, Kypreos, why don't you go back to the minors?" When I got back to the bench I said to the guys, "Did you hear that? Mario knows my name!" I was so excited. We were winning the game 4–1, and with just seventeen seconds left in the third period, all hell broke loose with four different fights on the ice. I paired off with Gord Dineen and both of us received a five-minute major and a game misconduct. In all, there were almost 100 penalty minutes, and six game misconducts.

Four days later in Detroit, I scored my first NHL goal—I'd had to wait a whopping 15 games into my NHL career for this moment. It happened early in the third period, in a game we were controlling with a 2–0 lead. I was in the high slot when my teammate Doug Wickenheiser attempted a wraparound. I crashed the net whacking at the rebound and the puck went right up under the crossbar, beating Sam St. Laurent.

I loved my goal for so many reasons. First, my mom and dad were there. Second, it was against an original-six team. Third, it was assisted by the late Doug Wickenheiser and Alan May, both of whom I had a ton of respect for. Last, I fought for every inch of that goal, driving hard to the net. I kept the stick and gave it to my dad. The Caps presented me with my first-goal plaque a week later. But the fact that it took 15 games to happen was very frustrating. Being in and out of the lineup was equally frustrating. I went from a guy who could score at the Junior and AHL levels with consistency to virtually nothing in the NHL. I understood it was the hardest league in the world to score in, but that never made me feel better. Even today, that hasn't changed.

The Capitals were midrange in the NHL, a kind of a meat-and-potatoes team, and were struggling with a 9-11-4 record. But once I got that first goal, I started to get a bit more confidence. In my next 10 games, I had 3 more goals and 3 assists.

We started our first game of 1990 on New Year's Day in Washington against the Los Angeles Kings. It was my first chance to play against Wayne Gretzky. I remember seeing the Kings bus come in underground and there was a buzz because Gretzky was in town. When the Kings equipment was off-loaded, Wayne's sticks were separated from the rest of the team's. L.A. trainers would personally carry his four sticks to the dressing room like they were carrying nuclear launch codes. In the history of the game, no trainers treated sticks better than the L.A. Kings did Wayne's Easton sticks. He had just started a new stick deal, leaving Titan's wooden stick and changing to the Easton aluminum. Everyone talked about that silver Easton hockey stick. It reminded me of the movie *The Natural*, where Roy Hobbs had a bat nicknamed Wonderboy. There were photographers and tons of media waiting to talk to the best hockey player in the world.

I scored our second goal early in the game, helping us to a 4–1 lead. But then in the third period the Great One took over. The Kings scored six unanswered goals, including two by Wayne. L.A. won 7–4. Although it was a tough loss, I was one of the three stars that night along with Gretzky. That was a highlight for me.

Two days later we were in New York playing the Rangers and I got into a fight with Kris King. It was a good fight, though I probably took more than I gave. The next day at practice our coach, Bryan Murray, couldn't skate over to me fast enough. He was really pleased with what I did against Kris. I guess Lou Franceschetti's comments from that game in Toronto were still ringing in his ears—we were still lacking some pushback and other teams were taking a lot of liberties with us.

Bryan Murray was a no-nonsense hard-nosed coach. He'd sometimes chirp other players a little too much, but that's just how competitive he was. One time we were playing Boston and Ken "The Rat" Linseman had had just about enough of Bryan Murray yelling at him. Just before the second period started, as Bryan was walking on the ice towards our team's bench, Ken gave him a good whack in the back of the leg with his stick—not hard enough to start a melee, but hard enough to make us laugh. We could hear Bryan yelp! But Bryan never made a big deal about it.

I was thrilled that I had received good feedback from my coach and made it a point to give the Capitals more of the pushback they needed. The next home game, the Canucks' Garth Butcher and I were both given a ten-minute misconduct in the first period for some pretty serious chirping, and I got five minutes for fighting Ronnie Stern in the second period.

While that part of my game was ramping up, the rest of it was on a downswing. My knee was strong, but beginning to bother me as I started to feel an uncomfortable clicking. We discovered that some of the staples from my surgery were starting to loosen up, so I had a procedure to remove the staples. My knee was sturdy enough without them. That shut me down for a little bit, though. Then, when I was ready to resume play, Bryan Murray was fired as head coach. I was told to go get some playing time in the AHL in Baltimore and expect to come back.

Doug MacLean, formerly my Capitals assistant coach, had recently been named head coach there. He'd replaced Terry Murray (Bryan Murray's brother) when he had been brought up from the AHL to take over the head-coaching duties in Washington. Bryan Murray had been fired after 46 games. The Caps had been struggling with an 18-24-4 record when the organization made the changes. What a family dilemma. Fire one brother and hire another, but it probably made for some interesting Thanksgivings.

It worked out well for me in the AHL after my surgery, though, because I enjoyed playing for Doug. All the young guys in Washington had enjoyed Doug MacLean as a coach. He had the perfect temperament and sense of humour to play off a very emotional Bryan Murray. That's why they were lifelong friends well after their years in Washington. Years later, Doug and I worked together for Sportsnet. We always had a great rapport and often laughed about our time together in Washington and Baltimore. He was a great coach and very approachable. Many coaches are not. He kept the guys light when it was needed, but could also bring the hammer down to get the best out of his players. I'm not surprised he had twenty-five years in the business as either an assistant coach, coach, general manager, or president.

MacLean told me right away that he knew I wouldn't be there with the team for very long—that the Capitals would bring me up again. But you don't know how these things will work and I just tried to stay in the moment. I was starting to have fun there. After being in and out of the lineup with Washington, it felt great to play fifteen to eighteen minutes a game and get some power-play time. It was a good group of guys, too. Mark Ferner, Bob Mason, and Doug Wickenheiser set a nice tone for younger talented guys to feel at ease. Mike Richard, Chris Felix, Steve Maltais, and Tyler Larter were all top Junior scorers. John Druce had 15 goals in 26 games before lighting up the NHL playoff world. I totaled 6 goals and 5 assists in 14 games, which brought us to the end of the season and the playoffs.

We finished third in the South Division. In the first round we faced Adirondack—it seemed I was always squaring off against them. This time it went our way, in six games. But I didn't get to see it through. One game into the next round, against Rochester, Doug told me I was being called up by Washington, along with goaltender Bob Mason. I had four goals in those seven playoff games and felt good again. Now I was on my way to Madison Square Garden to join the Capitals in their second round of the playoffs. The New York Rangers had finished first in what used to be called the Patrick Division, 7 points ahead of Washington. The Caps had defeated New Jersey four games to two in the opening round of the playoffs to get here. Since becoming head coach, Terry Murray had guided the Caps to an 18-14-2 record in 34 games, including two wins over the Rangers for their last two regular-season matches. Everything was set up for a tough series. The Capitals had lost the first game of the series 7–3 when they called me back up.

This was a big opportunity for me. Everybody was watching this series on TV, and some games were on *Hockey Night in Canada*. Playing my first Stanley Cup playoff game was as memorable as my first-ever NHL game. It had a different emotional tension compared to the regular season. MSG had great energy. It had been fifty years since their last Stanley Cup victory and the crowd was wild. I hit everything with a Ranger jersey that moved. I knew what I was there to do: provide some pushback so that our skilled guys weren't getting as run over as they had been in Game 1. I guess it worked well enough because we won the next four games, taking the series in five. I also got to witness a playoff phenomenon called "Druce on the Loose." A scoring stretch that was one of the best in Stanley Cup history: 9 goals in 5 games against the Rangers. In total, 14 goals in 15 playoff games. A once-in-a-lifetime run that most players could only dream of. The Capitals enjoyed the notoriety John Druce gave our team with features in *Sports Illustrated* and *Hockey Night in Canada* covering his spectacular goal streak.

Unfortunately, we lost Dino Ciccarelli and Kevin Hatcher to knee injuries for the third round and that cost us dearly in the conference final against Boston. The Bruins had finished first overall in the conference, more than 23 points ahead of us, and had beaten us in two of three regular-season games. We had another uphill battle ahead, but this time we couldn't get it done. Boston beat us in four straight. I scored my one and only Stanley Cup playoff goal in the final game, but clearly it wasn't enough. I did, however, stay in the lineup after getting called up, playing every playoff game, which would help to set me up for a good following season.

It's always disappointing to lose, but I did come away from the experience with something valuable. I learned how much everything is magnified in the Stanley Cup playoffs. The energy on the ice, the intensity. Every player's focus increases tenfold. It is a sprint, at a high level, fueled by desperation to win the next game. As a kid, I'd dreamed about getting to that place, but until you are there, you can't imagine what it's like.

And there was a silver lining to the end, also. Even though we'd been eliminated, the Capitals had gone further than ever before in the franchise's history. Once the disappointment subsided, we could be proud of ourselves. We had a team celebration two days later at a bar in Georgetown. We all arrived in limos, enjoyed some drinks, and everybody seemed to have a good time.

The limos were waiting for us afterwards and I remember jumping in one of them. There were four of my teammates already inside and a young woman they had met at the bar. Everything seemed to be fine, nothing out of the ordinary. We were waiting for some other teammates, so I hopped out to grab some food. When I got back with bags of chicken, the woman was still there. Everyone was laughing and having a great time. We ate and then left to go home. That was it.

Two days later, there was a story on the front page of the *Washington Post* reporting that several of my teammates were facing allegations by the woman in the limo. It didn't seem like it was real. While I was there I saw nothing like that. Several people, along with me, were asked to testify in front of a DC Superior Court grand jury to determine if there was enough evidence to indict. The entire thing was surreal. I couldn't believe that our night in Georgetown had become front-page news.

I was summoned into the office of General Manager David Poile and he was clearly troubled. I didn't know what to say, but I tried to tell him that somehow we would get through this as an organization. But it was a mess. The night that started as a major highlight in Poile's career had turned into his worst nightmare. There were thousands of angry letters addressed to the team. Fans turned on the Capitals overnight, calling the players pigs and wondering why we had shamed the city of Washington, particularly after our magnificent playoff run. David told me he was aware that I had been in the limo and that I needed legal representation immediately. I was also told not to speak to any of my teammates. The entire thing was devastating for everyone involved.

Because I had been interviewed by the police and was going to be asked to testify in front of a grand jury, I couldn't go back to Canada, where I spent my summers. Horrible letters were left for me in my mailbox where I was living. It's not that hard for people to find out where you live. Media from tabloid magazines and TV shows camped outside my building, waiting to see if they could get me to say something. My mom was calling me every day wondering what was happening. I had to reassure her everything would be fine.

I testified in front of about twenty-five people, many of them women. I told them I was there with the players and the woman in the limo for a short period of time before I went to get some food, and didn't witness anything wrong. I didn't hear the woman scream for help or hear her say she wanted to leave, nor did she appear uncomfortable. I told the jury if I knew any woman was in trouble, I would have helped her. Even in the presence of veteran players, of course I would have done something to help.

Then things got even stranger. The *Washington Post* erroneously reported that I told an unnamed source that I had gotten into the limo with a "bucket of chicken" and left when I saw the woman struggling with the players. The headline was "Capital Says He Witnessed a Struggle." This could not have been further from the truth and I have no idea how they got that information. Because I was not allowed to communicate with any of the players, I couldn't tell them the story wasn't true. I wanted to call the newspaper and set the story straight, but was advised not to. The Caps just wanted the attention to go away.

I had letters from women who had read the article praising me for testifying against my teammates, which I didn't do. I felt bad about how people had been misled by the story. The entire thing was a disaster.

Ultimately, the grand jury declined to move the case forward due to insufficient evidence. Afterwards, I was finally able to talk to my teammates. And as an organization, we started to heal. But it was clear that irreparable damage had been done to our team, on and off the ice.

In the off-season, the St. Louis Blues made an aggressive offer on Scott Stevens, who was a restricted free agent: a four-year deal worth more than $5 million, including a $1.4 million signing bonus. It made him the highest-paid defenceman in the NHL. He had been the heart of our team. The Caps decided not to match the offer. It was a lot of money, of course, but I believe there had been so much turmoil that, for a number of reasons, the Caps stepped aside. We still had Rod Langway, our captain and a two-time Norris Trophy winner, but we were shocked. If you ask me, letting Scott Stevens walk was perhaps one of the worst decisions in NHL franchise history. Our team never really recovered from losing him. Scott Stevens should have retired a Washington Capital.

It was the strangest off-season of my career, but I did my best to focus on the future. I went into the 1990–1991 season feeling confident in my game. I had some great playoff experience under my belt and felt I was ready to be an everyday player, and make a difference. I also had a new roommate this year, Steve Leach, a great guy. He loved when my parents visited because he got to eat amazing homemade food. He got a kick out of watching my parents preparing meals. My mom would send my dad out to get groceries, but then would have to send him right back to the store for items she'd forgotten to mention. This would always happen. My dad would joke that he couldn't even take his coat off and Steve would laugh. He'd say, "You guys sure take your meals seriously." Steve claimed he gained five pounds every time they visited.

I knew I would have to fight more this year to secure my place on the team. It didn't take long for that to happen. In our second game of the season, against Detroit, I scored a goal and registered my first fight, this one against Joey Kocur, one of the all-time toughest fighters in NHL history. Dale Hunter warned me to always be careful with Kocur: "He cracks helmets with punches." Joey and Bob Probert on that Detroit team were known as the Bruise Brothers. As we squared off, I was just thinking, *Please, don't let him get started.* I just got in tight, made it look good, and got the hell out. There are some fights you just don't look forward to. Kocur and Probert could go down as the toughest one-two in hockey history. At the time you're thinking the only upside to fighting either one of them was living to tell about it. But of course it was more. As long as Kocur doesn't embarrass you, the upside is a lift for your team. Dale Hunter reminded me of that after the second period.

A good fight had other benefits, too. If you weren't scoring, it was another way to get on the highlight reel. The hot sports show in Toronto at the time was *Sportsline* with Jim Tatti and Mark Hebscher, which showed highlights of all the games. I knew they showed the fights, so I wanted all my buddies to watch. It was all good. I didn't back down from anybody, despite giving up size and weight compared to the heavyweights. I fought Todd Ewen, Gary Nylund, Darin Kimble, Lyle Odelein, Jay Caufield, Mark Janssens, Scott Stevens, Ken Daneyko, Mark Tinordi, Jim Kyte, and Shawn Cronin that season. It helped me gain a bit of a reputation, which in turn bought me some room on the ice. I finished the year playing every single game that season with the exception of one. I had nine goals, three of them game winners. It was no surprise my penalty minutes went up significantly with 196.

I remember the Scott Stevens fight in particular. It happened the first time we played the Blues that season. Going into that game, Coach Terry Murray was worried that Scott was just going to own us. Terry didn't want us to be buddy-buddy with him and show him any respect. I knew I was one of the guys he was talking to. How did I know? Well, for one, he was staring right at me when he said it. I had a ton of respect for Scott— who didn't have respect for him? But your allegiance is to your hockey team. So when early in the second period, with the score 2–1 in our favour, Scott and I went shoulder to shoulder in a corner, I couldn't back down. We bumped each other again before we dropped gloves and threw three or four good shots at each other, wrestling until the linesman broke it up. I had just battled one of the toughest defenceman in the league, a guy who bled for the Washington Capitals, and now he was bleeding for the Blues. Scott was in a very different situation from me. He spent eight years fighting for the Capitals and in one split second he's fighting them for his new Blues teammates. Pretty good message to a team who just made him the first million-dollars-a-year defenceman in history. From the box, I snuck a glance at him. He gave me a little grin and winked because he knew I had to fight him. It was a nice moment, having a character guy like Scott recognize me for doing that. That part of the game doesn't make the highlight reel. The game ended in a 3–3 tie.

I also remember the fight against Shawn Cronin, who was nicknamed "Cronin the Barbarian" for fairly obvious reasons. Midway in the first period of a game in Winnipeg, on March 8, 1991, Jets forward Brent Ashton was coming up the boards and tried to cut inside of me. I dropped my shoulder and hit him. He spun in the air and landed face first on the ice, blood streaming from his nose. As soon as play resumed, Cronin fought me as a response. I was later told by our assistant coach, John Perpich, that Ashton was in surgery to repair a broken jaw. I felt sick to my stomach. By the end of the game I had the whole Jets team chasing me. They were fuming and I was apprehensive leaving the building, to be honest. TSN was broadcasting the game and I was told Gary Green was screaming that it was a vicious, dirty hit. I guess referee Paul Stewart could tell I was rattled and he really helped me out. He told me even though it was a high hit, it was with my shoulder and not an elbow. Years later, Paul gave his version of the hit in a column he wrote for the website *Hockey Buzz*. He said that it was a clean hit by the standards of the time, though today it would be considered a head shot. Right after I fought, Winnipeg's Laurie Boschman hit one of our guys, and our coach demanded Paul do something about it. According to his article, "although Kypreos's hit was clean and I had told the Winnipeg side as much, the Jets' response was exactly what was to be expected. They hadn't crossed the line yet, either." We won the game 2–1. I called Brent a few days later to apologize and, man, it was a tough call to make. He wasn't very happy with me and I understood that.

One of my better memories that season happened around Christmas in a game we played in Chicago. There were a whole bunch of autograph seekers waiting for Dino and Rod Langway, but a kid came up to me and asked if I would sign a hockey card of myself. I told him I didn't have one, that one didn't exist.

"Yeah, you do," he said.

"I'm pretty sure I don't have a hockey card," I said again. Then he shows me an O-Pee-Chee card of myself.

"Oh my God, I've got a hockey card!" I said. I gave the kid twenty dollars and kept the card.

That was a huge moment for me, having my picture on an O-Pee-Chee card. That year there were a whole bunch of card companies that started to compete with O-Pee-Chee, but the O-Pee-Chee cards with the bubble gum inside were what I remembered most as a kid growing up. I still love the feeling, even thinking about it now.

After Christmas our season continued to not go well and there was a threat we'd miss the playoffs. In late January the Flyers rag-dolled us 6–1. Despite Alan May and me fighting our way consistently to the penalty box, our team had the second-fewest penalty minutes in the league and David Poile wanted us to get tougher.

Right after that game, Poile traded a draft pick for John Kordic. The Leafs had run out of patience with him battling alcohol issues and fighting with his own teammates. We had all heard the stories coming from the Leafs players. This was so unlike Poile. He was one of the more conservative GMs in the league. Coming off the limousine incident, when public perception was so important, why Poile would gamble on such a troubled player was beyond my comprehension. Kordic was a train wreck, but desperate measures for desperate situations.

David and Terry met with the entire team before Kordic came and reassured us that he was focused on resuming his career and that he'd add a dimension to our group that would elicit fear in the other teams. We just weren't sure if the risk would outweigh the reward. But as a team, we were willing to give him a chance.

When Kordic came to the Caps, he was polite and outgoing. He brought a good balance to the dressing room, which had been generally low-key and reserved before. He addressed our team about his challenges and rehab, about trying to get better, and asked us to be patient. How could you not give a guy like that a chance?

Kordic did everything Poile had hoped; he fought early and often. In the 7 games he played he had over 100 penalty minutes. Two weeks after he was traded we went up against the Flyers again and needed to make the point that we weren't going to be bullied anymore. That game is considered one of the more violent games in hockey history, with almost 300 penalty minutes given. It was one brawl after another. Alan May, John Kordic, Al Iafrate, and I accumulated over 80 penalty minutes on this Sunday-matinee game in Washington. Thousands of Philly fans made the trip to watch the reckoning. There were fights in the stands, too. The coaches were screaming at each other. When Dale Hunter threw an elbow into Gord Murphy, my old Hershey Bears roommate, the tone was set.

In the 7 games that Kordic played, we only lost once. But things started to derail for him. He started showing up for morning practice with the same suit he'd worn to the previous night's game. His clothes were disheveled and torn, almost as if he had been fighting in his suit. He also made it a point to ask certain players, including me, to lend him some money. When that happened, we knew it was over for him. Washington released him. Sadly, less than two years later, John Kordic died in a hotel room of a heart attack due to drug use. He was just twenty-seven years old.

We made it to the playoffs, and through to the second round before we were knocked out. I had an assist in 7 games and 38 penalty minutes. Because of who I had fought that season, I knew I had established myself as a good middleweight enforcer. The coming year would carry an expectation to continue to fight. Once you gain a reputation, it's hard to lose it, one way or another. Heading into the 1991–1992 season, I was on the final year of my contract and knew I'd have to continue doing what I was doing to earn another. We began the season with an 8-2 record and continued playing well. We finished second in our division, 7 points behind the New York Rangers. But we were upset in the first round by Pittsburgh, which went on to win the Cup.

In 65 games that season (I had missed some here and there with injuries) I finished with 4 goals, 6 assists, and 206 penalty minutes. By the end of the season I felt pigeonholed on the fourth line. I asked Poile for more ice time. But with Kelly Miller, Randy Burridge, and Todd Krygier as left wingers it didn't look like there was going to be much room for me to move up. The team was also hoping Jeff Greenlaw, a first-round pick, would pan out. I knew I had an uphill climb if the Caps were ever going to see me as anything other than a fourth-line player. But I didn't have to wait long to find out if I was going to make an impact in Washington.

CHAPTER 5

Traded to Hartford

Not long after the playoffs ended I got a call from Caps GM David Poile. He told me I had been traded to the Hartford Whalers—the Caps were getting Mark Hunter and future considerations. My first move, from Philly to Washington, was on waivers. This was my first official trade.

The Whalers had a new GM in Brian Burke and this was also his first trade. He had worked for the Vancouver Canucks for five years as director of hockey operations and signed with Hartford as president/GM. He called me just after David and told me that I was his type of player and he was looking forward to having me on the team. Burkie liked tough hockey—he made that pretty clear. I went from making $110,000 to $300,000, which was just under the average for NHL contracts. I was happy to find another spot on a team and my focus was to go to training camp in great shape.

The Caps had a solid fan base, but that was not the case when I came to Hartford. The Whalers owner, Richard Gordon, had essentially just dismantled the franchise the season before, trading away fan favourites Ron Francis, Ulf Samuelsson, Mike Liut, Joel Quenneville, and Dave Tippett. Quite simply, Gordon wasn't popular with the fans because of these moves. Whatever Gordon was planning for the club, it was struggling in the short term. Once Francis and Samuelsson were dealt, the onus was on John Cullen and Zarley Zalapski to become the team's new superstars. It didn't happen. By the time I arrived, the crowds had dwindled from fifteen thousand a game to a mere eight thousand.

As the new GM, Burkie had his work cut out for him. One of the first things he did was change the Whalers uniforms from a bright green to the dominant blue colour that went back to the team's days in the World Hockey Association. It sounds like a trivial thing, but as players, we liked the change. It felt like the team was turning a corner. And it signaled to the fans that this was a different team. The second thing he did was change the cheer song for games. For years it had been "Brass Bonanza." It dated back to the WHA days. Our captain, Pat Verbeek, told him many of us supported the decision to get rid of it. I told him it sounded like the beginning of a game show.

In Washington I was seen as a one-dimensional enforcer, which made it challenging for me to contribute in more than one way. I was never on any specialty teams, but in Hartford I had a chance to kill penalties. Burke wanted my toughness, but with everything else ramped up. He encouraged me to take on a bigger role offensively with some time on the third line with a skilled player, Terry Yake. It was exactly what I wanted, more of an opportunity to see if I could still score.

We already had a tough lineup. Jim McKenzie, our heavyweight, had a reputation as one of the toughest guys in the league. It was a bit of a relief that I wouldn't be the only one called on to fight the big boys around the league. We also had physical players Mark Janssens, Doug Houda, Pat Verbeek, Randy Ladouceur, Adam Burt, and Jim Agnew. This tough-as-nails lineup was an introduction to Burkie's style of play. In his words, "Pugnacity. Testosterone. Truculence. And Belligerence." We were the first of his teams to have these qualities. Even our goalie, Sean Burke (no relation to Brian), could throw a good punch.

Our coach was Paul Holmgren, who had just been Philly's head coach for four years and assistant coach for three years before that. I knew him because of my time in the Flyers organization. He was a tough player in his career and a tough coach. He expected the same from us.

The toughness was there, but our team struggled all year. We lost our first 4 games, and after 10 had a record of 3-7. It was a harbinger of the rest of our season. We just did not have a very skilled team. In this situation you know that in the big picture you're not very good. But still, before every game you think, *This is going to be the one where we catch the opposition on an off night.* We didn't go into games thinking we were going to lose. We played hard and just tried to work well within the team concept. Sometimes, when teams aren't doing well, there can be selfish players. Maybe they're part of the problem to begin with, or maybe they think they can at least make themselves look good—that wasn't the case in Hartford.

Some fans let us know that they weren't happy with our performance. The dedicated, hardcore Whaler fans stood by us, but even they couldn't hide their disappointment. It became a bit of a joke among us players that every game felt like a road game, even the ones at home. But it wasn't funny—playing in a half-empty building is deflating. We tried to do everything we could to help boost attendance. I was always doing community events and volunteered in the community as much as I could. I made good friends away from the game. Local firefighter Dan Nolan and restaurant owner John Carbone were great to me. It doesn't hurt being friends with someone who can open up fire doors to the busiest bars, or the owner of the best restaurant in town. I was given the Fan Favorite Award. That was a big deal because in previous years it had been won by the team's stars, such as Ron Francis.

Hartford was a young team and a lot of the players were single. Jim McKenzie would organize NFL pools for Monday nights and a big group of players would watch together. My roommate, Geoff Sanderson, would be among us. He became the top scorer on the team with 40 goals. He was part of a new generation of players who could fly on the ice and was über skilled.

Brian Burke had hired Pierre McGuire as Paul Holmgren's assistant coach. Pierre had come from the Penguins and tried to play the good cop to Paul's bad cop. In a game in Hartford on New Year's Eve, against the Quebec Nordiques, we got off to a terrible start. A young Mats Sundin was owning us. Starting from puck drop, we had barely touched the puck for two periods, and were down 4–0. During the second intermission Holmgren went ballistic. He stood in the dressing room and insulted every single one of us. "Way to bring in the New Year with all our fans, playing like garbage," he said angrily.

Then he threatened that there would be changes in the lineup. He was so disgusted he stormed out. Pierre sat idle during Paul's rant. Then he attempted to rally the troops and put a positive spin on the situation.

"Fellas, this is what we're going to do!" he said. "Down four goals, we are going to break up the third period in four segments. Every five minutes we will score a goal, tie the game, and then win in overtime! Now who's with me?"

Frank Pietrangelo answered under his breath, "That's one helluva plan, Pierre." He knew Pierre well from their days in Pittsburgh, where they won a Cup together. But what happens next? Michael Nylander scores three and half minutes into the third. Pierre is ecstatic. He starts patting everyone on the back. "Way to go, guys! We are *way* ahead of schedule." Being the smart-ass that I am, I couldn't let that go.

"Pierre, should I rag the puck and slow down the clock a little to get us back on schedule?" I asked.

I'm not sure if he laughed, but we were howling on the bench. Things didn't quite go according to Pierre's plan after that and we lost the game soundly at 6–2. That's the type of year it was.

As the season went on, in much the same way, we grew to expect Holmgren's wrath in the dressing room. His favourite thing was to grab a hockey stick and walk around the room just slapping it in his other hand. You could hear the snap of the wood striking his bare palm. It wasn't a very comforting sound. It was like Buford Pusser in the movie *Walking Tall*, who walked around carrying a bat. It was scary (and I guess that was the point). Mark Greig, a first-round pick, would whisper to me, "I think he's gonna hit me with that thing."

As far as being a physical player, when I was in Washington, Dale Hunter had given me some advice about the role. He told me that getting suspended wasn't the worst thing in the world. I asked him what he meant by that and he said, "It keeps them guessing. And when they are guessing what you're going to do, that's the split second that you can hold on to the puck a little longer, get a little bit more room. They are less focused on winning the game and more focused on keeping an eye on you."

At this point I had quite the reputation for being unpredictable, and this nearly caused a big problem. In February 1993, we played in Winnipeg and I had a really good offensive game, scoring twice and receiving only 4 penalty minutes. But what I remember most about that game is Jets rookie sensation Teemu Selänne scoring twice as well. He was well on his way to a historic rookie season. Right at the final buzzer, I made a beeline for him. My team was wondering what the hell I was doing and Winnipeg pounced on me thinking I was going to try to take a run at their prized rookie. I just wanted to ask for his stick. I don't know why, but I remember thinking he was going to be a huge star and it would be neat to have one of his sticks from his rookie year. It caused a real commotion.

Needless to say, things got a little stressful late in the season. Late one night, outside a bar on a road trip in Tampa, I had a brush with death when I bumped into Coach Holmgren. I had just scored my seventeenth goal of the season, which turned out to be my career high. We had won the game 4–3 that night and I was feeling particularly good. The team, however, was out of playoff contention—we'd already lost over 40 games at that point. For Holmgren it had clearly taken its toll, and we'd both had a little too much to drink. I honestly don't know why I thought it would be funny to chirp my head coach. Holmgren was one of the toughest players, with seventeen years pro and over 1,600 penalty minutes. I told him, "I don't think you ever fought a good lefty in your whole career." Like I said, in all my wisdom I thought he'd laugh. It was, of course, the furthest thing from the truth. He'd fought everybody, lefty or righty. But his face turned to stone.

"Oh, really? How 'bout we put that to a test right now, right here in the parking lot," he said. He grabbed my shoulder and strong-armed me. I grabbed his shoulder and strong-armed him back. There we are, squaring off outside, and slightly off-balance, but that didn't matter. Now he is throwing some playful jabs my way. I throw some jabs his way. His jabs start to sting a little, so I decide to push back a bit harder. Paul Holmgren is a very big man. I had to look up as we started to push and poke one another.

It was getting ugly fast. His eyes got squirrelly and I knew he felt long overdue for a good fight, maybe from his tough playing days. We were at the point of no return when, by sheer chance, my teammate Randy Ladouceur suddenly shows up in a cab. He sees us with our fists ready to coldcock each other and slides across the hood of the cab, just like in an old episode of *Starsky & Hutch*, screaming, "Noooooo!" He jumped in between us and pulled us apart, just in time to stop our coach from crushing my face. Ladouceur probably saved my career and my life. The next day it was as if nothing happened.

Sometimes players have a tough time managing their adrenaline. That's what happened when you played that type of role back in the nineties. It doesn't leave you with a lot of time to rationalize decisions. The game is so fast, and back then it was an eat-or-be-eaten mentality, so there was not a lot of time for reflection. I didn't make the brightest decisions at times, but neither did a lot of other guys. Is this a good idea? Should I go at him at this angle? You just react. The game today is so much different. Everybody is more levelheaded. That wasn't our world back then. It was pure survival.

That season I was on pace to score 20 goals. It would have been a milestone for an enforcer who also had 300 penalty minutes. I only needed three more and had 9 games to play. Only six players have ever done it: Tiger Williams, Paul Holmgren, Al Secord, Chris Nilan, Bob Probert, and Dave Schultz. I was on pace for joining that list.

On April 1, in a game against Pittsburgh, I pulled my abdominal muscles in a fight with Grant Jennings. It felt as if someone had harpooned me from the stands—the pain was so intense. The next morning, I tried to lift myself out of bed and couldn't. I forced myself to play one more game, but I was in so much pain I barely played. I then shut it down, missing the final 7 games.

Even though my season ended early, it ended on a high note. Brian Burke had created the Heavy Hitter Award for the player who best demonstrated persistence, determination, and a consistent hard work ethic each game. At the end of the year I had earned it the most times, which meant I received a new GMC truck. I'd been working for this all year so I could give that truck to my dad. Brian wasn't stupid: you get the mouse on one side and the cheese on the other. Lead them to the cheese. He wanted his players to hit, and he offered a great reward for doing it well. Trying to earn that award made me do some questionable things: high-sticking, hitting late, blindside hits. Things my Greek mother wasn't exactly proud of, but it got me the reputation as a heavyweight. I was top four in the league in penalty minutes, right behind Tie Domi, Marty McSorley, and Gino Odjick.

Brian Burke left after the season to take on the NHL's new role of vice president of player discipline. He had had enough of owner Richard Gordon. There had been a challenge in team management. Gordon was really good friends with a tennis legend, Ivan Lendl. Somehow, Lendl, who had won eight majors, had Gordon's ear on the hockey team and that created a weird dynamic. We would see Lendl every once in a while, like he was part of the organization. Lendl insisted that Richard Gordon fire Paul Holmgren after Paul started five rookies in overtime versus the Rangers. This is how some owners run NHL teams when guys who have no experience in hockey get involved. Understandably, it grated on Brian's nerves. His line was "There's two hands on the steering wheel, and if I see a third one, I'm gone"—which is exactly what happened.

That year the NHL salaries had risen significantly and contracts were now being disclosed publicly. Back when I started NHL salaries were not publicly available. The lack of knowledge meant franchise players like Wayne Gretzky, Mark Messier, and Mario Lemieux were hugely undervalued. But the players' association's new president, Bob Goodenow, and his lieutenant, Ian Pulver, were insistent that salaries be transparent.

Goodenow and Pulver built the association into one of the most powerful unions for athletes in the world. Pulver was one of Goodenow's first hires, in 1990. As the new heads of the union, they had to start from scratch and repair the tremendous damage that disgraced lawyer Alan Eagleson had left behind. Eagleson used fraud, embezzlement, and intimidation in running our hockey union.

But the new leadership did a lot for players. Goodenow and Pulver's insistence on salary transparency was the single-most-important decision for players since Ted Lindsay first formed the association in 1957. Once the salaries for franchise players were available, it allowed a more fair distribution of team money. Knowing what Gretzky made helped Lemieux better understand what his true value should be.

Just two years later, in 1992, Eric Lindros was traded from Quebec to Philadelphia for a bunch of players and $15 million. He briefly became the highest-paid player in the league—before he even played one game in the NHL. It set the tone for Wayne, Mark, and Mario. Until then, there had been no true understanding of how much money teams had and were willing to offer good players. Top players could now work off of each other and help pull up everyone underneath them, too.

For a player, knowing how much others made gave you great leverage in negotiating. If another guy was making more than you, but maybe you had more goals or points, it was hard to argue you had a fair deal. It could also be so funny to watch guys look at the *Hockey News*, or any paper that published salaries. "Oh my God," they'd say, "that guy is making that much? I'm way better than him. That's crazy." Or, on the team bus you might hear, "That guy can't even stand up! Why is he making more money than me?" With salaries disclosed, it was clear the dam had broken.

With Burkie gone, Paul Holmgren took over as GM and head coach. I had a one-year contract with Burke and my agent, Harry Francis, was able to use my strong offensive numbers the previous season as leverage and I signed a contract worth $525,000. It almost doubled my salary. For depth guys who played my role, I was now among the higher paid. Harry and I had set a goal of between $500,000 and $600,000 a year. At the time, the average NHL salary was about $700,000, so the Whalers got creative in order to save money. If we won the first round of the playoffs, I'd earn an extra $20,000. It escalated to an extra $30,000 if we moved past the second round, $40,000 for the third round, and $60,000 for winning the Cup. Not bad considering four years earlier my yearly salary was only $110K. It was a long shot to attain all those bonuses, but I was pretty happy that the Whalers had padded the contract.

When the next season started, however, it seemed those bonuses would be a pipe dream. We started off horribly again and I wasn't scoring any goals. I wasn't even getting good scoring chances. I felt that I'd recovered from my abdominal strain, but I wasn't sure if it was holding me back. Then, in late October, I was late on a hit on Dallas's James Black. The impact of my shoulder on his face split him open right across the forehead. There are two or three hits I made during my career that I really regret, and that was one of them. Dallas's Mark Tinordi went bal-listic and came after me under the stands, as our benches were on the same side. Security had to get between us. I would have done the same thing if someone had hit my teammate late like that.

I knew right away I was in hot water, but I hoped Brian Burke, in his role as head of NHL Player Discipline, would be fair because of our history. He ended up slapping me with a five-game suspension that cost me $40,000. In hindsight, it was the right decision. As I sat out those games, thinking about how I could salvage the season, I had no idea that I had played my last game as a Hartford Whaler.

CHAPTER 6

Life in the Big Apple

For the second time in just two seasons I was traded. On November 2, 1993, I was involved in a multiplayer deal involving three teams: Hartford, Chicago, and the New York Rangers.

Mike Keenan, the new coach of the Rangers, wanted high-scoring, solid two-way winger Steve Larmer, who was in a contract dispute with Chicago. But it became tricky for Rangers GM Neil Smith because Chicago wouldn't trade with New York. Keenan had previously coached the Blackhawks and after three seasons did not leave on good terms. In addition to coaching, Keenan wanted more authority as a GM, but the Hawks wouldn't give it to him, so they parted company in November 1992.

With that history, Smith had to work with Paul Holmgren in Hartford to get Larmer. It was a three-way trade. The Whalers acquired Larmer and Bryan Marchment for Patrick Poulin and Eric Weinrich. Then Smith traded James Patrick and Darren Turcotte to the Whalers for me, Larmer, Barry Richter, and a sixth-round draft pick in 1994. The crux of the trade was sending Patrick and Turcotte to Hartford for Larmer. But Hartford was on a tight budget, and to make the deal work, their ownership wanted more money off their books. Because I almost doubled my salary with my new contract, it made the most sense to trade me. Such is the life of pro sports behind the scenes. At least now I had a legitimate chance at realizing my dream of winning the Stanley Cup.

Players always want to know who they've been traded for, what their perceived value is. We'd all like to think our new team would pay a king's ransom for us, that they see us as an integral part of the organization. I didn't need to be a genius to know I wasn't a key piece in this trade, but it was still fun being part of a deal of this magnitude. Since Neil traded Tie Domi and Kris King to Winnipeg, they were looking for more toughness. The Rangers organization knew I was never going to be a top-six player in their lineup, but I was a guy who could play hard and compete. They also knew my reputation as a good guy in the dressing room. For teams to win championships, the bond between players has to be authentic. Getting along well with my teammates could go a long way to helping in our quest for the Cup. That can't be underestimated.

As soon as Holmgren told me I was heading to the Rangers, I couldn't stop thinking about the possibility of winning the Cup. Most role-players wouldn't spend much time in October or November thinking about their team's chances of winning the holy grail of hockey. But when you're playing on a bottom team, like the Whalers were then, it's demoralizing knowing early on how your season will likely end. With my trade to the Rangers, this changed overnight. Now my hopes for a contending season jumped tenfold.

With that thought came another realization. I had an unusual contract with tremendous upside if I moved to a contending team. Remember, my contract was back-loaded with bonuses for a strong playoff run. If the Rangers won the Cup, I could net an extra $150,000. Four years earlier, my salary was $110,000. I could make more than that on bonus money alone if we went all the way.

In the end, everyone got what they wanted. Keenan got Larmer, whom he had coached in Chicago, and I was acquired to add even more toughness to a Rangers team that already boasted Joey Kocur and Jeff

Beukeboom. These were guys who could drop their gloves in a split second. Most teams had two guys who could take on most heavyweights, but after examining the roster, I wondered how much reinforcement was really needed. Apparently, to end a fifty-four-year Stanley Cup drought, two tough guys weren't enough. Add in Mike Hartman and Jay Wells, who could still eat nails, and we had guys who could more than hold their own.

There was plenty of muscle to go around and I was fine with that. We also had plenty of extra skill in Eddie Olczyk, Phil Bourque, Peter Andersson, and Mike Hudson. Guys knew ice time was going to suffer, but somehow it felt different than in the past. The Rangers had the kind of money that bought lots of insurance. This was the last season the team would be controlled by Paramount Communications. Their mind-set was "we're going to win the Stanley Cup and we don't care how much it costs us." Even though I wouldn't be given the same opportunity to contribute as a more rounded player, like I had in Hartford, it was a welcome trade-off for being in the mix for a championship season. From Eddie Olczyk right through to Glenn Healy, we all felt the same way. Win this year and walk together the rest of our lives. I assumed I'd just go in, play hard, and create havoc whenever I could. Just give them what they want.

During my career, I was never shocked by being traded. I knew how expendable a guy in my position as a role-player was. The truth, though, is that this holds true for 90 percent of the league. On a moment's notice anyone could experience a sudden move, unless they're one of the rare superstars. Even then there is no real certainty.

I always knew I wouldn't play for one team my entire career. I tried not to think too far ahead, instead focusing on the present. There are always guys who worry about being traded, but I felt comfortable enough that I'd be in New York long enough to see a legitimate run for the Cup. The first thing I wanted to do when I arrived was to try to find a way to fit in. Unfortunately for me, I had to wait to play because I was still in that five-game suspension for the late hit on James Black. It was a disappointing way to start my Ranger career.

On hockey teams, though, the things that you do and say off the ice have almost as big an impact as what you do on the ice. I did my best to be around as many new teammates as I possibly could and tried to create good energy. To play a tough guy and a fighting role, you first must gain the trust of your teammates. That means you make it your business to connect in some way with everyone. Cliques are often dangerous in the dressing room and the Rangers that year fortunately did not have a problem with this. I loved making my teammates laugh. I always valued humour in the room. I was never a practical joker, though, because that can escalate quickly.

My humour often left me most vulnerable. Our practice facility at Rye Playland had a strange layout in that Keenan had to walk through our dressing room to get to his office. When he arrived before practice, most of us were usually already getting ready. Anyone who knows Mike Keenan is aware he always took great pride in his appearance. Italian shoes. Designer jeans. Crisp white shirts. One day he came walking through with a bright red cashmere scarf wrapped around his neck, the long end flowing behind him. Halfway through his trek across the room, I grabbed a red hockey sock, wrapped it around my neck, and followed right behind him. Some of the guys were starting to snicker when Keenan does an about-face and totally busts me. He didn't laugh. He had no expression. I've seen guys get traded for less, and everyone pretty much said goodbye to me. I had a few healthy scratches in the games that followed, but Mike never mentioned it and I never brought it up.

The truth is, I felt the team could maybe use some positive energy. Hartford was more than a hundred miles away from New York and it was big news that the Rangers had had a shaky start to the year. We'd heard that Iron Mike, as he was known, was getting into battles with some of his players. Turcotte, Patrick, and Brian Leetch had all been on the receiving end.

"You're no Chelios," Keenan would tell Leetchey (in reference to the Hawks' defenceman Chris Chelios). It was obvious Keenan was trying to get into Leetchey's head by comparing him to the star player he had coached in Chicago. Never mind that Brian had won the Norris Trophy as the NHL top defenceman in 1992. By the time I arrived, the Rangers had started to sort out those early season issues and come together as a team, but that tension was still there.

I sensed right away there was an immense pressure on the Rangers to win the Cup. That was made abundantly clear when they traded for Mark Messier in October 1991, in a deal that sent Bernie Nicholls, Steven Rice, and Louie DeBrusk to Edmonton. The Rangers wanted Mark to lead them to a championship, which he had done five times with the Oilers. Mark had already had great success in Edmonton, winning MVP and five Stanley Cups. His first year in New York he won another MVP and made the playoffs, but the second year was a disaster. Fans were starting to think the team was too old. Roger Neilson was fired halfway through the 1992–1993 season. Mark and Roger had different philosophies when it came to ice time and shuffling lines. As I said, teams that win have to get along, and being on the same page is crucial. Keenan took over the following year, the year I was traded to New York.

As soon as I arrived, it was like going from the minors to the big leagues. I left a small town in Connecticut, known more for insurance than hockey, for the bright lights of Manhattan. In Hartford fans had turned on the Whalers and the ownership group, and the arena was quiet for many of our home games. Now I was playing in one of the most famous arenas in the world with die-hard fans.

A few days after I had arrived, I walked down Fifth Avenue and a New York Police squad car pulled up right beside me, literally squealing to a stop. *That's it*, I thought. *I'm going to jail before I even get a chance to step on the ice as a Ranger.* The officer stepped out and extended his hand, welcoming me to the city. He wished me the best of luck in bringing the Cup home. And that, in a nutshell, is NYC. A city that celebrates the Yankees and Mets, the Giants, Jets, and Knicks. It amazed me just how big a slice of that sports fandom the Rangers had. With over seven million people in the city, it became clear to me how important the Rangers' success was to New Yorkers.

Rye Playland, where we practiced, was an amusement park right out of the 1920s. This setup actually seemed a little strange for such a big-market team. I'd first seen Rye years before in the movie *Big* with Tom Hanks. On the day of my first practice session, Mark Messier walked over, extended his hand, and welcomed me. Even watching him approach was quite intimidating. First and foremost, the man looked like he was chiseled out of stone. Everybody talked about the way he looked. The guy reeked of intensity even when he smiled. There was no escaping it. He asked me to tell him a little bit about myself, whether I was married or not. I told him I had no wife or kids.

Most guys on the team with families were living in Westchester. Mark, Brian Leetch, and Mike Richter all lived on the Upper West Side. Mark said that's where I should be, too. Experiencing what the city had to offer was very important to the captain. Prior to his arrival, it was considered better for guys to live away from the pull of the city because management thought it had too many distractions. Mark changed all that. He felt that soaking up the culture of New York was good for the players' connection to the fans. While others avoided it in the past, he embraced it. Losing focus never entered his mind. If you were committed as a player, living in the city would never affect your ability to perform.

Mark's attitude was, if you wanted to live in New York City, the Upper West Side was the place to be. That sounded good to me. I asked him what it would cost for a decent two-bedroom apartment near the

guys. He said $3,000 a month. My jaw absolutely dropped. For some-
one who was coming from Hartford, where my rent was $650, this was
incomprehensible. But it wasn't so bad in the end. Keenan and GM Neil
Smith made a deadline deal that brought Brian Noonan to the Rangers.
I had a small, temporary apartment in New Rochelle, but when Brian
came along I had found my roommate. All the single Rangers lived
within a few blocks, on the Upper West Side. Brian and I split $3,200 a
month and it was worth every dime.

Hanging out in Manhattan with Mike Richter, Brian Leetch, and
Mark Messier wasn't the worst thing to ever happen to me. We all developed a really good relationship because of the time we spent together
going to and from practice. And going to dinners and shows with these
guys—it was often an education for me to hear their thoughts on how
they felt we could be better and bring the team together.

The energy in New York was never-ending. And it struck me that so
many of the people there were striving to do something special. Actors,
artists, singers, songwriters, producers, athletes, Wall Street bankers—
you name it. If you want to become something, New York is the place.

When we got to the rink, fans would be waiting for us. They'd watch
us go into the building and then wait for us to come out afterwards to
sign autographs. Much like with the Leafs back when they were playing
at Maple Leaf Gardens, most of the original six teams had an older fan
base who passed on the love of their team to younger generations. Even
though half of the Rangers fan base hadn't been alive long enough to
fully appreciate the long Cup drought, they inherited a deep longing for
a championship. It's similar to what players go through. The moment a
player is traded to a team, he becomes emotionally, physically, mentally,
and spiritually invested in the team. He inherits all that team's history. It
didn't take long for me to feel it. These people were bleeding and they
just wanted to stop New York Islanders fans from chanting "1940!"
every time they played them. That year was the last time the Rangers

won the Cup. The Islanders started out as an expansion franchise in 1972 and quickly won four consecutive Cups in the eighties. It was hard for Rangers fans to watch. They wanted redemption and it was easy to understand their pain.

Our team had a lot of depth. A lot of the guys had been solid players with other teams and were now being asked to take a lesser role—Eddie Olczyk, Mike Hartman, Doug Lidster, Glenn Healy, myself, and others. Because the Rangers were in a position to collect all these high-end contracts, they didn't care how much it cost or how many guys it took. We were all in the same boat and we looked after each other. I had known Glenn Healy from my Toronto summer skates since I was seventeen years old. I had a rapport with him and his wife, Suzie. Glenn's philosophy in life is do what you can within your control and forget the rest. He liked to play chess on the road. It wasn't the easiest thing for him to carry around a chessboard the size of a kitchen table on our plane, but he did. Sometimes these games would get so intense that if we couldn't finish upon arrival, we needed to find a safe spot on the plane so that no one would touch the board. There is a *Seinfeld* episode where Kramer and Newman get into a wicked game of Risk and run into the same problem. It was getting ridiculous how competitive we got over chess. One night our charter flight had waited to fly us back to New York. After a tough 3–1 loss that night, Glenn and I tried to wait the sufficient amount of time dwelling on the loss before we pulled out the chess set to finish our Karpov vs. Kasparov classic. I suggested to Heals, "We need to wait one hour." He said to me, "Are you crazy? In twenty minutes Keenan will down a few beers and won't remember if we just played the Dallas Stars or the Dallas Cowboys." So, we get the board down from the overhead compartment and start to play as quietly and respectfully as possible. But Keenan didn't fall asleep as fast as we expected. It was just the opposite. We can see him stewing as he paced back and forth. Then he does something he has never done: he walks towards the back of the plane, staring straight at us. I whisper to Heals, "Oh my God, ditch the chessboard." Heals said, "No, just keep playing." Sure enough, Iron Mike stops right beside us and just watches us play. Not one word spoken. Just Keenan with one hand holding his beer and the other one on his chin as if to anticipate my next move. The next thing you know, Mike took his free hand and swiped all of our pieces onto the floor, then casually walked away. That was Iron Mike.

One night we were playing the Leafs at MSG. I was really hoping to play this game, but I was told that morning that not only was I not playing, I wouldn't be taking warm-up either. Usually there is an extra player in warm-up on the long shot that someone got hurt. Mike Hudson was the extra player on this night. When Joey Kocur's back started to spasm, Keenan, for whatever reason, decided he didn't actually want Hudson to play. He rushed into the dressing room and asked where the hell I was. Eddie O said, "We haven't seen him yet but if you are looking for an extra player, I'll play." Keenan looks at Eddie and tells him, "No, Kyper's playing when he gets here." Eddie called me at home and told me to get to MSG as soon as possible.

"Eddie, what?" I asked. "I wasn't even in warm-up. I've just had two bowls of chili and three beers this afternoon." He said Keenan didn't care. I needed to get my ass there. I jumped in a cab and frantically told the driver to take me to MSG as quick as he could because I was playing hockey tonight for the Rangers in twenty minutes. He replied, in a heavy New York accent, "It's a special night for both of us; I'm singing later tonight on Broadway." Clearly he didn't recognize me, but he got me there fast. Eddie waited for me downstairs and held the elevator for me. That's the type of teammate he was. I hit the ice with no warm-up and threw up chili after the first period.

In all honesty, if there were guys with less character in those depth roles, guys who had bad attitudes or were selfish, it would have been enough to sink the whole ship. Even one bad seed can have a huge effect in the dressing room. And the opposite is also true—one great character can make all the difference. In my opinion, Steve Larmer changed the dynamic of the whole team because he was such a good two-way player. He was very responsible and could play with Mark Messier or switch off to another line. Sometimes numbers tell the story best. Steve had a streak of 884 consecutive games played, which only ended because he wanted out of Chicago. It was just time for him to move on and that was more important than any individual record. Keenan knew that a player like Steve could really add the depth he was seeking.

Steve had another season left on his contract after the 1994–1995 season with the Rangers, but he was battling a bad back. He decided to retire in '95 and left something like $1.4 million on the table. They begged him to come back and play however many games he could or wanted to, but his attitude was, if he couldn't earn his salary playing healthy, he didn't want the easy money. That's the type of character Steve Larmer has. Guys like him are rare.

I didn't know where Keenan truly stood with me, so the best I could do was wait patiently to try to earn any amount of respect from him. And then I got some. I remember this one fight with Quebec's Chris Simon at MSG, in March 1994. Simon was one of the toughest guys to ever play the game. A nasty, vicious fighter who ended up with two of the longest suspensions ever handed down in NHL history. He had been chirping me the last few games we played against one another and I just felt if I didn't finally stand up to him this one time, things would never change. We squared off at centre ice and he just missed me with his first punch—I swear it gave me a windburn. He then connected with his next two lefts, right to my face, which should have finished me off. I somehow managed to throw the next two punches. The second one buckled him. When I saw blood streaming down his right eye, I knew I'd landed the one punch I so desperately needed to. But he was still on his feet and I went into full survival mode, both of us bleeding above our eyes. Just before the officials could completely separate us, Simon told me, "Good bout, you're tougher than you look." I gained some respect from the big man and he never chirped me again. That fight earned me some respect from Keenan as well. I remember Keenan raced into the dressing room as I was lying on the medical table getting stitched up. He patted my shin pads and said he loved it. It felt good to be singled out like that. I must admit that Keenan never really challenged me at all like he did other players, but he was a master at crawling into people's heads.

Sergei Zubov learned that. I dressed beside the future Hall of Famer. "Zubey," as we called him, had a great career on defence. He led our team in total points that season with 89. But before that, Keenan didn't like the way he played in training camp, or the shape he was in when he showed up, so he sent him to the Rangers farm team in Binghamton to start the season. He missed the first three games. I don't think there is another player in history who started the first week in the minors then ended up leading his NHL team in scoring. That tells you all you need to know about how talented he was.

One time when he was not happy with Zubov's play, Keenan had a trainer summon him and the other three Russian players. Zubov and I had the last two stalls in the dressing room next to Keenan's office, so we talked often. Keenan didn't hold back. He tore a strip off all of them. He mentioned Don Cherry's theory about Russians—that they don't play at this time of year and you can't win with them. He was just giving it to Zubov, chewing him out. Eventually, Zubov came back to his stall to finish tying his skates. He was quiet and then looked a little perplexed. Finally, he asked me, "Who is this Don Cherry guy and why doesn't he like Russians?" I said, "Zubey, you don't need to worry about Don Cherry."

I'd never seen anyone with Keenan's type of personality before. My first-ever NHL training camp was with Keenan, back when I was trying out with Philadelphia as an undrafted rookie, in 1984. He had just been hired as the head coach. We were on a run in Atlantic City, on the boardwalk, and Keenan was jogging beside us yelling, "Philadelphia Flyers coming through! Philadelphia Flyers coming through!" Guys would roll their eyes. You could just see and feel his strut, confident and arrogant. There was a lot of ego in Iron Mike, but call it what you will, it clearly didn't hold him back, based on his early success.

The one guy Keenan never messed with was Mark, which made sense. Messier had five Stanley Cups, after all, and Keenan had none. He'd also gone through Canada Cups with Keenan, so Mark was the guy we all hoped could talk him off of the ledge. Mark Messier was one of the very best leaders. I believe he had the greatest sense of understanding a team's makeup—more than anyone I've ever played with. Mark believed in empowering his teammates. He'd had all this success and yet, when he walked into the Rangers dressing room, you would never have known. He knew for the Rangers to really learn how to win, he needed to start from scratch. And the first thing you do is start to earn the trust of your teammates.

Two weeks into my trade to the New York Rangers, Mark took me out for lunch. "Mess, I've never seen you wear any of your Cup rings," I said to him. "If I were you, I'd have two on each hand and one as a nose ring. Why haven't I seen you wear one?"

He paused, then said, "Why don't you wear yours?"

I wasn't sure if he was playing with me or had me confused with someone else, so I just replied, "Mark, I don't have one."

"I know," he said. "I'll tell you what. I'll wear mine next season when you can wear yours."

Well, if I didn't feel like I just got shot out of a cannon right then and there. Mark understood that a team is only as strong as its weakest link. He viewed a team like a jigsaw puzzle. No picture is complete until that last piece is placed, regardless of its size or where it ultimately fit.

He was a big energy guy, too. And by that, I mean he could sniff negative energy three miles away. If a player was feeling down, he would make it his business to know. He built relationships with teammates that would lead to trust over time. Hockey isn't like most other team sports. Mark understood that even superstars only play roughly twenty minutes each hockey game—they can only influence one third of the game. The rest of the time they're on the bench. Mark often said, "I need my teammates more than they need me."

It didn't take him long to gain our trust. So when he needed to stand up in the room and ask for more out of each and every one of us, we gave it to him. That doesn't always happen with other leaders.

There was something special about wearing the Rangers jersey. I think it's one of the nicest uniforms in the history of the NHL. One game I did an interview in between periods and I wasn't wearing my jersey because I always stripped down and changed my shirt. So I did the interview in a T-shirt. Later, Mark told me that when we do an interview, we always wear that jersey with pride.

Madison Square Garden is a unique building because the arena is on the fifth floor. Most anywhere else it's at street level. As soon as you walk in the building, there are photos of New York greats—and not just hockey players. Walt Frazier. Billy Joel. Madonna. Hulk Hogan. Some of the biggest entertainers featured in one of the most famous buildings in the world. You'd look up in the stands and there was always going to be a star. I got into an elevator one time with Christopher Reeve, before his tragic injury. I thought, *Holy shit, I'm in the elevator with Superman.* He was one of the biggest Rangers fans I met that year.

MSG is a great building in which to watch events, and when we weren't playing, we caught as many as we could. A handful of us went to Michael Jordan's first game at MSG, after he had returned to basketball from his attempt at a pro baseball career. The security guards took folding chairs and put them on court level for us, right beside the Bulls bench. We watched Jordan score 55 points. It was a masterful performance. And because we were so close to the action, we also got to see the dynamics between MJ and his legendary coach, Phil Jackson.

The game was tied. When Chicago took a late time-out in order to change the lineup, Jackson pointed to one of the Bulls and looked over at Jordan. MJ shook his head as if to say no. Then Jackson pointed to another player and got the same signal from Jordan. On Jackson's third attempt, this time pointing to Bill Wennington, Jordan gave him the nod. MJ was helping to orchestrate how the final minutes should be played. He had a feeling for who was needed on the floor. A good captain has that sort of relationship with his coach. I believe that is exactly the sort of dynamic Mark had with Keenan.

It was fun going to MSG as a fan, feeling the buzz. I always spent the first quarter scouting the famous faces in the stands before focusing on the game. There were always stars to see. Peter Jennings, Spike Lee, Madonna, John Cusack, Robert De Niro—you never knew who you might see.

The Rangers set me up with Knicks tickets four rows up from the floor, and this particular game I wound up sitting beside a famous award-winning actor named Michael Zaslow. Michael was a talented actor who gained fame on Broadway and for playing Roger Thorpe in *Guiding Light*, the daytime drama show. I was embarrassed when I had to admit I didn't recognize him. I apologized and said if he was on *The Young and the Restless* it would be a different story. He laughed. I told him, "My mom watches *Guiding Light* and would certainly know who Roger Thorpe is." I couldn't have met a nicer guy that day. We talked most of the night about the Knicks and, of course, about the New York Rangers. He spoke of the discipline of acting and how he was able to draw inspiration from the athletes who found ways to show up every night. He was then kind enough to invite me to a taping of his show later that week.

When the day came, they actually plugged me in as an extra in a scene. The producers didn't have a speaking part for me, but they had me sitting at a bar, then cutting in on some guy's girlfriend on the dance floor. I kidded with Michael that Wayne Gretzky got a speaking part on *The Young and the Restless*. I asked Michael, "I don't have to take a punch in this scene, do I? I have enough of that in games." He and the whole crew laughed. And that was it—the extent of my daytime acting career.

After that we'd meet for a coffee on occasion to talk sports. He spoke highly of Greek people he had met in his life, including his costar at the time, Melina Kanakaredes. Melina went on to *CSI: NY* fame. Michael was one of the nicest, most charismatic people I met in NYC while playing for the Rangers.

A short time later he was diagnosed with Amyotrophic Lateral Sclerosis (ALS), a debilitating and fatal condition also known as Lou Gehrig's disease. He had called me one last time to let me know he was in a battle with this disease. It was tough to hear this, and I felt for him. He made quite an impact in my life in a very short period of time.

There was also the legendary China Club, which was known as the most famous club in New York City. Sure, Studio 54 had international recognition in the disco days, but no club in NYC history could touch the China Club's run as the hottest place to be on its signature Monday nights. Over a thousand people would jam into the club in hopes of seeing movie stars, top athletes, and, if you were really lucky, a jam session from an impressive musical lineup that could include Bruce Springsteen, Prince, or Rod Stewart. You never knew who might jump up onstage.

Early in my career with the Washington Capitals, we arrived in NY on Monday for a Wednesday-night game. About ten of us raced to the China Club and there was mayhem at the entrance. We were hoping they'd let us in because we were, well, you know, "pro athletes." We designated Dale Hunter as our China Club captain and sent him to talk to a well-known front doorman named Johnnie B. He told Dale to have us wait a little while and he'd get us in. Close to an hour later we were still waiting outside. Dale blurted out, "Boys, let's buck up. We'll grease him and he'll let us in." So we chipped in fifty bucks each and gave the doorman the money. He graciously thanked us and said that it wouldn't be long. Damn if we didn't wait close to another hour. So, dummies that we were, we greased him again. All in all, it took over two hours to get in. Funny, though, not one of the guys waiting bailed. It was worth the wait.

A couple of years later, I go to the China Club as a New York Ranger, with Messier and Leetch. Think we had to wait, or grease any doorman? Not a snowball's chance in hell. Is there anything better than that? As soon as we arrived, a doorman escorted us in and showed us to a table in a roped-off area. We got a ton of respect, which anyone that rides Mark Messier's coattails can come to expect. Johnnie B. was still working there and showed up at our table. "Moose, I got the St. Louis Blues here waiting outside. What do you think?" Mark just looked at his watch, then at Johnnie B., and said, "A little bit longer." *Wow*, I thought to myself, *that's how it works. It's a Rangers city.* To this day we are all still close friends with Johnnie B.

Life in the city was great, but I was in and out of the Rangers lineup. It was disappointing, but finishing the season as a first-place team made it a little easier. And we honestly felt we were working towards a championship, so it came down to having a good attitude. The Rangers were paying us in full to be there for them when needed. When it's asked for, you give it to the best of your ability, and when it isn't, you wait patiently. You can't control when the coach wants to play you or doesn't want to play you, and that's how you get through a year with a team that is stacked with talent. Be the hardest player at practice, work the hardest in the gym. That's all I tried to do. Mike Hartman, Mike Hudson, Eddie Olczyk, and Glenn Healy got through it that way also. It's what gave our team the best chance to win.

Management made some trades at the deadline that brought in even more depth—Glenn Anderson from Toronto, Craig MacTavish from Edmonton, and Stéphane Matteau and Brian Noonan from Chicago. I didn't overanalyze the impact of the trades, even though Eddie Olczyk, Glenn Healy, Mike Hudson, Doug Lidster, Mike Hartman, and I had constant hotel-lobby roundtable discussions. The truth is, we were Black Aces, a term that refers to extra players on a hockey team. Even some media had called us that. We'd contemplate who the next guy to get back in the lineup might be. We'd talk about who Keenan liked—and didn't like. We'd sit in the lobby and guess at what in the hell we would be doing in twenty years. Someone would point to Eddie and Heals and say, "You're going to be on TV as a broadcaster"—which they both became. As for me, they thought I'd own a nice little Greek restaurant in Greektown Toronto. The King of Souvlaki is what they said I would call it. I don't think I've ever laughed as hard as I did during those talks.

Even sitting out some games, finally being part of a winning team was amazing. And there were cash incentives from management that we started to collect. Every player, whether in or out of the lineup, was eligible for team segment bonuses. There was a bonus for gaining a minimum 6 points out of 10 available in a stretch of games. Power-play and shorthanded numbers could also earn cash. Even a team shutout earned us $1,000 each. It was crazy to watch guys blocking shots with their faces with less than a minute in the game in order to protect a 6–0 lead. Today, players can't earn one extra penny in this salary cap era. It's a shame because those bonuses brought us even closer as a group. It was one of those years when all the stars aligned. We finished with 52 wins in 84 games and won the Presidents' Trophy for most points, with 112. Our segment bonus wins may have cost the Rangers' owners at the time, Paramount Communications, over $1 million—which was loose change in the couch for them.

I played 46 games that regular season, but one in particular towards the end stood out. We were finally able to beat the Islanders in their home arena, which was the first time in nearly five years for the Rangers. For some reason it felt like a good omen for the closing of the season. There was a playoff atmosphere and we were fighting for much more than just a win. With the score 2–2 after a hard-fought first period, Mike Keenan decided to pull Richter forty-five seconds into the second period after he gave up the go-ahead goal to Pierre Turgeon. We were all dumbfounded. We asked each other "What is he doing?" just loud enough so the next guy on our bench could hear. Glenn Healy, who had been a fan favourite playing for the Islanders the year before, got his chance to close out a very important game for us. Healy went in for Richter and then got pulled after giving up just one goal in eleven minutes on a wraparound by Benoît Hogue. The score was only 4–2. It was a crazy thing to pull him at that point and Glenn was furious. He relentlessly yelled at Keenan, things I wouldn't tell my worst enemy. I've never heard anybody go at a coach on the bench like that. The tension was unbearable, not to mention distracting, as Richter went back in. Alexei Kovalev got us within one in the second period, and then in the third the blue line took over and Beukeboom scored, tying it 4–4. The arena was insane. Late in the third Zubov scored with a minute to go from the point. With so many Rangers fans the crowd erupted. And we broke a five-year losing streak in the Nassau Coliseum. It was the last meaningful shot in the arm we needed to go on to win the Presidents' Trophy for the top team during the regular season. It was a good test of character in the midst of some Keenan controversy. We felt if we could get through that and find a way to win, we could get through anything.

We opened the playoffs against the New York Islanders, who finished 28 points behind us, in fourth place, in the Atlantic Division. There was plenty of bad blood between the teams. Back in 1979, Ulf Nilsson of the Rangers got hurt pretty badly in a game when Islanders captain Denis Potvin nailed him with a clean, hard check. Nilsson got a skate caught in a rut and suffered a broken ankle. The Rangers had hated the Islanders ever since. It seemed almost destiny that our road to the Cup would go through the Islanders. We wanted to win these first games and silence any doubt that the Cup was in our sights. With home ice advantage, we won the first two games at MSG by 6–0 scores.

We went to Long Island for the next two games feeling good about how we'd started the series, but well aware that although the Rangers had finally beaten the Islanders in the regular season in their arena, they had not beaten them in the playoffs. Islanders fans didn't let us forget it either. Sure enough, when Game 3 got under way at Nassau County Coliseum, we heard the old taunt from the fans: "1940, 1940."

I dressed for both of these games and we won 5–1 and 5–2. Steve Thomas played on that Islanders team and I remember talking to him after the series. He said he couldn't remember ever skating in a playoff game when his team didn't touch the puck. For our team, that alone was a small victory to celebrate. And beating them in their own barn was a big obstacle to overcome on our way to the Cup.

We played Washington in the next series, who had finished 24 points back of us, in third place. Even though the Capitals still had some players from when I played there, notably Dale Hunter, I had long since moved on, literally and figuratively. I was now a New York Ranger. Hockey players are so loyal: when a team signs you or trades for you, they become the team you bleed for. That season we played a game at Northlands Coliseum in Edmonton, where Kevin Lowe, now a Ranger, had won five Stanley Cups with the Oilers. He was coming off the ice and some Oilers fans started chirping him. He just stopped and started giving it back to them, to the point where it became heated. I couldn't believe it. This had been his home and now he's giving Edmonton fans the FU. He didn't give a shit. I realized that this was how badly Kevin wanted to win a Stanley Cup for the Rangers. Those five Stanley Cups with the Oilers were gone. The next one was all that mattered. I thought about Mark Messier, never wearing his Cup rings.

Our team was healthy and Keenan didn't want to change the lineup, so I didn't play against Washington. It was tough. Although I had been a big part of the season, it's the playoffs that really count. The energy on the ice is incredible. After winning the first three games against Washington 6–3, 5–2, and 3–0, we lost the fourth one 4–2. But we rebounded to clinch the series with a 4–3 win. We stayed healthy, which is rare so deep into the playoffs. We had swept the Islanders and had six days off between the first and second series. Then we only lost one game against Washington and had another five days off before we faced New Jersey.

We had 8 wins in 9 games, and were executing our game plan well. We beat the Islanders and the Caps handily with a balanced attack, scoring from everywhere. There was a discipline that Mark and Kevin Lowe brought from Edmonton. There is no other way to explain it. Our specialty teams were on fire, but it never went to our heads. We just kept pushing forward. We played six consecutive games where we scored five or more goals, which is unheard of in the playoffs.

But all that mattered was what came next when we faced New Jersey in the third round. The Devils were a powerhouse. My old teammate Scott Stevens patrolled the blue line and punished anyone who crossed it. And Martin Brodeur, only twenty-two years old, had firmly established himself as a star. Along with Scott Niedermayer, Stéphane Richer, Valeri Zelepukin, and some other very skilled players, they had some guys who could really move the puck. They had a lot of similarities to the Rangers in playing styles. They played hard.

The series was set up to be a tough contest when it began at MSG. Sure enough, that first game proved there'd be no easy wins when it went to double overtime—we lost 4–3. In Game 2 we were able to establish ourselves and control the play well enough to earn a 4–0 win, but then, when the series moved to New Jersey for the third game, we had another double overtime. This time it was decided with a goal by Stéphane Matteau, giving us a 3–2 win.

Things were looking up but then all hell broke loose in Game 4. There are many versions of what happened in that game. This is what I remember. Coach Keenan started his mind games sixteen minutes into the first period, benching his best players. We were only down 2–0 at that point. Then Iron Mike swapped goaltenders, pulling Mike Richter for Glenn Healy. That was a very strange strategy considering we entered the game with an overall playoff record of 10–2.

We didn't have typical goalies with Mike and Glenn. Sometimes goalies can be a little bit nuts. You'd have to be in order to stand in front of a net and withstand 100-mph snapshots aimed at your head. But both Mike and Glenn were incredibly down-to-earth and we felt solid playing in front of either of them. Still, this was a strange move for Keenan to make with such a good record.

Apparently pulling Richter wasn't enough of a wake-up call either, so Keenan started giving Brian Leetch's ice time to Jay Wells. Wellsie couldn't believe it and begged Keenan to get Brian back on the ice. Matteau scored to make it 2–1 in the second period, but it got even more ridiculous when Keenan still refused to put Brian Leetch on a late-period power play. As if that wasn't disturbing enough, for unknown reasons he decided to skip Mark Messier's regular ice for a few rotations. We lost 3–1.

Keenan spent a good part of the postgame interviews telling reporters that Brian Leetch was hurt, but Brian wouldn't have anything to do with it and denied having any sort of injury, which was true. As far as we knew, there was no injury.

There was a feeling inside our dressing room that the whole thing was unraveling—that this was the beginning of the end. Leaving New Jersey, we felt that Mike had lost Brian and many other players. It would have been easy for Mark Messier to go into Keenan's office kicking and screaming—I bet a lot of guys wanted to. That wasn't his style, though.

Mark is a very methodical guy and everything he does and says has a purpose. Mark needed to reach our coach like no one else had before. If Keenan was going to lose, he had this tendency to go down on his own terms. He always wanted his best players to know they fell short. That was his mentality.

Mark wholeheartedly disagreed with it. His job as captain was getting everyone back on board with the team. Mark doesn't really ever talk about it, but we knew that he had put the onus back on Keenan. "If we lose this series, let's not lose it eating our own." Mark knew he had to mend the fractured relationship Keenan had with the team. He encouraged Keenan to address us and told him there was plenty of time to turn it back around.

But nothing changed, and whatever problems we were having, Mike didn't address them. We lost the next game 4–1. We were down 3–2 in the series and Mark took complete charge.

What happened next became hockey history and solidified Mark as one of the game's greatest leaders. He addressed the media and said, "I know we are going to go in and win Game Six and bring it back here for Game Seven. That's exactly what we are going to do in Game Six." We didn't know about that comment until the next day when the tabloids had a field day. "BOLD PREDICTION: WE'LL WIN TONIGHT!" No one on the bus really mentioned it on the way to New Jersey, but Leetch and I were the last two guys off the bus. An issue of the *New York Post* was lying on one of the empty seats. Leetch read the headline then turned to me and said, "Well, I guess we're gonna win tonight."

Game 6 is still the most incredible game I've ever seen. A few things stood out to me, aside from Mark's bold prediction. Mike Richter was spectacular in net. He made acrobatic saves and stopped a handful of two-on-ones in the second period. Even Mike Keenan, despite all the negativity around him, rose to the occasion. He made an in-game adjustment that helped save the series, moving Steve Larmer off the Messier-Graves line and adding Kovalev. Together, they changed the energy.

Maybe it was just a chemistry thing, or just the time to change things up, but it felt like it opened up the dam. We were down 2–0, but a late-second-period goal gave us new life going into the third. Then Mark had a magical third period. He had three goals that felt like our own miracle on ice. The final score was 4–2. The Rangers and Mark's bold prediction kept our season alive. As ecstatic as we were, we couldn't celebrate knowing we had a Game 7 hurdle back at MSG.

The next day we had a practice at Rye Playland, back in New York. Something had really changed in Mike Keenan. We waited for him on the ice, but he never came. We were summoned back to the dressing room where we saw him more vulnerable than we ever had. He was hunched over as he sat in one of the dressing room stalls. He began the meeting by addressing his behaviour in the series. His tone had totally changed. He asked us to forgive him for some of the coaching decisions. He was near tears. He lifted his head up and said, "I made mistakes, I lost it, and I'll be better next game." With that, it seemed like the impossible had happened. Iron Mike showed us a human side that we didn't know existed. Years later many of us on that team have debated whether the speech was sheer brilliance or just theatrics, but it was enough to salvage our playoff run.

Game 7, in MSG, after a whirlwind of emotions. It was a tough game, with lots of good scoring chances. Brian Leetch opened the scoring, with a full 360-degree turn from behind the goal line, stuffing it past Brodeur. It was the only goal for nearly the whole game, and just when it looked as if it might be enough, Valeri Zelepukin banged in a loose puck with just seven seconds left in regulation. MSG was deathly silent. A few of us were waiting in the dressing room ready to celebrate for a path to the Stanley Cup Final only to go into another overtime. As the guys started walking into the dressing room, a few broke their sticks in sheer disgust. Then veteran Stanley Cup experience took over.

Kevin Lowe walked into the room, sat down, and smiled. "Isn't this fun, boys?" he said. "If it wasn't so hard, more people would win." This somehow settled the room.

We held them in a scoreless first overtime, and for the third time in this series, a second overtime period was needed. Before that last period, Stéphane Matteau asked Eddie O for some good luck before heading from the dressing room to the ice. In typical Olczyk style, he kissed Matteau's stick. I guess it worked. Early in that double overtime, Matteau beat a Devils defender to the puck in the corner, made a quick turn towards the net, and scored a wraparound goal, giving us the 2–1 win and a series victory to take us to the Stanley Cup Final.

Howie Rose, who called the game on MSG radio, chanted the now famous "Matteau, Matteau, Matteau, Stéphane Matteau! And the Rangers have one more hill to climb, baby, and it's Mount Vancouver!" After the game, Matteau commented on his goal in an interview. It was a bit of an odd bounce—he didn't have the time or the space to get all the way around, so he just put the puck to the front of the net with a few guys bearing down on it, and it snuck in off Brodeur. He said, "Overtime goals, they're not pretty, but they count."

It was utter relief in the dressing room. But there was also a sense—I don't know if it was destiny—that we were going to find a way to win the Cup. We had these guys who had won it before—Mark and Kevin along with Esa Tikkanen, Craig MacTavish, Jeff Beukeboom, and Glenn Anderson—all telling us they were going to find a way. That *we* were going to find a way. How do you not believe them when they've won so many championships? How do you not trust that?

We had four days to think about it before our first Stanley Cup Final game against Vancouver in MSG. Pat Quinn coached the Canucks and he was an intimidating figure. His team had a tough physical presence, much like him. Greg Adams, Shawn Antoski, and Gerald Diduck were big and heavy, and did a good job of insulating The Russian Rocket, Pavel Bure. Kirk McLean, whom I had grown up with—the same kid I got kicked out of typing class with—was their star goalie. This team defied odds by coming back from a 3–1 deficit against the Calgary Flames to win the next three games in overtime and clinch the series. It had never been done before and set the tone for a tough matchup between us.

This series, which started in New York, began much the same as the previous one against New Jersey. Game 1 went into double overtime, where we lost 3–2. Even though we had four days' rest, emotionally we were spent after the Jersey series and just couldn't seem to match the intensity of the Canucks. But we came back for Game 2 more settled. Doug Lidster, who had been in and out of the lineup that year, stepped in for Alexander Karpovtsev when he got injured. Lidster, who was an ex-captain of the Canucks, scored the first goal, which was symbolic for us. We won 3–1.

This was about the same time we heard rumours that there were problems between GM Neil Smith and Coach Mike Keenan. They were at each other's throats. Keenan, apparently, was already in talks with other teams, like Detroit, who was looking for a new coach. But as players, we had to focus on what needed to be done, and block out everything else.

The series shifted to Vancouver, where we won the third game 5–1, and then the fourth game 4–2. They won Game 5 in New York 6–3, and when we returned to Vancouver for Game 6, they took that one, too, with a 4–1 score, to tie the series at three apiece. There were riots and looting in the streets that night. Canucks fans went insane when their team tied the series. It was actually pretty scary to watch. What should have been a twenty-minute ride back to the hotel took us almost two hours. I remember being on the balcony with Tikkanen and listening to the fans going nuts. The sky was lit up from fires. I had never witnessed anything like it. *If that's what happened when their team won,* I thought, *imagine if they had lost.*

As we returned to New York, only one thing was certain: the next game would decide everything. Keenan wanted each of us to write a letter to him on the flight home about what we were going to do to change Game 7. I wrote that I thought I could bring good energy and maybe a subtle change could make a difference. I thought I was the guy to do it with a hit, or I'd get in on a forecheck and maybe force a turnover—one of the things I had done well during the season. I didn't take bad penalties or turn the puck over, but I created havoc and forced pressure on the defence.

When we returned home, Keenan wanted to take us to Lake Placid to get away from it all, but Mark and Kevin said no. They wanted us to go to our homes, sleep in our own beds, eat the food in our refrigerators, and relax. They were convinced everything was going to be fine and they wanted us to believe it, too. Keenan listened, and that shows you just how much respect he had for Mark and Kevin.

There were, however, plenty of distractions. The *New York Post* had come out earlier in the series with an article about Keenan possibly leaving to become head coach and GM of Detroit. Keenan had to quash the rumours before Game 7, declaring, "I'm going to be the coach of the New York Rangers unless someone tells me otherwise." Again, we had to put all of that crap to the side and focus on what was ahead.

Game 7 might have been the most important game in Rangers history, but for us the plan was simple: this was still the same game we'd played over and over. We knew what we had to do on the ice. Those veterans who had been there before reminded us that whether it's Game 7 of the Stanley Cup or the first game in the preseason, it's still the same routine—you do whatever it takes to get the job done. We watched the veterans go about their routine, business as usual, and there was something comforting about it. Messier made a speech and it wasn't long. "Boys, sometimes in life you've got to slay the dragon, and tonight's the night." That was it, and all that was needed.

I didn't get much sleep the night before. I was excited about the possibility of winning the Cup and at this point I wasn't sure if I would play. It was naive to feel so confident, but I just kept thinking I'd been through so much since I began playing hockey at the age of seven, the rejections and injuries. It was as if everything I had been through in my entire life boiled down to this one game. I was going to find a way to play what would be the most important game of my life.

As luck would have it, on the day of the game, I had developed an enormous pimple right in the middle of my forehead. Not surprisingly, the guys were teasing me. *I can't win the Stanley Cup with this thing on my face*, I thought. I was so confident we would win the Cup that I sent Corey Hirsch, one of several players called up from Binghamton, to go to a pharmacy to get some cream to cover it up. God bless Corey, he didn't hesitate. He came back with some Clearasil cover-up cream. I was getting ready for my close-up.

All day I had been told to be ready. Joey Kocur was hurting and the team was looking to make a change. As I sat in my stall, Assistant Coach Colin Campbell came up to me and said, "You're in!" with a big smile, knowing how much it meant. Normally, you'd never change a winning lineup, but when you've lost a couple games in a row, you've got to change some of the energy. I was the only lineup change for Game 7.

I have never heard a louder building in my life. John Amirante, the Rangers' longtime anthem singer, was drowned out by the crowd. All season long you could hear the organ and the singer clear as a bell, but as the anthem escalated, the crowd noise ramped up until Amirante's voice was not even audible. The din was piercing, one of the most amazing sounds I've ever heard at a sporting event.

I remember taking shifts and trying to hit everything that moved. On one play I lined up a hit on Dave Babych, but missed and went headfirst into the boards. I probably concussed myself a little bit, but at that point I wasn't about to say anything to anybody. Brian Leetch opened the scoring midway through the first period on a fantastic three-way passing play. Then Adam Graves made it 2–0 on the power play at 14:45. All of our best players showed up early in the first period. We were feeling good, but kept reminding ourselves that there was still a lot of work ahead of us.

We got an early power play in the second period, but Canucks Trevor Linden scored their first goal shorthanded at 5:21. Giving up a shorthanded goal is deflating, and the other team gets a big boost of adrenaline—it completely changed the momentum. But when we got another power play later in the period, Mark Messier made good on it, scoring at 13:29. We headed to the dressing room after two periods with a 3–1 lead. A good position, but far from secure, especially against such a talented team. The Cup was still twenty minutes away.

In the third, Trevor Linden again got his team going, scoring on a power play at 4:50, and narrowing our lead to one goal. With the stakes that much higher, you could feel the crowd's energy change—more on edge. It stayed that way till the dying seconds. There was a close call when the Canucks' Nathan LaFayette hit the goalpost with about six minutes to go. Afterward, CBC announcer Harry Neale declared, "The post and the crossbar will get a lot of votes for the Conn Smythe Trophy."

Sometimes you need a little luck! With just seconds left, we cleared the puck from our zone, and as it crept down the ice we started celebrating—but too soon. With just 0.4 seconds left on the clock, we had an icing call. Some fans were already cheering and others weren't sure what to do. When 1.2 seconds were added back on the time, the tension grew. So little time left, but is 1.6 seconds enough to score a tying goal? After fifty-four years of not winning a Cup, even the smallest seed of doubt can creep in.

I remember pausing and taking a look at the building. I watched all the police line up in the front rows, by the glass, with riot gear on, locking their arms together in a human chain. *What the hell is going to happen here in less than two seconds? Are they going to jump on us?* I remember the scene from the 1977 World Series, Reggie Jackson running in from right field and having to bulldoze his way through the crowd after the fans charged the field. Maybe it was going to be like that for us trying to get to the dressing room.

I didn't have to wait long to find out. Craig MacTavish took the face-off for us, one of his specialties, and he got the puck back, away from any Vancouver player. In just 1.6 seconds, the third-period buzzer goes off and we end the fifty-four-year drought.

We went crazy on the ice, jumping up and down and screaming. Brian Leetch and I were just looking at each other. "What do we do next?" I asked. And Leetchey said, "I don't know, let's go ask Mark." But we weren't done celebrating and we found a new pile of teammates to jump on. Sure enough, the New York fans were amazing and the police just stayed where they were.

The Stanley Cup was brought onto the ice by two members of the Hockey Hall of Fame, wearing white gloves. This was the first year that happened. It was Commissioner Gary Bettman's first full season, and afterwards he decided it would become a tradition. After thanking the Rangers and Canucks organizations, he congratulated our players. This was followed by another tradition he began, inviting the captain of the winning team to accept the Cup. "Captain Mark Messier, come get the Stanley Cup!" Tina Turner's "(Simply) The Best" blared over the loudspeakers. Mark raised the Cup and nodded for us to come over. When the team surrounded him, I leaned over and snuck the first kiss. The Cup was passed from player to player—it's usually done by seniority. I remember getting the Cup from Mike Richter and trying to lift it over my head (it was way heavier than I thought, thirty-six pounds, to be precise), and then directing it towards the crowd. This whole thing was like an out-of-body experience. We came together for the traditional team photo with all of us lying down or kneeling. It was something started by the Edmonton Oilers when they won their first Cup in 1984, and I was in the front row.

After the team photo, we took turns holding the Cup again. The following year there was a hockey card of me raising the Stanley Cup over my head. That was a huge moment for me, even better than when I first saw a hockey card of myself, from my rookie year. When I had the Cup back, I skated over to the glass of section 72 and lifted it. Some of the fans there reached over to try to touch it. I remember all those fans throughout the year saying, "Please, please." A few rows behind, Steve Zaretsky and his father, Dave, who had been a season-ticket holder since 1972, held up a sign that read NOW I CAN DIE IN PEACE. *Sports Illustrated* snapped a photo of it, which became a signature moment in Rangers history. It was closure for Steve and all Rangers fans. I had seen that sign in Game 5 and I had to take the Cup to where he was sitting. *Here it is, Steve*, I thought. *This is cool, touch your Cup.* Steve later created a website called NowIcandieinpeace.com.

My father and my sister Stelle and brother-in-law Glen were there for the final game. My mother stayed back to take care of her first grandchild, Ally. It was so special to have family there. Players are allocated tickets and my family sat in my seats. That night my father got to sit beside a true die-hard New York Rangers fan, Steve Romano. Steve found out they were my family and when there were only a few minutes left to go in the game, he left his seat to go buy my dad one of the championship T-shirts that were made available to the fans for after the game. The vendor told him there were strict rules to not sell any before the game was over. Steve then explained that he was sitting beside my dad and bribed him with fifty dollars to sneak one out of the box. My dad had a Rangers Stanley Cup Championship T-shirt when the game was still undecided.

My family made their way down to the packed dressing room and literally soaked up the atmosphere with all the champagne spraying everyone. There's a photo of my sister soaking wet. My buddy Jim Mandala was at the game, too. I spotted him standing outside the dressing room and invited him inside. At that time celebrating with family members took place in the dressing room. Now family is allowed onto the ice after the game. The Zaretskys had also been invited and were there as well. Steve left the sign outside the dressing room and it was gone when he came back out. The Hockey Hall of Fame wanted it for a display, but it was never found. At least *Sports illustrated* had taken a picture of it.

We didn't get out of the dressing room until around 2 a.m. That's when the real party started. We went to a bar called the Auction House, which was owned by our old friend Johnnie B. It wasn't a big place, but it seemed like half of New York wanted in there. Actor Tim Robbins, whose movie *The Shawshank Redemption* had just come out, was there. He told me he never dropped his name to get into places, but did so this time because he wanted to see the Cup. As for the China Club, a few days later we took the Cup there, too.

That night, Mark Messier became the only hockey player in history to captain two different Stanley Cup championship teams. That's still true today. And as he promised back at that lunch we had together at the start of the season, he only wore a Stanley Cup ring once the rest of his teammates could wear one, too. That is true leadership.

CHAPTER 7

After the Cup

Three days after the series ended, we met at our practice facility at Rye Playland to get ready for the Stanley Cup parade. We had no idea what to expect or how many people would attend. It started at Battery Park, where there were floats for the players, the coaching staff, and management. It was determined who would be on each of the floats, and the beauty of it was they allowed our parents to be included. My mom had flown to New York to celebrate with us. The NYPD assigned each player two police officers for the day.

New York knows how to put on a show. The city is famous for its parades with ticker tape floating down from the tops of buildings. I remember when our float turned up the Canyon of Heroes near the World Trade Center. The roar of the crowd hit me in the face—powerful enough to move hair. I'd never experienced anything like it in my life. There were people jammed on the roadsides and hanging from ledges from buildings high above. I couldn't believe they were allowing this. There was confetti coming down from everywhere. We made our way up to city hall, where recently elected New York mayor Rudy Giuliani gave us each a key to the city. For whatever reason, after the parade was over, Glenn Healy and I were left with the Cup. All we were told was to make sure we brought it to Mayor Giuliani's house for dinner. Glenn wanted to make a stop on the way: McSorley's, the oldest pub in New

York City. We went there in a police squad car. We were still wearing our jerseys from the parade as we pulled up to the front of the pub and got out with the Cup. The first thing we noticed was everyone else had jerseys on, too. The Cup was taken out of the car and the place went absolutely bananas. We barely got through to the front door before the Cup was taken out of our hands and passed through the crowd, jumping ahead to the front of the bar. Then the same thing happened to us. I couldn't even touch the ground or move—I was just being held up by the pressure of the people. It was one of the craziest things I have ever been a part of it. We spent about an hour in McSorley's and it was total mayhem.

We went to the Guiliani home and met his eight-year-old son, Andrew, who wanted to be a goalie. So, we offered to give him some training. He was wearing goalie equipment and we were just firing shots at his head, and he loved every second. Guiliani's son had turned into somewhat of a celebrity back in January when he was spoofed on the *Late Show with David Letterman* and *Saturday Night Live*.

The four Russian players on our team—Alexander Karpovtsev, Alex Kovalev, Sergei Nemchinov, and Sergei Zubov—became the first from their country to win the Cup and that was a big deal. They put together a party for the team at a nightclub in Brighton Beach, which is a Brooklyn community where many Russians live. They had a twelve-course meal with caviar and live entertainment. Kevin Lowe showed up in flip-flops because he thought Brighton Beach meant we were going to the actual beach. It was a great night and my mom really got into it. Our "black-eyed beauty" was dancing on a table until three or four in the morning. She said the Messier family was heading out to another party, but I had to get her out of there because I was tired and wanted to go home.

A week later, I received a call from Mark Messier and he asked me what I was doing. I told him I was probably going to get a haircut and he said that was too bad because he and Brian Leetch were going to throw out the first pitch at the New York Yankees game and wondered if I wanted to join them. I told him I could probably reschedule the haircut.

On the way, Mark and I went to Columbia Presbyterian Hospital to visit Brian Bluver, a thirteen-year-old who was in dire need of a heart transplant. He had been on a list for a while and only had a few days—at the most—left to live, unless he got a match and a heart was donated. We had the Cup with us and it was very emotional. Mark told Brian that he'd get the heart transplant and do great, and he promised Brian that he would be there with us when we raised the Stanley Cup banner at the start of the next season.

If anyone else had said it . . . I don't know. But just a couple days later, Brian Bluver would get his heart transplant. Miraculously, he recovered fully. And true to his word, Mark had Brian there at MSG for the banner raising. The story doesn't quite end there, though. Brian's heart surgeon was Dr. Mehmet Oz, who in later years became famous for appearing on *The Oprah Winfrey Show* and then starring in his own, called *Dr. Oz*. In 2018, I attended the Super Bowl in Minnesota and Dr. Oz was there. When I saw him at the game, I had to talk to him about this amazing experience we'd shared. He didn't remember me at first, but then he thought back to his young patient and how Mark and I had gone into the hospital with the Cup. Dr. Oz said Mark's visit that day had done wonders for Brian.

After that visit to the hospital, we took the Cup to Yankee Stadium, where they dressed us up from head to toe in pinstripes. Pitcher Steve Howe taught Leetchey a few tricks. It turned out that Leetchey could throw a ball ninety miles per hour, so during batting practice Mark played catcher and I hit.

After batting practice we went to the clubhouse. Don Mattingly, the captain of the Yankees, asked the three of us to sign a hat for him. Mattingly, arguably the best player in the mideighties and unquestionably my favourite baseball player, asked me to sign his hat! To use a *Seinfeld* phrase, it is a bizarro world.

The energy before that baseball game was drastically different from what we were used to. Before a hockey game, the room becomes quiet and intense. Typically, hockey players are at the rink three hours before puck drop. Someone is always in charge of the music and it is played pretty loudly up until about an hour and a half before the start of the game. Once the music is turned off, all horsing around stops, game faces are on. Every player has a different way of preparing, but it's anything but relaxed.

After we finished eating from a massive buffet at the Yankees clubhouse it was a little over an hour until the first pitch. We wanted to let the ballplayers get focused for the game, like we would have, but when we tried to leave they told us we needed to stick around for their kangaroo court.

It wasn't a metaphor. Wade Boggs comes in and he's got a judge's robe and wig on. He sits down at the front of the room and waits to hear all the cases. Danny Tartabull was called to the front. He was accused of not knowing the number of outs during an inning. Typical baseball stuff. He pleaded his case, was found guilty, and owed the court $200. He had to pay the money to a fund that would be used at the end of the year. One young player was then accused of being late for a team bus. He walked to the front of the room, pleaded his case, was found guilty, and fined $100. Then Wade Boggs says, "Next case: the New York Rangers." Leetchey, Mark, and I had no idea where this was going. Boggs explained that in celebration of Bernie Williams's game-winning home run a few nights earlier, he was feeling pretty good about himself and went to the China Club to celebrate. But unfortunately, all the attention that was expected to be lavished on Williams was lost when the Rangers brought in the Stanley Cup.

"You guys stole Bernie's thunder. How do you plead?" he asked.

Brian and Mark shoved me to the front of the room. I had to think pretty quickly. I told the kangaroo court that we were, of course, not guilty. I then stated our case.

"I remember security did an excellent job of making a clear path down the stairs," I began. "As we entered, we carefully scoped out the room. I saw the entire room, but, unfortunately for Bernie, there were no girls within thirty feet of him. I'm sorry to say that Bernie Williams had no game that night, so there was no thunder to be stolen."

The whole room broke out in laughter. Boggs slammed his gavel down and declared us not guilty. I've never heard that kind of laughter just before a hockey game.

About three weeks later, Brian Noonan and I went to MTV's *Beach House*, which was a one-hour show with a bunch of really good-looking girls on the beach. We brought the Cup. I'm not sure the girls really enjoyed it that much—as it had done before, the Cup took all the attention.

Every member of a Cup-winning team is allowed to take the Cup home with them for a day or two. Mike Hudson, Glenn Healy, and I were the Toronto players and it was delivered to us on August 2. We decided together where it would go first: the Hospital for Sick Children. It was the first time the Cup had ever been taken there. As Toronto guys, we, of course, had to apologize that we weren't from the Toronto Maple Leafs, who had not won the championship since 1967. But I think our gesture was still appreciated.

After that we went to my dad's restaurant, Peter's Steak House. We made the rounds and then took it to my mom's brothers' restaurant, Pops. The cover of the *Toronto Sun* featured my uncle Jim and uncle Steve with me at Pops in front of the Stanley Cup, which they were thrilled about.

My buddies and I decided to stop at the House of Lancaster, a popular striptease bar. While the girls were up onstage, all the eyes of the patrons in the back of the room were glued to their cameras, taking photos with Lord Stanley's Cup. It's fair to say that a few of the dancers weren't so happy that the attention was off of them, so we got out of there pretty quickly.

My cousin George Kallinikos suggested we do a party on Danforth Avenue, the heart of Greektown. I definitely wanted to do something for all the people that I grew up with who had supported me, but wasn't really sure what to do. George did all the planning. The next thing I know people are donating balloons, ribbons, ice, a DJ—you name it. We ended up having the party at a place called Ouzeri with about three hundred people dancing until the sun came up. My buddy Jim Mandala was at the door checking names off the guest list. Some people tried to lie their way into the party, but Jim made sure that wouldn't fly. It was the best night of my summer. The Cup has such an effect on people who are able to see it for the first time. Twenty-five years after that party I still have people telling me their stories about being there. One guy stopped me just a few weeks before writing this to show me a picture stored on his phone. It came from an old photograph from that night that showed him hugging the Stanley Cup. For true hockey fans it means everything.

Because I was showing up everywhere with the Cup, Eddie O nicknamed me Forrest Gump. I was soaking it all in. The NHL head office in New York saw me enjoying it so much that they asked me to do a few more appearances with it. When I was back in New York, the Rangers also asked me at the last minute to replace Mike Keenan at an event for Canali, an Italian menswear company.

Keenan couldn't make the appearance because of something that had been long rumoured: He had been negotiating with Detroit during our playoff run, trying to get out of the Rangers coaching contract with GM Neil Smith. Keenan and Smith had been fighting the entire year and we weren't surprised to hear the rumour confirmed. The story was actually broken by my ex-coach and future television colleague, Doug MacLean.

He'd been given the inside information from someone in Detroit. He inadvertently mentioned it to someone back in his home on Prince Edward Island. A radio station got wind of the story, leaked it, and the NHL was pissed. Discussing possible employment with another team while still under contract is strictly prohibited. It might happen, but seldom do people get caught like Keenan did.

Because Keenan wanted to keep a low profile after the conflict, he chose not to go to the Canali event, so the Rangers sent me instead. It worked out well. When I showed up I was introduced to George Tsaganeas, who ran the Canali division in the eastern U.S. at the time. Yes, he is another Greek. Besides getting a great Italian suit, I made a lifelong friend in George. In fact, he baptized my second son.

The one thing I will always remember is my father's advice when I first went to Philadelphia. He told me that life was about connecting. Reaching out and meeting people, connecting them to each other, and developing relationships. During the hockey season I was pretty tame and focused on the game, but with all the celebrating the summer after winning the Cup, I truly felt this advice take root. Glenn Adamo, who was the NHL's vice president of broadcasting, encouraged me to continue to get out there and market myself. In an indirect way he had a great influence on my future career in broadcasting. Glenn put me on an MTV game show with Snoop Dogg hosted by VJ Lisa Kennedy. My teammates thought I was nuts, but honestly, being on TV was the most fun I'd ever had outside of hockey. I was accused of "milking it" a little too much, and the truth is I did. But the seed was planted for my future. Much like star defenceman P. K. Subban now, I didn't shy away from opportunities. P. K., however, is a machine. He has the energy to be "on" 24/7. In my opinion, he is a natural performer. My TV talent took a little bit more work.

Meanwhile, the Keenan situation progressed until he eventually signed with the St. Louis Blues as GM and coach. Things fell through with Detroit. He claimed the Rangers did not pay him a bonus, which violated his contract, and this allowed him to leave. The Rangers disputed it, and the press had a field day. The *New York Post* branded Keenan a "Benedict Arnold." One article said he was a "Traitor! Like a Rat, Keenan Jumps Off Ranger Ship." New Yorkers don't mince words.

NHL Commissioner Gary Bettman heard submissions from both parties and nine days later made several rulings. This part blows my mind. Bettman allowed Keenan to sign with the Blues but fined him $100,000 for conduct detrimental to the league, and suspended him for sixty days, so he couldn't begin work until September 24. Gary Bettman did something unusual in dealing with the Keenan fiasco. For tampering, the Blues were penalized for their part and had to give the Rangers compensation. That compensation ended up coming in the form of the trade of the talented young centre Petr Nedvěd, in exchange for Esa Tikkanen and Doug Lidster. The Rangers had to pay Keenan a $608,000 bonus and, in turn, he had to pay the team $400,000 for not fulfilling the remainder of his contract. And there's more. The Rangers had to pay the NHL $25,000 for filing a lawsuit against their coach, which is against league rules. With that, Keenan agreed to drop his countersuit. Detroit was also fined $25,000 for negotiating with Keenan. And this all happened in a hugely successful Stanley Cup championship year. I can't imagine what would have happened in a bad year.

When the word came down that Keenan was now with St. Louis, about 70 percent of the team was at Adam Graves's wedding, in Windsor, Ontario. Some guys let out small cheers. Others were completely ecstatic and relieved.

Just a month after we won the Cup, we no longer had a coach. Two weeks later, GM Neil Smith announced that Colin Campbell, who had been an assistant coach with the team for four years, had been promoted to head coach. Colie did an unbelievable job of being a buffer between Keenan and the players. He had put out a lot of fires. I was glad they were able to give it to him. Colie kept Dick Todd as his assistant and hired Mike Murphy as another assistant.

There was a lot more turmoil coming, however. With all this going on, the NHL and the NHL Players' Association were involved in a battle over a new collective bargaining agreement and it was looking more likely that the season would not start as scheduled, and could even be shut down completely. The big issue was that the owners wanted to implement a salary cap and the players were against it.

The summer ended with no resolution in sight, but we returned as a group for the start of training camp. We were happy at least to be working with a coach that would be much easier to play under than Keenan.

During a team stretch before practice I mentioned to a few of the guys that a friend of mine was hosting a dinner party with a group that included Joan Lunden, the host of *Good Morning America*. Well, didn't some of the guys start giving it to me when they heard this. Kevin Lowe made me well aware that Joan had interviewed presidents. "Kyper, what are your thoughts on world issues?" To which Mike Richter replied, "That will be the shortest conversation she'll ever have." Not to be left out, Glenn Healy chimes in: "Remember, the Middle East isn't Thunder Bay."

Despite the encouragement of my team, a group of us met for dinner that night and we ended up in a New York nightclub. Two days later the story ran like wildfire. Page 6 of the *New York Post* started with a mention of Joan and her new boyfriend. Then Howard Stern and his sidekick, Robin, had some fun with it. Things got a little goofy when the media started appearing at our practice facility. One young girl in particular was hanging outside and asked me if she could take a picture of me alone. I declined—something seemed a bit off. Then Mike Richter said, "Why don't I take the picture and you appear in it with Kyper as well?" That was a great idea of Ricky's. We both figured if she had other intentions for the photo, she couldn't do much with it because she was in the shot. We thought we were brilliant.

A few days later that exact photo showed up on the cover of the gossip tabloid *Star Magazine*. She had cropped herself out and spliced in Joan Lunden. The cover *of Star Magazine* read: "Joan Lunden Dumps Costner for Toyboy." She had recently divorced and there were stories that she had been dating actor Kevin Costner. I certainly wasn't expecting to be on the cover of tabloid magazines because of that photo. Guys on the team had an absolute field day. We were travelling through California on a packed commercial flight and I happened to be the last guy to jump on the flight. What I didn't know was that Mess had bought the whole team a stack of *Star* magazines at the airport and handed them out to half the plane. When I boarded the flight everybody held them up. We all had fun with it, including me.

The team fun didn't last long, though. The NHL and the NHLPA couldn't come to an agreement, which led to a lockout and the regular season was put on indefinite hold. The NHLPA advised the players to take a break and get away from hockey because the likelihood was the lockout would go on for a while. The PA had a contingency plan to pay us, but it wasn't anything significant, just enough to tide us over for what we thought would be a month or two. It stung, but I rationalized it. I wasn't just losing money; we were doing this for the future of the players.

Mike Hudson, Brian Noonan, and I decided to go to Cancún for a week to have some fun. The last thing the NHLPA or Executive Director Bob Goodenow wanted was guys fretting over whether we were going to be getting back to work tomorrow.

Because we had just won the Cup, it was kind of a big deal that three of us from the New York Rangers were vacationing in one of these resorts. It's impressive to be part of any NHL team, but it was a big difference in 1994 to be a member of the New York Rangers rather than, say, a member of the Tampa Bay Lightning, or a franchise that didn't yet have a huge following or history. People may not have known all the teams in the NHL, but they knew the New York Rangers, so we got a bit of extra attention in Cancún. The only thing missing was the Cup. We were three single guys with not a care in the world, knowing this lockout would be settled or fixed one way or another.

I returned home to Toronto after the vacation and began skating with some other NHL players. There were so many of us living in the city. The lockout didn't seem to be ending anytime soon. We figured if we did return to work that season, it would be shortly after Christmas. Any later and the season couldn't be salvaged. Even so, we were skating every day, as it was important to try to stay in shape and be ready. We had a really good core of guys. Peter Zezel of the Leafs would lead the charge of finding us ice time and getting good skates going. Besides Peter and myself, the group had Detroit's Kris Draper and some Maple Leaf players, including Tie Domi. We set up a charity game at Varsity Arena to raise money for the Hospital for Sick Children. Lots of people were working to keep hockey alive. A Toronto FM radio station organized an event with the NHLPA, Bryan Green from Plain and Simple, and DJ Joey Vendetta, who helped secure some sponsors, for what became the Q107 Cup. It was a lot of fun.

When the lockout finally ended it was January 11, 1995, 103 days after it started. Much of the season had been lost—468 total games, including the All-Star Game. After all the negotiations, there were some big changes to the arbitration system and a salary cap for rookies. And the new deal was a six-year agreement, giving us that long before we'd potentially have to go through this again. Those lost games cost me $250,000, basically about half a year's pay, which I would never recover. But, at least for the time being, we'd avoided a general salary cap. We believed strongly that salary caps would never be a good thing, and today's players have found this out. Good players that can still play the game are now forced to retire early. Because their contracts are too high for the value that they provide, the contracts no longer match the value placed on them by the cap. Vincent Lecavalier was a prime example of this when the Flyers let him go. Although no longer a superstar, he had more strong years to play, but his contract made him untouchable. So our being able to hold off on a cap for at least a few more years was an achievement.

A 48-game schedule was drawn up that would begin on January 20 and extend into May, the first time the regular season would go beyond April. To accommodate this change, there would only be intraconference play, meaning Eastern Conference teams would only play against one another and the same in the Western Conference.

It was great to be back in New York with the guys. The David Letterman show requested ten Rangers for his famous top ten list. Barry Watkins and John Rosasco from the Rangers PR department had a tough time picking which of us should do it. Letterman's show was at the height of its popularity and ran late-night television. I got chosen, along with Glenn Healy, Mike Richter, Jeff Beukeboom, Joey Kocur, Eddie Olczyk, Adam Graves, Mike Hartman, Brian Leetch, and Mark Messier.

Letterman started the monologue that night by asking the audience, "How many of you are here tonight only because you could not get Rangers tickets?" We each then explained the "top ten ways the Rangers spent their time off." We had so much fun. Glenn Healy said he went joyriding on a Zamboni. The always reserved Brian Leetch said he spent his time "keeping my stick waxed, if you know what I mean." Mike Hartman was substituted for by a four-hundred-pound stand-in who said he spent his time eating during the lockout. My line was, "You know that adorable skating bunny in the Ice Capades? That was me." Mark ended the top ten list with "eating Stanley Cup–size Jell-O shots." New York has to be one of the best cities to play in.

We had a few practices and then it was back to playing. Some stars, such as Doug Gilmour, got invited to Europe to play. Gretzky took a group of high-level players and did a tour of games in Europe as well. But once the lockout ended, the Rangers looked forward to raising the Stanley Cup banner at our home opener at MSG.

That night we were hosting the Buffalo Sabres. Game-day operations told us how the ceremony would unfold. I have to admit it was well thought out. This was one of the first times the Stanley Cup was brought back for a regular-season game. If it had been done before, it had not been this late in the year. The ceremony, which was emceed by MSG Networks' John Davidson, who is now the president of the team, began with Ranger greats Rod Gilbert and Eddie Giacomin walking on the ice to participate in the raising of the 1993–1994 Eastern Conference champions banner. Rod saluted us on the bench. He was followed by Eddie, who was serenaded with chants of "Ed-die, Ed-die" by the crowd. He also pointed towards us as if to say, "You guys did it."

They were followed by a video replay of our Stanley Cup run, beginning with Howie Rose's memorable Matteau call. The camera then pointed to Stéphane. I don't think he was expecting that. He just said, "Wow, thank you," and then he raised an arm to salute the crowd. The place went wild. Once again the fans were shown a video of us hoisting the Cup that night over seven months prior. Five longtime season-ticket holders, representing all Rangers fans, were paraded onto the ice. Then came a video replay with a montage of the final seconds of Game 7 of the Stanley Cup, and Howie's call: "And the waiting is over. The New York Rangers are the Stanley Cup champions. No more curses, and it's unbelievable." The video included footage of us celebrating wildly on the ice, and me taking the Cup over to the fans to let them touch it. Then we saw some of the celebration in midtown New York back in June and part of an interview with Adam Graves, who said, "The bottom line is that Ranger fans and the people of New York will never, ever, ever have to hear '1940' ever again."

The arena lights were shut off and the Cup lowered from the rafters, surrounded by dry-ice fog with lasers firing. We all stood around the centre ice circle as part of the ceremony, and watched the Cup drop perfectly onto a stand. It was maybe a little over-the-top, but the fans were still so excited after having waited fifty-four years. Everything is just a little bigger in New York City.

With all of this going on, I'm not sure how many people noticed that we had a special guest on our bench that night. Watching it all from the best seat in the house was Brian Bluver, the boy Mark and I visited in the hospital while he was waiting for a lifesaving heart operation. Mark had promised he'd be here, and here he was. For Mark and me in particular, having him there was the best part of the whole thing.

The fans started chanting "Let's go, Rangers." The organization asked Mark to re-create the celebration in June by raising the Cup and then having all of us skate around with it again. They replayed Tina Turner's "(Simply) the Best."

Raising the banner was a proud moment, but I couldn't shake the feeling that we'd been denied something—this was all seven months after the fact, and felt a little awkward. We had gone through a long-drawn-out affair with the lockout. The Ranger fans loved it, but it would have been nice if we'd been able to do this much earlier and with a normal start to the season. In the end we were back to work, where we belonged, and our job was to focus on winning. After all the fanfare we lost that night to Buffalo.

With Colie Campbell as our new head coach there was a significant difference from when Mike Keenan stood behind the bench. Mostly, things were calm. I think we enjoyed playing without all the drama we had gone through with Keenan. Plus, I felt with Colie as coach I might have a bigger role. However, we didn't get off to a good start to the 48-game season, losing 4 of our first 5 games. The Stanley Cup hangover was real, as many of the first-time winners soon found out. Colie liked my work ethic and there were times throughout the season when he moved me up in the lineup. At critical points in a game he would put me on a line with Alex Kovalev and Sergei Nemchinov, both skilled scorers. We worked well together.

As the reigning champions, we visited the White House during that season, in March 1995. It is customary now, but at the time we were only the second NHL team to be invited. Pittsburgh was the first team to go, back in 1991. We took a charter flight to D.C., and when we arrived there was a bus waiting to take us to the White House. As we were waiting on the tarmac for the bus, I noticed oil dripping off the plane's wing onto Brian Noonan's shoulder. He was looking great in a nice suit and tie, with one exception: a huge grease stain down the front of his jacket. We all had a laugh, including Brian.

In recent years, athletes going to the White House—or not going, in particular—is seen as more of a political statement. But at that time there was no question as to whether we would go. There weren't the same political tightropes to walk like there are today.

President Bill Clinton welcomed us. He was the head of the most powerful nation in the world and was simply honouring a team for a great accomplishment. Clinton was an impressive statesman. There was an aura about him and most of the team was in complete awe. He even managed to make light of the lockout that year, saying, "We have been trying to make this visit happen for some time, but what's a few months compared to fifty-four years?" He shook each of our hands and repeated each of our names. Apparently, he has a photographic memory, so this was maybe part of his process. I met him again in Toronto about fifteen years later and he remembered everything about that day. He referenced names and details that even I had forgotten. I was blown away.

Our team sat in the Oval Office for a while and then the ceremony took place in the Rose Garden. The president officially welcomed us and congratulated us on our achievement. Just before we took the team picture with him, I told Noonan we had a bad position and we needed to move from the back to the front, but he didn't want anything to do with it because of the grease stain. I figured, suit yourself, and I jockeyed up to the front row. Two months later we got the team photo, and just as I suspected, all you could see of Brian Noonan, buried in the back row, was his right ear. I told him the good news was that no one could see his grease stain.

That visit to the White House was the highlight of the season up to that point. By March, the abbreviated season was proving to be a tough one, overall. We struggled and underachieved, and ultimately finished with a record of 22-23-3. I don't know who was more disappointed, us or our fans. But this is not what anyone expects from a championship team.

It wasn't really the same team, though. The Rangers had banked on Petr Nedvěd to be a difference maker, and he was a talented guy, but he just never fit in that year as the ideal second centreman behind Messier. Sometimes that can happen, and it's not anyone's fault. Not only did we have a new coach, but we made significant changes to our lineup, which is not unusual, even after winning the Cup. Pat Verbeek, my teammate in Hartford, was acquired at the trade deadline in March for Glen Feather-stone. Nathan LaFayette, who almost tied the game for the Canucks in the seventh game of the Cup Final, was acquired a couple weeks later for Corey Hirsch. All great guys, but in a shortened season we just never clicked as a team. And on top of everything, Steve Larmer's health was deteriorating because of back issues. It was devastating. He was in a lot of pain. I remember watching him barely able sit down at times.

We were playing okay and battling to make the playoffs. I remember a game we played at home against Washington in April. I made one of the most memorable body checks of my career, against my former Capitals teammate Calle Johansson, that left him looking like Disney's Bambi on ice trying to get up. It was a textbook hit that checked off all the right boxes: elbows down, full-body contact, and my feet never left the ice.

Right after the hit, Caps defenceman Mark Tinordi started to chase me on the ice during the play. It created enough havoc that Brian Noonan was left to score to make it 2–0 for us. Caps head coach Jim Schoenfeld went ballistic, which resulted in us getting another power play. Zubov scored to give us a bigger lead. But that hit earned me a lot of accolades from my teammates, my coaches, and the NY press, too.

Even with our poor record, we secured a playoff spot as the eighth and final seed. We were hot in the last month but never found the consistency we had the year before. With one game below .500, we barely squeezed into the playoffs. Going into the postseason, we still felt like we could compete at a high level. We were eager to prove we could. We opened the first round against Quebec, which had finished with the best record in the Eastern Conference. We'd finished almost 20 points behind the Nordiques. No one gave us much of a chance against that first-place, highest-scoring Quebec team. Emerging star Peter Forsberg and the highly talented Joe Sakic led the team in points. Wendel Clark was also a Nordique. The team was talented but young and unproven.

We lost the first game in Quebec 5–4. Then won Game 2 in Quebec by a convincing score of 8–3. Petr Nedvěd had a big third period. I assisted one of his goals. Game 3 was back in New York with momentum on our side, and we won 4–3, with Brian Leetch scoring the game winner.

Game 4 is remembered as one of the most controversial for the Nordiques. Referee Andy Van Hellemond decided to waive off a first-period goal by Joe Sakic. It was an odd decision. Quebec defenceman Craig Wolanin had slashed Kovalev hard across his back and Kovalev fell to the ice. With Brian Leetch caught pinching, Joe Sakic was sent in against goalie Glenn Healy, and Sakic scored to make it 3–0 Nordiques. After a lengthy delay while the officials huddled, Andy Van Hellemond decided to discount the goal despite no whistle on the play. He waived the goal off because of the injury to Kovalev. Even we were shocked at the call. Something like that would never happen today in the NHL.

John Garrett, who was working for *Hockey Night in Canada*, was calling the game. He suggested that the Rangers were leading a "charmed life" because of the bad call. I don't know about that, but we did come back to tie the game 2–2, then won in overtime. Nordique fans were furious. After the game we could hear Nordiques GM Pierre Lacroix screaming at the top of his lungs at the officials. He waved an NHL rule book in their faces. I was on the line with Kovalev, who took a lot of heat for falling on the play, but he was by far the most talented player I've ever had on a line.

Despite the controversy surrounding the slash, Kovalev was the best player in the series. And I was playing my best hockey as a Ranger. By this time, Colie Campbell had put me on a regular line with Nemchinov and Kovalev.

When something like that call on the Sakic goal happens, it can create a lot of ill will. Game 5 was in Quebec, and, with their team facing elimination, the fans were angry. After we lost the game, they were throwing things at us while we were still on the ice—we had to duck out of the way. I was pelted with a mustard container that exploded after bouncing off my shoulder and my whole jersey was covered. I didn't even know it at the time because there was so much chaos. The game was over, but not the night. When we boarded the bus, the Nords fans started rocking it.

Game 6 was back in New York. We started strong, with three goals in the first period. With about seven minutes to go in the game, Chris Simon, who I had fought earlier in the year, took a five-minute major for hitting me headfirst into the boards. There was no concussion protocol back then. Jim Ramsay, our new head trainer, came to me on the ice and kept asking me the score. When I finally got it right, they let me back on the ice. I had been down for quite some time and Jim told me not to rush. Clearly the longer I was down on the ice the more pressure mounted on Van Hellemond to eject Chris Simon from the game. And that is exactly what happened. I was groggy, but there was no way I was going to take myself out of the lineup—probably not the smartest thing. But my line with Nemchinov and Kovalev scored three of the four goals. We won the game, and the series, that night, in what was the Nords' final run in Quebec. Shortly after, the franchise was moved to Colorado. Ironically, the Colorado Avalanche won the Stanley Cup the following year.

But overall, it was a good moment for us. Knocking out the first seed the way we did had the media thinking we had a good shot at repeating a Stanley Cup championship. Ultimately, Andy Van Hellemond was fined by the NHL. Gary Bettman said, "It is clear that Van Hellemond erred in judgement when he disallowed an apparent goal." It was probably little comfort to the fans in Quebec.

We faced Philadelphia in the second round. The Flyers had finished second in the Eastern Conference, and with good reason. They were a hard group to play against. They had the Legion of Doom line of Eric Lindros, John LeClair, and Mikael Renberg. There was no stopping Lindros, who was playing his best hockey. We were swept. The Flyers lost in the next round to New Jersey, who went on to win the Cup, sweeping Detroit.

When it was all over, we knew there were going to be further changes in the lineup for the 1995–1996 season. In the off-season, Nedved and Sergei Zubov were traded for Luc Robitaille and Ulf Samuelsson. And Larmer retired. Doug Lidster was reacquired in a trade for Jay Wells. Wayne Presley, my former teammate with the Kitchener Rangers, signed as a free agent after playing with Buffalo. Bruce Driver was also acquired as a free agent—he came from the Cup-winning Devils. With the season done, and our team being dismantled, I wondered what my future in New York would be.

CHAPTER 8

Home to Toronto

Early in the next season, there were rumours I was going to be traded to Buffalo for Bob Sweeney. In fact, I was sure I would end up with the Sabres. From what I'm led to believe, a deal had been agreed on, but it fell through when somebody from the Sabres was injured. I stayed on with the Rangers for 1995–1996, knowing that my time there was likely coming to an end. Christmas passed and still nothing. The season was going fairly well and it looked like we'd make the playoffs.

Much like in 1994, we had a great new group of guys on the team, which now included Luc Robitaille and Ulf Samuelsson—great teammates. We were on the road in Philadelphia, and for some reason the Spectrum arena had placed the Flyers wives' room directly across from the visitors dressing room. The caterers would always leave their carts of food for the wives in the hallway right opposite us. It drove Ulfie nuts. He used the hallway to do stick work and the carts were always in the way. He told me, "I'll teach the caterer a little lesson for leaving that cart right in my way." He took the blowtorch used by players to curve sticks and heated the handle to the guy's cart. Not warm—hot. Seconds after he was done, the caterer came out; as soon as he attempted to push the cart he let out a screech like I've never heard before. We were never short on laughs with Ulfie.

In early February I was a healthy scratch before a home game. I went out with some teammates to a charity event and had a twenty-minute conversation with a woman there. She had flown in from Frankfurt from a modelling job, was exhausted, and only stayed at the event for forty minutes. Timing is everything. What I didn't know then was that I had just met my future wife, Anne-Marie. It's a good thing we met when we did, because my time in New York was nearly at an end.

Two weeks later, on February 29 , 1996 (it was a leap year), Rangers GM Neil Smith called me at my apartment to tell me I'd finally been traded. "I'm sending you home to Toronto," he said, "and hope you are happy." I knew something like this was coming, but to play in my hometown, for my childhood favourite team—to say the least, I was happy. The Rangers acquired Bill Berg and Sergio Momesso in exchange for Wayne Presley and me.

Back when I was in Junior, as a member of the North Bay Centennials, I remember playing in Kitchener, against the Rangers, for the first time. I checked a rookie pretty hard, and Presley, who was on that Rangers team, came after me to fight. I dropped my gloves, one-punched him, and knocked him out. It was unfortunate. Wayne was not really a fighter—he had a 63-goal season that year—but thank God he is easygoing. When we became teammates in New York, we had some laughs about that fight. Now we were both going to the Leafs.

But the truth was I had mixed feelings. For many NHLers, playing for the Leafs is overwhelming. I grew up understanding the fixation the city has on their team. The media and fan attention are so concentrated it is truly like living in a fishbowl. In Toronto, anything you do, good or bad, gets blown up ten times bigger than in other hockey markets— even New York and Boston. At the time, the Toronto Raptors NBA team was just getting started and the Toronto Blue Jays baseball team was a distant second in popularity, despite winning two World Series in the early nineties. With all the pressure the city put on the Leafs players, it felt like hockey was the only game in town.

I liked being a Ranger and all that came with it, but the decision was made. My parents, of course, were happy. You never truly know how things are going to turn out—that was always their philosophy. So, they didn't throw any big party or celebration for my coming home. They were just hoping things worked out for me. I was told I was the eighty-eighth Toronto-born player to ever play for that team.

After being traded, players always want to know what they'll be landing in. The Leafs were struggling with a 25-28-10 record and were mired in a six-game losing streak when I arrived. But they had a potent lineup that included Doug Gilmour, Félix Potvin, Todd Gill, Kirk Muller, Dave Gagner, Jamie Macoun, Dave Andreychuk, and Tie Domi, among others. Pat Burns was the coach. I was going to a team that had made it to the conference finals in 1993 and 1994, but was now on the decline. There was talk that Pat Burns was going to lose his job, and there was a lot of turmoil. Clearly, I wasn't going into a very healthy Leaf environment and it was incredibly demoralizing.

I left New York and arrived in Dallas, where the Leafs were playing two days later. When I checked into the hotel where the Leafs were staying, Howard Berger, of Toronto's all-sports radio station, the Fan 590, was waiting for me. Within hours of my arriving, the Toronto media wanted to know about the new guy. This is the type of media attention Toronto fans crave. Even as big as the Rangers were, New York media did not have this type of appetite.

Gilmour, who was the Leafs captain, had the same command of the room as Mark Messier did with the Rangers. This was his team. But while Mark had that deep intensity, Doug was more relaxed. No matter how bad things were, he always found a way to make coming to the rink fun. He enjoyed a good laugh and was a great practical joker. He would put baby powder in the hair blowers and the guys would go crazy when they dried their hair. He'd cut teammates' hockey sticks halfway through for practice, so on just one slap shot the stick would easily snap right in half.

I remember my first morning skate on that Dallas road trip. We were on the bench waiting to take to the ice during a drill, and as we were sitting there talking, Gilmour was bending down pretending to tie his skates when in fact he was untying one of mine. My turn comes up for a line rush and I jump over the boards. Within a few feet I start wobbling and then my boot almost falls off my foot. I looked around and saw Doug laughing his ass off. This guy was going to be a lot of fun to be around.

I knew I was brought in to add some support and heart, and not let other teams take liberties with our key guys. The Leafs already had Domi, who was one of the toughest guys in the league, but this was my role with every team I played for: keeping other teams honest.

When I pulled on the Leaf jersey for the first time, I was a kid again. To this day, I can actually feel myself pulling that blue Toronto Maple Leaf jersey over my head, knowing I'm actually going to be playing a game for this team. It was the same feeling I had at the age of nine when I first put on a Darryl Sittler jersey that my parents had given me for Christmas. It was really weird, but I'm sure any Toronto kid who played for the Leafs had that same feeling. It was probably the same for Eddie Olczyk, a Chicago kid, when he got to play for the Blackhawks.

Unfortunately, in my first game as a Leaf we lost 5–1 to Dallas, but I did my job, fighting Bill Huard. When we played Colorado the next night, our losing streak was extended to eight consecutive games. Going into Colorado, I remember Pat Burns's pregame speech that sounded more like a goodbye. He told us that it was on us as players, there was no more "we." It was more like "you guys" have to find a way to get through. It seemed beyond him at that point. He spoke as if he knew his ship had sailed. We lost 4–0.

I didn't get to play under Pat Burns for long—he was fired upon returning to Toronto. The story goes that Burns wasn't going to resign, but GM Cliff Fletcher reluctantly made the move to try to shake the team up. He was really close with Pat. The two had gone through the Leafs' amazing playoff run in 1992–1993 and came so close to making it into the Stanley Cup Final. The move was made after the game, but we weren't told about it. We found out when we returned home and went to the Gardens for practice. There was a message in the dressing room on the board from Pat wishing us well. It read, "Good luck, guys. Burnsie."

Burns had already packed up his things and gone home to Quebec. Nick Beverley, the Leafs director of pro scouting and player personnel, took over on an interim basis. Pat was well respected and loved. Even though I wasn't around him long, I got the feeling he was a demanding coach who simply couldn't squeeze any more out of the team.

It's tough to come to a team with something like this hanging over it. Because of the losing streak, and the likelihood that Burns would be fired soon, I probably did not enjoy playing my first games as a Leaf as much as I thought I would. A player coming to the New York Rangers inherited the team's history and its desperate need to end the Cup drought. Overnight, it becomes a part of you, the weight of that history. It was similar joining the Leafs. Their losing streak became my losing streak. You want to be the guy who comes in and makes the difference, and sets the team on a new path, somehow. But that's not really how these things work. It takes time, and vision—a lot of soul-searching as a group. It's a lot to adjust to. And sometimes, the team simply isn't good enough.

We finally snapped our eight-game losing streak with a 2–2 tie against the New Jersey Devils. Not a win, but an improvement. It was good to get that monkey off our backs.

Being home gave me some unwanted pressure. I wanted to get tickets for friends and family, but the players were only given two tickets for each game, and we had access to buy only two more. I had to make it clear that it would be hard to make everyone happy. I would have loved to have been able to get tickets for everyone, but that wasn't possible. With more than thirty first cousins and sixty people in all, including aunts and uncles, I had lots of people who wanted to come support me. They were actually great about it and understood.

Seats at Maple Leaf Gardens were a big deal. The Gardens had an unusual design in that fans were very close to the ice. At the time, there was no separation between the player benches and the rows of seats behind them. It was quite common for season-ticket holders to walk right behind the bench en route to their seats, or to be sitting on benches at ice level, on either side of the players' bench. Players would spit their water out and hit a spectator's shoes. There were lots of apologies, especially by visiting teams who weren't used to the setup. It was a strange design on both benches. I can't recall another team bench where a fan could walk directly behind the players with no barrier.

The team put me in a hotel in Toronto until I could find a place to live, which is standard procedure for traded players. I stayed at the Sutton Hotel, but I also went home to my parents' place sometimes for some quiet and, of course, a really good meal. It wasn't like I moved in with them, but because we were so close as a family, it was easy to go back anytime I wanted. My room was still there. It was a home base for me, a safe haven. I would go out with the guys from the team for dinner, but other than that, I stayed at home. Meanwhile, Anne-Marie and I spoke almost every night. She had a busy travel schedule, so it was hard to see each other. We joked that it was like we had become pen pals.

Two weeks after the Leafs traded for me, they swung a six-player deal with the New York Islanders. The main player in the deal was former Leafs captain and fan favourite Wendel Clark. He had the offensive skills and toughness that Cliff Fletcher wanted. Nine games after that trade,

I scored my first goal for the Leafs. It was against the Red Wings in Detroit, and I scored on Mike Vernon in the second period to give our team a 3–2 lead. But we ended up losing 6–5.

Our second to last game of the season took place in Chicago, which was always a tough place to play. Bob Probert, one of the most devastating punchers in the game, was playing for the Hawks at that time. Luckily, I tangled with other players that night instead. Early in the first period, I was going after a loose puck by the boards when Jim Cummins, who was one of the true heavyweights at the time, breaks my nose with a roundhouse elbow. I started bleeding profusely. My eyes were watering and I could barely see my hands in front of me. Cummins was given a five-minute major.

There was no question I was concussed, but I got back on the ice. About seven minutes later, I got into a fight with Cam Russell. Then, early in the second period, Cummins and I were both given unsportsmanlike penalties. Ten seconds after we left the box, there was a face-off. We lined up against each other. I took my stick and rammed it right across his head. We fought, again. In addition to our fighting majors I was given a two-minute minor for unsportsmanlike conduct, and another two minutes for (if you can believe it) elbowing.

In the dressing room, Coach Nick Beverley addressed our team, and said about me, "Why is this the only kid who looks like he cares?" We lost the game 5–2. My nose was on the other side of my face, but sometimes these things give your team a spark. Other times it won't make a difference.

When we flew back to Toronto my nose was a mess. I decided to go home and sleep in my own bed rather than at the hotel. It was early in the morning, so I tried to get through the front door quietly. But I could hear my mom waiting for me on the other side. She'd watched the game and I wasn't looking forward to explaining why I felt the need to fight so much. She turned a bunch of lights on, grabbed my chin, and tilted it a couple times, looking at my nose. To my surprise she didn't get upset at me. She said, "Tonight, Chicago found out what we are made of." And then she went back to bed. At the end of the day, that was *always* what mattered. I was not the biggest guy in the league, and probably lost more fights than I won, but for me it was always about showing up.

Despite the early struggles, we finished well enough to go to the postseason. We opened up the playoffs against the St. Louis Blues, where Coach Mike Keenan was now in his second season. The Blues had tied with us in points, but we had beaten them overall in head-to-head play, so the series opened in Toronto.

The Blues had Grant Fuhr as their goalie. Fuhr was part of the Edmonton Oilers in their dynasty years and for a time was considered one of the top net minders in the league. Keenan had signed him in the off-season as a free agent and figured Fuhr could regain his form and once again be one of the best goalies. He had played an astonishing 79 games that season, the most he'd ever played in a single season in his career.

The Blues had another star from those famed Oilers years. Wayne Gretzky had been acquired in a trade in February because Keenan was looking for depth. Before the series began, Doug Gilmour said in a team meeting that he was looking forward to getting another shot at Gretzky in the playoffs. Gretzky was infamous among Leafs fans for cutting Gilmour with a stick in the playoffs in 1993 (while he played for L.A.), though it was missed by referee Kerry Fraser. Gretzky then singlehandedly eliminated the Leafs from the series with monumental efforts in Games 6 and 7. Gilmour said, "That guy got me in '93 and I don't want that happening again."

The narrative for us in the series was to get in Fuhr's face and create traffic, but in Game 1 he backstopped his team to a 3–1 victory, stopping thirty-three of thirty-four shots. When we played the second game two days later, our strategy was the same: create chaos in front of the net. About seven minutes into the first period I followed a puck in towards Fuhr. I was in tight and gave him a stick to his glove hand, searching for the puck. Goalies hate it when you get in their face. Except Grant Fuhr was probably one of the calmest and most focused goalies ever to lace up. He had ice in his veins. I knew Blues defenceman Chris Pronger would respond and I wanted to get his blood boiling. Pronger came in and cross-checked me hard. I figured if he was crazy enough to give me a shove, it could play well for us; maybe I could draw a penalty. But Pronger's cross-check did more than I intended. When I fell on Fuhr, it didn't appear that I injured him.

To his credit, Fuhr shook it off and continued to play. Pronger was given two cross-checking penalties and I was given one for slashing Fuhr's glove hand. What I did was create some energy, plus I got Pronger to take an additional penalty that led to a Mike Gartner goal for us, the first one of the game. The havoc in front of the net did what it was supposed to. My teammates and coach were the first to tell me I had done a good job. But later in the period Fuhr struggled off the ice with the help of a trainer. When he hobbled to the dressing room, I had a huge pit in my stomach.

On the CBC telecast, analyst Harry Neale said I had no chance to avoid Fuhr because Pronger had given me an awful shot. Sitting there in the box, there were two ways to look at it: we should be able to win it facing their backup goalie, Jon Casey, but there was also the thought I might have just injured a future Hall of Famer, one of the greatest goalies in the history of the game. That was a terrible feeling. It didn't help that Blues heavyweight Tony Twist did not take kindly to it. He told me I was a dead man.

That kind of play was not new. It was something that had been done a thousand times before at the NHL level. And it makes sense. If somebody is going to knock you from behind, into his own goalie, land

My parents, George and Dorothy, with me and my sisters, Stelle and Tess. For some reason, Mom always dressed me in sailor outfits when I was young. If you look closely, I have my dad's car keys in my hands. Letting me hold them was the only way they could get me to stand still for the photo.

My mom playing keep-away with a toy boat. She did whatever she could to try to contain me.

My Wexford minor hockey team. I'm at the far right in the back. It gives you an idea of how big our team was when I'm one of the smaller guys.

Everyone wants to play for the big club, but if you're going to be in the minors for a while, the Hershey Bears organization is the best place to be. Lots of great memories there.

In 1988, our Hershey Bears team finished first in the league and then had a perfect 12–0 playoff record to end this historic season and win the Calder Cup. A couple of battle scars on the face, but worth every drop.

There's nothing like putting on that NHL sweater for your first regular-season game. I was proud to start my NHL career as a Washington Capital.

This was a charity game with a bunch of NHLers, led by my dear friend Peter Zezel, at Birchmount Stadium in Scarborough, Ontario. Peter, Craig Woodcroft, Tie Domi, and Wendel Clark are in the back row and I'm in the front with Mike Ricci. On the far left is Brian Budd, who was a famous pro soccer player and an extraordinary athlete.

There were some challenges playing for the Hartford Whalers, but there were some great moments too. Here I am battling with Brad McCrimmon and Steve Yzerman. This photo was taken by Mike Hartman's father, John. Mike and I played together in North Bay and New York.

Being traded to the New York Rangers was one of the best things that ever happened to me. And my family loved to visit me there! Here I am with my dad's mom, my yiayia Anastasia, at a practice. She rarely got to see me play, so this was a special moment.

My whole life I dreamed of winning the Stanley Cup. But as much as it meant to me and my family, it was even bigger for the great fans of New York. I just had to skate the Cup over to where these guys were sitting. You can make out Steve and Dave Zaretsky's sign: NOW I CAN DIE IN PEACE. After a fifty-four-year Cup drought, it summed up what a lot of fans felt.

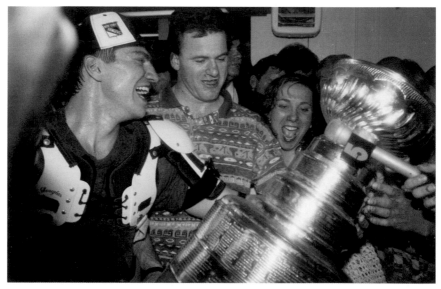

The party was just getting started in the dressing room and it was extra special to have my sister Stelle and her husband, Glen, there with me.

My mom and dad were also in New York to celebrate with us. This was at the Waldorf Astoria hotel, where the Rangers put on a spread like you've never seen. My parents partied as hard as anyone. I appreciated the celebrations so much more because they were there.

I had a blast visiting Yankee Stadium with Mark Messier and Brian Leetch. Even though I'd been in New York a year, I'd never had a chance to go. What a way to visit for the first time. The team and the players were great hosts.

Back home my friends organized an amazing party in Toronto's Greektown, the Danforth. That's my buddy Jim Mandala wearing one of the T-shirts my friend Bryan Green made for the event. There's my mom on the left with my cousin George Dizes, and second from the right is my cousin Stella Dizes.

This fight against Chicago's Cam Russell wasn't the prettiest. But even a broken nose didn't stop me from dropping the gloves three times that night. When my mom saw the damage to my face, she just said, "Tonight, Chicago found out what we are made of."

Creating havoc in front of the net was part of my role. I'd done it just like this many times, but I've always regretted that Grant Fuhr got hurt by a similar play in the playoffs.

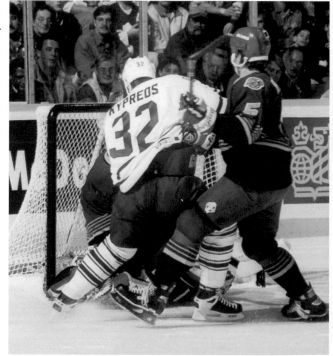

I wanted my proposal to Anne-Marie to be special, and the middle of the ice at Rockefeller Center during Christmas, in front of a packed crowd of evening skaters, seemed just right. It would have been a tough skate back to the bench if she'd said no, but I had a good feeling.

A lot of my teammates and hockey family came to our wedding, but only one, Glenn Healy, played the bagpipes. I often joke with Glenn that he's better on the pipes than between them.

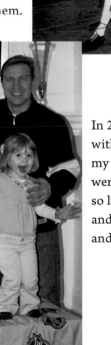

In 2007, I got to spend a little time with the Cup again, this time in my own home with my family who weren't around when I won it. I am so lucky to have them: Anne-Marie and my children, Zachary, Theo, and Anastasia.

An early promotional shot of our broadcasting team at Sportsnet. I was with them from the beginning and it was both a huge learning curve and great challenge to help build Sportsnet into the giant it is today. From the left, Greg Millen, Craig Simpson, me (no jacket required), Darren Dreger, and Jim Hughson in the front.

RICK MADONIK/TORONTO STAR VIA GETTY IMAGES

When Rogers began broadcasting *Hockey Night in Canada*, I found myself on the panel every Saturday night of the season. I'd watched *HNIC* all my life, and it was such an honour to be on the show with these guys, Ron Mac-Lean, Kelly Hrudey, and Elliotte Friedman, among others. A lot of hard work and preparation goes into the broadcast each week.

on him. He is probably the softest guy there with all his equipment. I'd done that a few times over my career, but I had never taken out anybody's knee because of it. I am highly competitive and can honestly say there is a short list of players that I wouldn't mind seeing limp off the ice. But under no circumstances would any of us intentionally hurt a goalie. It is like a code. Billy Smith may be the only exception—he was a vicious player and used his stick as a weapon, but he was long before this time. Grant was the opposite. When Casey came out to replace Fuhr, we finished the period with a 3–1 lead.

During the intermission on CBC's *Coach's Corner*, Ron MacLean announced Fuhr was done for the series with a torn medial collateral ligament in his right leg. Don Cherry replied that it was a "dummy defenceman" move that caused it and that "Chris thought he was doing a good thing."

The Blues were down, but far from out. They battled back with two goals in the second period to tie the game 3–3 and then took the lead on a power-play goal at 10:44 of the third. But a few minutes later we got our chance to come back on a power play of our own and Kirk Muller tied it. The game went to overtime, where another power play led to a goal. The Blues were assessed a two-minute minor for too many men on the ice at 2:52 and Mats Sundin put the game away for us.

Keenan went ballistic after their loss when he spoke to the media. "Kypreos deliberately tried to make contact with [Fuhr]," he said. "It's unfortunate that he decided [to do that], maybe his coach did, I don't know. Unless the coaching staff devised it, the player took it upon himself to employ that tactic. If you look at the cross-check, [Kypreos] defied all laws of gravity because Pronger cross-checked [him] away from Grant."

He added there was no excuse for it and pushed the league hard to suspend me. Coach Nick Beverley, in turn, fired back at Keenan, saying he had lost respect for him based on suggestions that the Leafs coaching staff lobbied deliberately for players to injure an opponent.

———

"We want to win, yes, but anyone who knows me and my charac-ter . . . to be called on the carpet so to speak in front of the media in that manner was thoroughly disgusting in my view and I take great exception to it," he said.

When I was asked by the media about what Keenan had accused me of, I told them what I knew to be true: "He's a very intelligent man who uses every tool that he has to try to benefit himself and his hockey club."

I had played for Keenan when we won the Stanley Cup and he put me in the lineup for the pivotal seventh game. But now, after the fact, he couldn't care less about me. It's as if we hadn't shared anything together. It was more of "what have you done for me lately?" I was just another guy he was attacking.

There were three days before the next game and the situation esca-lated. Feeling the heat, Brian Burke, the NHL vice president director of discipline, suspended me for one game. He said there was no doubt that I had been cross-checked from behind, but I had the opportunity to avoid the collision.

Not everyone agreed with the league's decision. On TSN, Bob Mc-Kenzie said as far as he was concerned, the suspension was a joke. He said the NHL had "rabbit ears" and was making a "furor, pardon the bad pun" out of the situation. He said it wasn't going to be a big deal suspending a player such as me who wouldn't be a huge factor in the series.

Keenan tried to make it seem like Fuhr would return for Game 3, but that was him playing mind games. On TSN, Pat Burns, who was doing analysis of the series, said he doubted Fuhr would be back to play the Leafs. He thought it was simply theatrics by Keenan to psych us out.

We played the third game in St. Louis and I travelled with the team, even though I was suspended for that game. They had to book me under an alias because the Blues fans were furious. I had death threats.

Thankfully, there was no social media then because I would have gotten buried. We lost the game 3–2 in overtime on a goal by Glenn Anderson, with Wayne Gretzky providing one of the assists. I was told to stay in the dressing room and not go through the arena to the press box. That night I did an interview with ESPN from underneath the stands. It was the only interview the Leafs allowed me to do in St. Louis.

I was back in the lineup for Game 4, which the Blues won 5–1. There were no fights and the Blues were hit with more penalties than us (seven to our four), but the real difference was when they scored two short-handed goals. Shayne Corson and Brett Hull scored on our power play, which effectively neutered our offence.

Down 3–1 in the series, we still felt positive going home. We were leading 4–3 late in the third, but with just thirteen seconds to go St. Louis scored on a power-play goal. Facing elimination, we showed our resilience and won in overtime. I drew a holding penalty on Murray Baron and Mike Gartner then scored on the power play.

We felt good heading back to St. Louis, but I still had to use an alias. Wendel opened the scoring with a power-play goal in the first. It was the only goal until early in the third period when the Blues tied it up. When they added another one, it proved to be the game winner and the end of the series. We just couldn't find any good rhythm overall and simply didn't play well enough.

In the off-season, I spent time in New York with Anne-Marie, going to the Hamptons and Cape Cod on weekends. We went to Brian Leetch's summer home for July 4 with about thirty other people and had one of the best weekends of the summer.

Later that summer I got a phone call from HBO. They wanted me to play the part of a hockey player named "Guy Fondue" for a new Robert Wuhl TV series called *Arli$$*. I'd been an extra that one time on *Guiding Light,* but this was a stretch to say the least. They flew me to L.A. for a day of taping in an episode that included Stellea Stevens and a young basketball player named Kobe Bryant.

I was responsible for an on ice skating scene where Robert's character, Arliss, a sports agent, judges my workout and then informs me he can no longer represent me because he was about to become an NHL owner. It was an intimidating acting experience. I spent the majority of the day talking to a relatively unknown Canadian actress from Montreal named Sandra Oh. She of course went on to nighttime fame with *Grey's Anatomy*. She helped calm my nerves.

In my episode, Arliss spoke of his new hockey franchise landing in either Carolina or Las Vegas. This was in 1996—a pretty good prediction, as both places now have NHL teams. It's maybe not quite at the level of *The Simpsons*, predicting back in 2000 that Donald Trump would run for president, but still impressive.

Anne-Marie, who had some acting experience on stage in small theatre productions in NY, helped me read my lines. She must have been a pretty good coach because my scene went so well that the producers, Michael Tollin and Brian Robbins, wrote me an additional scene at the end of the episode.

I also bought a house in Toronto that summer, and was excited about playing my first full season with the Leafs. They had hired Mike Murphy as their new head coach. I knew Mike because he had been one of Colin Campbell's assistants in New York after Mike Keenan left to go to St. Louis. Murphy had been a head coach in Los Angeles for two seasons in the mideighties and had been an assistant in Toronto for three seasons in the early nineties. But it didn't take long for my excitement about the new season and a new coach to turn to disappointment.

In November, in a game at home against Buffalo, I got into a fight with Matthew Barnaby. The fight turned into wrestling around and I suffered a spiral fracture in my right leg. My skate caught an edge and my foot stayed in place while my leg went in another direction. It sidelined me for ten weeks, and when I was ready to play again I was sent to the Leafs' American Hockey League affiliate in St. John's, Newfoundland, on a conditioning stint. I returned to the Toronto lineup in February. I don't know if it was harder watching the games from the sidelines when I was injured or returning to an organization that had lost its way. We missed the playoffs and it felt like we had hit rock bottom.

CHAPTER 9

Not the Way I Wanted to Go

I prepared for the new season as I always did. I trained with the same group of guys at the Fitness Institute. As with any team that misses the playoffs, there were personnel changes. The Leafs made some off-season moves, acquiring Derek King, Glenn Healy from my Ranger days, and Kris King. Both Derek and Chris were left-wingers like me, so it put more pressure on me to make an impact and keep my place on the team.

On September 15, 1997, the Leafs had an exhibition game back at MSG. Going into the final year of my contract, I knew I'd have to make a statement for the management to take me seriously. And it was no longer about just the Leafs. With the new additions to the roster, I knew I might be traded and I had to prove myself to any other team that was watching. As I said before, teams have short memories. Most likely a fight was in the cards for me, whether I liked it or not.

Studying the names on the "most likely" list wasn't hard in the nineties. On the Rangers lineup Darren Langdon and Ryan VandenBussche definitely stood out. At age twenty-three, Ryan was considered a young up-and-comer, looking for a full-time job in the NHL. I had fought players just under that weight class in the past. Guys like Lyle Odelein and Ron Stern come to mind.

For most of Ryan's hockey career, he had been an enforcer in the minors, annually racking up more than two hundred penalty minutes a season. He had played eleven games for the Rangers the previous year, recording four fights, including bouts with Stu Grimson and Dan Kordic, two of the NHL's true heavyweights at that time. Both were five to six inches taller than him and outweighed him by thirty to thirty-five pounds. VandenBussche was not afraid to take on anyone.

Knowing all of that as I did, he still didn't strike me as a true heavyweight. As a middleweight, I was bold enough to fight heavyweights like Marty McSorley, Chris Simon, Shane Churla, or Tony Twist. I knew deep down I had no business fighting guys so far out of my weight class, but I also knew the upside to holding my own. For me, this exhibition game in New York stacked up to feature a young, hungry kid who wanted to make a name for himself versus a veteran who wasn't quite ready to give up.

Early in the first period, Ryan and I were on the ice at the same time. I gave him a good shove after the face-off and we squared off. I initiated with two of the most famous fighting words in hockey: "Let's go."

Within a few seconds I knew I was in trouble. Although I initiated the fight, he was by far the aggressor with two lightning-quick punches. It felt like a jackhammer. I had underestimated my opponent. Like me he was a dominant left-handed fighter, but he could switch hands better. For centuries southpaws have caused opponents all sorts of trouble. Ironically, that was my advantage early in my career. But now it was lefty against lefty. I couldn't pick up the rhythm of Ryan's left hand, which put me on the defensive right off the bat.

With a strong third punch, Ryan didn't just knock the helmet off of my head; he sent it flying halfway across the ice. I've watched the fight on YouTube with friends. We joke that Ryan was like David Copperfield. One second my helmet is on my head, then poof, it's gone. But I have no memory of that happening.

The following left hook buckled my knees. The first person to notice was linesman Pat Dapuzzo. You clearly see in the video how close Pat comes in towards us while we're still in the heat of the battle. He wasn't attempting to stop the fight, but rather to check to see if I was still coherent.

"Kyper, are you okay?" Pat screams.

He follows it up with, "Do you want me to stop the fight?"

"No!" I yell emphatically.

At that moment Pat Dapuzzo backs off, raising his right hand as if to say, "Okay. Don't say I didn't try."

Many tough guys in my era had good relationships with NHL officials. Often TV cameras show light moments between referees and players in conversations that include a laugh or two. But I don't think the cameras often captured the bond between tough guys and the officials who needed to get in and break up the fights. Ron Asselstine was one of my favourites. The man known to all of us as "Bear" was one of the best at policing our fights. One night in Detroit, while digging through the bottom of the pile in an effort to find me, Bear asked me, "Kyper, what the hell did you eat last night? The garlic is coming right through your equipment."

That brought a smile to my face. And he wasn't wrong. I'd taken the guys out for Greek food the night before. I replied, "Bear, we went to the Pegasus. You gotta have the saganaki."

I know it broke Pat Dapuzzo's heart that I got hurt on his watch that night in New York. Years later he would come up to me and lament that he should have stopped the fight before it got so bad. It was nobody's fault. Linesmen have so much respect for what so many of us had to do. Pat allowed me to extend the length of the fight even though we all knew I was losing. He showed me respect by letting me dictate how it should have gone.

Earlier in my career with the Rangers I fought with Chris Simon, another lefty. He buckled me right at the start, too. Somehow I managed to bounce back with a flurry of punches to earn Coach Mike Keenan's praises after the game. Keenan's response in front of my teammates really impacted me. I suppose I was hoping for a similar ending with Leafs Coach Mike Murphy.

That night I couldn't get a good grip on Ryan's left arm because he was just too strong. I stopped throwing punches in an effort to regroup and I managed to gather myself enough to get my body position in tight on Ryan. It's the first rule in a hockey fight when you're on defence: bring them in close. Unlike his rock-drilling left that obliterated my helmet, I managed to pull his helmet off. I started throwing what he must have thought were Mighty Mouse punches to the back of his head—punches that do very little damage yet look respectable on a highlight reel. The fight should have ended then if only my ego would have allowed it. Instead, I held out for one more chance to throw a knockout punch. It was a career-altering mistake. Ryan caught me with two successive punches. The first grazed my right shoulder, but the second was square to my cheekbone.

How I escaped with half of my face not caving in I'll never know. The second hit to my head belonged to Madison Square Garden. Leafs winger Kelly Chase was close enough to see it. He told me I had passed out while I was still standing. I collapsed, falling forward. I was unconscious, without the ability to break my fall, and my forehead hit the ice full force. It is hard to know where the blood was coming from. I started to bleed all over the ice. My mouth was filled with blood, but I didn't remember any of that. From start to finish the whole thing may have lasted twenty-five seconds. I produced a finish all right, just not the one I had hoped for. And it certainly didn't prove to the Leafs that I could stand up and protect my teammates, let alone myself. That was the last night I tied the skates.

I was told that replays of my fight were shown that night by sports stations across North America. I was in no condition to watch television, nor did I want to see it. It would go down as one of the ugliest knockouts in hockey history. The sportscasters prefaced the footage by saying it was graphic. One of them warned, "If you don't like blood, turn away." Another said: "The fight made the chainsaw massacre in *Scarface* look like a pinprick."

Back in April 1996, in a game in Chicago, I had donated quite a bit of blood as a result of a vicious elbow from Jim Cummins. The jersey from that fight, with its bright red against the Leafs' royal blue, ended up being auctioned off for charity, to a collector, for a high bid. But that was nothing like the blood I lost at MSG. That jersey and the one at MSG got the two highest bids in auctions.

I sat on a medical examining table while the doctors asked me questions: "How many fingers am I holding up? Do you know your phone number? Where are you, Kyper?" They asked me to visually track a light. Anne-Marie, who still lived in New York, made her way down to the dressing rooms. As was the norm at the time, there was no real protocol for the type of head injury I sustained. With a horrible headache, I kept repeating the same thing over and over, not understanding exactly where I was. I had to try really hard to remember my phone number. I saw double.

Anne-Marie tried everything she could to get me to stay in New York and go to the hospital. But between my ego and the lack of mandated medical procedures for concussions, and with my insistence, I was allowed to fly home. My brain was bruised and I simply downplayed everything. At the time there was still a stigma around suffering a concussion, or, as we referred to them back then, "the injury no one can see." My attitude was "shake the cobwebs off, and I'll be fine."

My biggest concern at the time was how this was going to play out moving forward. As messed up as I was when I was lying on the medical table, I had enough brain cells left to know things might have gone past the point of no return.

The truth is, if I had paid attention I would have known Vanden-Bussche had the reputation for having a good left hook. Maybe I just didn't show him enough respect. Maybe I should have been more worried in the dressing room, puking from nerves like a lot of guys, instead of trusting that things would be okay. This fight would end up being a big feather in Ryan's cap; his stock soared. There's no question about that. My stock plummeted. With no crystal ball, I could only hope things would get better.

Back in Toronto, Tie Domi was really good to me. I had debilitating headaches. When I went on IR he was one of the few who would constantly check in. People see his 333 fights and 3,500 penalty minutes. They see a tough guy, but only a few people really know how sensitive he is at times.

Once, on a road trip in Arizona, Tie Domi, Kirk Muller, and I were in a taxi on our way to dinner. On a highway just outside of Scottsdale, Tie started yelling frantically. He got the driver to pull over to the side of the interstate. A stray dog was caught in the median while traffic whisked by on either side. Kirk and I watched Tie leap over lanes of traffic to steer the dog off to the safety of the shoulder on our side of highway.

Tie understood me more than most. Like all enforcers, he knew the risks we took. He was a confident guy when he fought, no question about that. But a good portion of that confidence came from a type of rage; a ruthless refusal to get hurt. His public image was that of a gladiator, but he was much more vulnerable than people ever gave him credit for.

After two weeks the headaches continued. I also had some issues with balance and short-term memory loss. The biggest tell that something was way off was when my appetite didn't return. Anyone who knows me is aware how much I love good food. I grew up in the restaurant business and come from a long line of healthy eaters. My uncle Pete Dizes was the only person I've ever known to be asked to leave an all-you-can-eat buffet.

With training camp over, numerous players, including me, needed to meet with Leafs Associate GM Mike Smith. The conversation with him couldn't have lasted longer than two minutes. He wanted to send me immediately to Chicago, to the International Hockey League, another Leafs affiliate team. I tried to talk to him about my ongoing symptoms, but it was like talking to an iceberg. I got no warmth from him. Not that I needed a hug, but it felt like he was being dismissive. I had to explain to him that I couldn't step back on the ice until my condition improved. He was eager to know the instant I felt better. As long as I was injured, the team couldn't waive, trade, or reassign me. But I made it clear I couldn't go anywhere until my condition improved.

Besides the physical symptoms, I also had to deal with the anxiety of not knowing what was going to happen next in my career. I started wondering what the team thought when they saw me around. I didn't want to be a distraction. All the unknowns seemed to feed more anxiety, and the anxiety fueled more symptoms. I was lethargic, had vertigo, and was slow to react. I had trouble with lights. I had never experienced anything like it before. I'd been punched squarely in my left eye by Dave Maley one night in New Jersey and couldn't see out of it. As I was escorted to the penalty box, I only had my right eye to guide me. Saying I was frightened I'd lose my eyesight would have been an understatement. I had my eye wide open and I saw nothing. It was pitch-black. Thank God my sight completely came back by the time I served my five-minute major. As for the concussion, it was sticking around.

When you break a leg or tear a knee or get knocked down in a fight, you are going to get your sympathy from your teammates, but don't blink because you may miss it. They'll say, "Hang in there, pal!" and pat you on the back, then off they go, while never really giving it a second thought. Sounds rather cold, but that's the way it has to be for the healthy players. You have to compartmentalize: It does you no good to start worrying about being the next casualty. And someone's bad luck could be your opportunity to shine for your team. There is no *I* in "team" but there is one in "survival." Players head back out on the ice, thankful that it's someone else on the IR instead of them. And let's not kid ourselves: selfishly speaking, most injuries are first seen by teammates as a chance for an expanded role. There is less internal competition for other players, especially when you play the same position. That's the truth inside the dressing room that's never discussed among teammates. Whether it is an injury, a trade, a reassignment, getting released, or someone retiring, your inside voice first asks the question: *How does it benefit me?* That doesn't make a player selfish. It makes him practical. Eat or be eaten.

All athletes understand the overwhelming odds of making it to the pro league and earning a generous living. Human nature tells us to get what we can before they kick us out. Not to be cynical about this—it's actually just the opposite. When we start down the path, we don't know whether our career will last twenty minutes or twenty years. Less emotion and more practicality was how most of the players saw things back then.

I will forever hold in high regard the fact that I showed up for my teammates and my organizations. As tough guys, we represented something. We're not going to get pushed around or be taken advantage of. We won't allow the opposition to take liberties on our teammates. My stance, my belief, is: if the other team is going to try to intimidate or embarrass us, I have to stand up to them. Who doesn't love a guy who will fight for you when you can't fight for yourself? Is it really that big a surprise to hear that Bob Probert, Joey Kocur, Tie Domi, and Rob Ray were among the most popular jerseys sold in their era?

In the NHL I had a role. It didn't start out that way. It just evolved. After every fight, I'd go to the penalty box and try to check off boxes.

Did I fight at the right time? Did I energize my team? Did I help sway the momentum of the game in our favour? The unfortunate part for enforcers is if you lose a fight, then you didn't do what you were supposed to. And if losing becomes a trend, you're done. The team would find someone else. Nobody wants a guy that just gets beaten up for his team. There is no pride in being a punching bag.

CHAPTER 10

A New Beginning

Along with the physical challenges of dealing with a concussion comes the uncertainty of what might lie ahead. All I could think about was what the Leaf management might be thinking in terms of my future. I had real anxiety for the first time in my life. I was an engine in a car that was always accelerating—anxiety made my fears rev so high that I couldn't calm down. There was no idle. And it increased the physical symptoms I already had.

I couldn't read a newspaper. Exercise was out of the question. Bright lights still caused headaches. Even the headlamps of a passing car caused so much discomfort I couldn't drive at night. I saw spots at times, and then it was as if a glossy film covered my eyes. That usually happened at the end of the day when my body felt even more tired. Although my neurologist assured me it would eventually go away, it was difficult to believe that. I was scared that this was how I would live the rest of my life.

I did a CT scan with the Leafs, something I had never done before. I was really worried after it was over; there was something about how the technician looked at the image that wasn't reassuring. In fact, he seemed more serious towards me after he looked at the screen. The images showed dark spots on my brain that represented lesions. These lesions were abnormal changes in the cerebral tissue. Darks spots can range from being harmless to life threatening. The five root canals back in Halifax paled in comparison to this. While the Leafs' Dr. Wallace said he didn't think I was in any real danger, he stressed that the lesions had to be considered if I played again.

I continued to go to the rink, hang out with the team, and do cranial therapy with the Leafs' physiotherapist, Chris Broadhurst. This type of therapy was new to me; pressure was placed at points along my skull to relieve the compression in my head, neck, and spine. Some doctors debated over its effectiveness, but for whatever reason I found it helpful given the physical and emotional stress I was dealing with. After months of frustration I finally felt some relief. I can't say enough about Chris Broadhurst and Brent Smith, who also worked as a team therapist. They gave me hope that things would eventually return to normal.

When you have more time on your hands than you want, your mind starts to wander. Months after my injury, serious thoughts about life after hockey entered into the equation for the first time, and it was a conversation I wasn't quite ready to have with myself. It's interesting. People approach athletes still in their twenties with business opportunities and try to have the "life after hockey talk" with us. Of course, most athletes in their prime want nothing to do with it. "That's a long way off," they say, and, "I've got plenty of time to figure it out." That's what you tell yourself. But the truth is, when the majority of players retire, they won't have $10 million in the bank to ease the financial burden of postcareer years. I certainly didn't. I had a good start at life with $1 million in the bank by the time I was thirty-two. I was able to do that by not living a lavish lifestyle as a single player. No big house, high-rise condo, or cottage. No Porsche, BMW, or Benz. I just had the thought of building a nest egg. At this point I did start to wonder, how would I pay the bills for the next sixty years? Fans see the references to millions of dollars in press releases and think how lucky players are. What they don't see is high taxes, agent fees, and the cost of living in metropolitan areas.

Add in a bad investment, and now a league-wide escrow tax to protect the owners' shared revenue, and it winds up being roughly thirty cents to every dollar you actually bank. My point is, the amount you read in the headlines isn't all that it appears.

During my recovery a lot of friends from my New York playing days reached out to me. The hockey world is a good group: a fraternity. I never felt like I was kicked to the curb. They had seen a video of the fight and knew the risks players take. At the end of the day business is business; however, the response I received from people I played with, including former coaches and managers, was exceptional.

When enough time had passed, the Leafs allowed me to go on the ice with discretion. I began to skate separately from the team with equipment manager Scotty McKay, who often worked with injured players. But things were not like before. My timing on the ice and hand-eye coordination were delayed. My brain was like the spinning-wheel graphic on a computer, always loading. I had to wait for things to catch up.

A lot of attention had been paid to the violence of the fight, and I knew I'd see the replay for myself at some point. I remember the medical staff asking me certain questions following the fight, but at the time I had no recollection of being on the ice, how it started, the warm-up, or even how I left. As I said earlier, I wasn't the type of player to race home to watch videos of the games I played in. I really only watched myself with coaches or with my team during video sessions to break down hockey plays.

I had a number of media requests wanting to talk about the fight. Let's not forget, violence has a tendency to sell stories. NY's *Inside Edition* came to Toronto to do a sit-down with me. They replayed the fight in front of me, which forced me to watch it for the first time. It wasn't easy. There will always be a part of me that is a little embarrassed about how hard I fell, and my motionlessness on the ice. It was as if I was watching someone else. It appeared that the blood on the ice came from my mouth and ears. I never did ask about where the blood came from nor did I ever want to know. As I watched the replay, the gravity of my injury sank in.

The late James Deacon eventually ran an exposé in *Maclean's* magazine on fighting in the NHL and whether the league was willing to stop the brutality. The cover was titled "Thugs on Ice." Not exactly the way I wanted to be remembered as a hockey player. After spending three days with me, Deacon wrote a separate story on my MSG fight entitled "Knocked Out." It was sobering to read James's take on the "stomach turning sight of Kypreos, unconscious and facedown in a pool of blood . . . to restart the age old debate over whether fighting . . . should still be allowed in hockey."

My health finally started to turn a corner and I felt well enough to travel. I had things to look forward to. On the last Friday before Christmas, in New York, I proposed to Anne-Marie, even though I had no idea about my future as a hockey player. Anne-Marie and I had met in 1996, just three weeks before I was traded to the Maple Leafs. While we were dating, she remained in New York and travelled back and forth to Toronto. Before my injury we spent time in the Hamptons and Cape Cod. I can honestly say that my time recovering from the injury was one of the lowest in my life physically, but in other ways it was also one of the best.

Before I proposed, I called Anne-Marie's father, Ray, and asked for permission to marry her. Luckily, he approved and helped me keep the secret. I flew to NY and took her ice skating at Rockefeller Center. The Christmas tree was over seventy-feet high, decorated with about twenty thousand lights, and weighed twelve tons. There is really nothing like visiting Rockefeller Center at Christmas.

I knew the staff that worked at the ice pad. After the general public was asked to leave so they could flood the surface, they let me skate with

Anne-Marie out to the middle of the ice. I dropped down to one knee and asked her to marry me. Now that I think about it, I was taking some big risks. I might have fallen flat on the ice in New York for the second time in three months, and even worse, she could have said no in front of a huge crowd. But some things are worth the risk, and she said yes right away. A packed Rockefeller Center gave us a huge round of applause.

Anne-Marie had watched what happened to me in the fight with Ryan VandenBussche and been unfailingly supportive afterward. She saw what I was going through and knew that I was probably at the end of a career. But it didn't matter to her, and ultimately it didn't really matter to me. Perhaps it was naivete or arrogance on my part, but I had a deep sense through Anne-Marie that whatever happened, whether I played or not, things were going to be okay.

By about January or February, I was still uncertain about whether I should try to play hockey again or find something to help me transition to another career. At that point I needed a second opinion from another concussion expert, but the Leafs didn't have one. Normally, you just took the team doctor's advice; in the good ol' days, what the team said was the only information you had to go on. But other players around the league, such as Pat LaFontaine and Eric Lindros, had paved the way when they sought second opinions regarding their head injuries. If a player wanted to see another doctor, teams were open to it. For the first time, teams started to publicly support it. The National Hockey League and the NHL Players' Association had launched a concussion study in 1997 to improve the understanding of the condition. The NHLPA strongly encouraged players to seek other opinions.

I wanted an honest assessment about the risks of playing again. A team doctor's chief mandate is getting the players as healthy as possible and back on the ice. I needed to hear from somebody who didn't stand to gain from my returning.

Dr. James Kelly, a neurologist at Northwestern University Medical

Center in Chicago, had seen some other NHLers. Although he never told me I had to retire, Kelly confirmed what I probably already knew. The lesions that were on my brain put me at much greater risk if I received another blow to the head. He made it abundantly clear that moving forward, even a small head injury could cause permanent damage. It could even be fatal. That was tough to hear. What in the hell could I do besides play hockey?

CHAPTER 11

A Rookie, Again

After we were eliminated from Cup contention by the St. Louis Blues in 1996, I received a lot of press because of the Grant Fuhr incident. It led to a call from a TV producer. Would I be interested in working with Tom Harrington from CBC on his show, *National Sports*, as a playoff analyst, along with Ken Campbell from the *Toronto Star*? I thought this was an excellent opportunity to get myself out there. While I had done plenty of local television in the past, it was not lost on me that this show went coast to coast. Tom considered me an articulate guy who didn't sound like a lot of other hockey players because I didn't "speak in clichés." He said he appreciated my blunt honesty and brought me in as an analyst. This may be where the first real seed was planted for broadcasting.

A year later, in the spring of '97, the Leafs did not make the playoffs and I had just recovered from a broken leg from a fight with Matthew Barnaby. Jorey Middlestadt and Mitch Burman approached me regarding a new sports cable channel launching called Headline Sports. Jorey, who had previously worked at TSN as a reporter for *That's Hockey*, had known me from the Leafs dressing room. He considered me a player with good insight and recruited me, along with journalists Steve Simmons of the *Toronto Sun* and Steve Milton from the *Hamilton Spectator*.

With the Leafs not qualifying for the playoffs, I was available to help launch Headline Sports that spring. Day one also included a very young

Elliotte Friedman, along with Greg Sansone and Brian Duff. We were so new and unknown that our own local Toronto cable provider didn't feel it necessary to show this station. I remember going to my parents' house and trying to explain why they couldn't watch me on TV when I myself barely understood why.

Part of the launch of the new cable network was a roundtable discussion on a show called *The Front Page*. Segments lasted an hour and a half with little to no commercial breaks. It was exhausting. I guess Jorey liked what he saw, though, because afterwards he encouraged me to consider broadcasting as a career, something I had never seriously thought about before.

In April 1998, Glenn Adamo, the National Hockey League vice president of broadcasting, called to tell me there was a new national all-sports TV and radio network starting up in Canada called CTV Sportsnet. It would begin its first broadcast the following fall. Sportsnet's goal was to rival TSN, which had already dominated the market for years. He suggested I might consider a role there.

Then, in early June, the NHL office called to offer me an opportunity to cover the 1998 Stanley Cup Final between Detroit and Washington for their international feed. I worked with the late Dave Strader as a sideline reporter. It was surreal to interview these players I had just competed against not long before. I found Sergei Fedorov in between periods and asked him, "What are your thoughts after twenty minutes?" A simple broadcasting throw, like "Back to you guys in the booth," was a struggle. I sounded exactly like the cue card I was reading. I took some solace in knowing it was an international feed; my work wasn't shown anywhere in North America because those broadcasting rights belonged to ESPN and CBC. Dave Strader and my producer Lisa Seltzer were great during this overwhelming experience. They were incredibly patient with me. Lisa constantly reassured me that someone watching in

Prague or the UK didn't really care if I made one small mistake. When it was over they were complimentary, but I was sure I didn't leave them thinking I was destined to do this for the next twenty years. The experience did, however, leave me wanting more.

After this, and on Glenn Adamo's recommendation, I was given an interview with Sportsnet's vice president, Scott Moore. He knew me as an ex-Leaf and a former member of the New York Rangers. His friend Lee Herberman of Headline Sports also suggested me to him.

Now, when I went to meet Scott, I assumed it was casual. I dressed like any typical hockey player, wearing a T-shirt, jeans, and flip-flops. Before we even got past the introductions, Scott said, "Is that what you wear to a job interview?" I replied, "I don't know. I've never been on a job interview before." Scott laughed and to this day he swears he almost tossed me out right then.

We talked a little bit about my background and my experiences in the NHL. Scott told me later that he immediately liked me. He told me then that for an ex-athlete, transitioning to broadcasting would not be a walk in the park; it would take hard work, and relying on my contacts in the hockey world would be important. He also told me that when he interviewed people, he didn't rely solely on their qualifications, but also their personality and attitude.

I left the interview feeling neither good nor bad. I knew of other people who were interviewing for that job: former New York Islanders captain Pat Flatley; my ex-teammate from the Rangers, Mike Gartner; and my former coach Mike Keenan, who was in between jobs. These names were far bigger than mine and I bet they didn't show up in jeans and a T-shirt, certainly not flip-flops. Truthfully, I assumed I didn't have much of a shot. I was later booked for a screen test, which I did with veteran broadcaster Rod Black. We went through some highlights and analyzed what we saw. I did the best I could.

A month or so later Anne-Marie and I were in New York. I received a call from Scott saying that I got the job and that he wanted to send me a copy of a contract. I was blown away. Anne-Marie and I talked about what we should do, but it was a pretty short conversation. Getting in on the ground floor of Canada's newest all-sports station with national rights was an amazing opportunity. I could have tried to play hockey and maybe hung on for a few more years; or, maybe if I was lucky, with some longevity I could broadcast for five or ten years. Broadcasting clearly had more upside. And, in theory, there would be fewer concussions sitting behind a desk. Plus, it gave me the chance to retire from the NHL and still have a good income.

So in August 1998 I officially retired. I played a total of one thousand hockey games between the CHL, AHL, and the NHL, and I can say unequivocally, my body felt every single one of them. Hockey had left me with five root canals, a three-inch screw repairing a separated shoulder, a reconstruction of my right knee, a spiral fracture in my right leg, too many stitches to count, and a concussion that ended my career. I was a far cry from my Junior coach's favourite line: "What's the worst thing that can happen to you in hockey? A black eye or a broken nose?"

Retiring was actually an easy decision. It would have been nice to end my career with another Stanley Cup over my head instead of face-down at Madison Square Garden, but most people don't get to choose how their career will end. I never thought that fight shortchanged me. I played 442 career games in the NHL—that was 442 more than anyone thought I was ever going to play. I consider myself extraordinarily blessed.

Right after my retirement in August, Sportsnet announced that I had joined their team. Then in September, Anne-Marie and I got married.

Greek Orthodoxy does everything in threes: the Father, the Son, and the Holy Ghost. On the day we were married our first steps as husband and wife were walking together three times around an urn filled with holy water. I told Anne-Marie if we ever got divorced we had to come back and walk the other direction three times. I'm not really sure how many guys joke about divorce on their wedding day.

The priest did half of the ceremony in English and half in Greek. Greeks don't have a best man or maid of honour—instead, we have a koumbaro and a koumbara who both have to be Orthodox. They become the godparents of the first child. Choosing our koumbaros was easy. It had to be Chris and Debbie Zourdos, whom I met when I played in Washington. They had become like family to me and Anne-Marie.

My big fat Greek family loved every second of my wedding with so many hockey players in attendance. Mats Sundin was one of my ushers. Glenn Healy played the bagpipes and led us into our reception. Of course he wore his kilt.

The majority of Anne-Marie's bridesmaids worked with her in the modelling industry, so it was a pretty good-looking bridal party, something confirmed by my teammates. Apparently, most of the married players were not allowed to come within twenty feet of the dance floor. We did in fact break a few plates. During the ceremony, there is a tradition that you have a split second to stomp on your betrothed's foot to show who will have the upper hand in the marriage. Before I had a chance Anne-Marie made sure she stomped my foot first. And she never really did officially agree to be a "handmaiden" during our ceremony. That little tidbit by the priest, implying that the men make all the decisions in a marriage, took her by surprise. She made it crystal clear from the very start that we were on equal footing, we were equal partners. None of this actually surprised me; it's the thing I admire most about her. I had a dream fifty-fifty partner in marriage and my life as a broadcast journalist for Sportsnet was about to begin. Things were starting to look up.

We flew to Bermuda after the wedding, then one week later I began my new career. In my first production meeting there must have been twenty-five people, many of them women. It was all so new. Anytime I had been with twenty people in a room, it was hockey guys: each one trying like crazy to get a word in, everyone trying to be funny, F-bombs flying, everyone talking trash. Insulting each other in a dressing room is just a form of entertainment. Clearly, stuff you wouldn't get away with in any other professional environment. While it wasn't necessarily uncomfortable for me to be around these experienced journalists, I had to be really careful. To this day it amazes me how some ex-player analysts talk on and off air as if they are in a locker room full of testosterone. Today, jobs get lost because of it. Although I knew the adjustment I needed to make, it was a constant exercise to remind myself.

This new work environment was a complete eye opener for me. I had to take direction from producers, directors, and camera operators, all of whom worked closely together to fill a live half-hour show. I was overwhelmed by the number of people needed for it to all come together. The first two weeks of rehearsal were an education, to say the least.

Darren Dreger was hired as the lead host. Although he wasn't known nationally at the time, he had broadcasting experience in Edmonton. I was working with former goalie Greg Millen, who was a seasoned broadcaster and had gained a reputation with *Hockey Night in Canada* for one day becoming the next Harry Neale. Jim Hughson and former NHLer Craig Simpson were also part of the team. Gord Cutler had a reputation for being a very talented producer. Everyone had some prior broadcasting experience and I was surrounded by talented people.

There's no doubt that from the very beginning people questioned Scott about my hiring, and I was well aware of it. I was not a Hall of Famer, nor had I scored 500 goals. I was a role-player. In New York I wasn't a major contributor in winning the Stanley Cup, or at least that was the perception. So the doubters were saying, "Why him?"

Greg Millen didn't overly embrace me, but maybe it was just his old-school player approach, waiting for "the kid to earn his stripes." I feel he made it pretty clear. Toronto is the biggest media hub in Canada, and the fact that I was from the city helped me. But working where I grew up and being an ex-Leaf would only take me so far.

Scott Moore gave me an opportunity and saw something in me that others couldn't. He was very good at finding talent: just look at the people he hired in 1998 and the longevity they've sustained. Dreger, Kevin Quinn, Daren Millard, Craig and Christine Simpson (siblings), and Jamie Campbell, among others. And the one constant with Scott was that he always advocated for his talent. He was like a proud papa wanting to trumpet the virtues of his employees, whether in front of or behind the scenes. I've always respected him for it. I'll also never forget that he publicly said I would be the "John Madden of hockey." To this day I don't know what he meant by it, but I knew the bar he set for me was high.

Before the season started, our producer, Steve Lansky, asked Scott if he could take a group of us in the hockey department out for dinner as kind of a team gathering. What Scott didn't realize is that Lansky booked a reservation at Morton's in Yorkville, the most expensive steakhouse at the time in Toronto. There were about twenty of us, many of them interns. Morton's happened to be one of the favourite restaurants for hockey players and I had dined there many times. While I have no recollection of being involved in the decision of where we ate, I admit now I may have made a strong recommendation for Morton's. Now here I am with a bunch of young, impressionable kids who had just been hired out of college and they're in their glory at Morton's. Unfortunately, I had the hockey player mentality that when the team's paying for it you order anything you want. The culture for NHL players is when someone else is paying, you're going to beat the pot—meaning you overindulge. I told these kids that it's not enough to just order a sixteen-ounce T-bone steak; we should top off the night with Cuban cigars. I ordered about half a dozen cohibas that cost around seventy-five dollars each. Later Scott told me he wasn't thrilled to begin with that we ate at Morton's; he thought the dinner would take place at Montana's or a Boston Pizza. So he called in Steve Lansky and gave him an earful for choosing the most expensive steakhouse in the city, then handed him a bill for $500 as his portion of the overall payment. Afterwards Scott brought me in and read me the same riot act for buying the cigars. He then told me my first-ever paycheque in broadcasting would be minus $500. *Great,* I thought, *already in the doghouse and I haven't even seen one paycheque yet.* That was my initiation into the broadcasting world!

On-air Scott had me doing a variety of things, including giving my thoughts on the half-hour pregame national show. The production staff helped shape the show for me based on what they felt was the strongest story line. My job was to dig deeper into their ideas; what I believed was going on in management or what was being said in the dressing room. For a hockey insider, this sort of insight really takes time to develop. It takes years to start feeling comfortable and for your player contacts and team contacts to trust how you will make them appear. When I started at Sportsnet, they told me to just be myself. What the hell is that? I knew who I was, but not in front of a million people. I constantly doubted myself.

As the season progressed, it became tougher for me. I just wasn't confident about what I was doing, and worried about what I might say next. I started to battle some anxiety because of it. I remember being in the makeup room, with these bright lights on me, and the makeup artist started applying makeup underneath my eyes with a brush. It made my skin crawl.

I went through a very difficult time after Christmas. I had to catch myself a couple of times on the air. There was a nagging part of me that kept saying, "I don't know if I am meant for this." It was really, really hard.

At that point I had no idea how I was going to get through the whole season. Scott and others knew I was having a tough time as well. Between getting married and starting a new job, I had taken on a lot of change all at once. And then, when I found out I was about to become a father for the first time, I had a whole new thing to stress about. Looking back, I probably bit off more than I could chew.

Things just started piling on and I was thinking I had to find a way to make this work, keep grinding away. I'd go in and spend time talking with more experienced people. The more they got to know me, the more I got to know them, the more comfortable I would be trusting them. Steve Lansky, Bob Torrens, and Darren Dreger would always support me. They'd often say, "Here are your strengths. Why don't you try it this way? Maybe emphasize this point because you seem to be very passionate about this." I listened to every word.

I remember getting advice from broadcaster Rob Faulds. I wondered if I would be better within a few weeks or months and he told me it takes years, and to just hang in there. It alleviated a little bit of the pressure I put on myself.

With my colleagues' help, I made it through the regular season. But before I could put that first season behind me, Anne-Marie went into labour; it took twenty-seven hours for our son Zachary to arrive. As a first-time father, I felt rather helpless knowing Anne-Marie was going through all that agony and there was really nothing I could do but cheerlead. It wasn't exactly like *The Flintstones*, where Fred paces outside the delivery room, but I gained a newfound appreciation for women and what they go through when delivering a child.

Days after Zachary was born, I went on the radio show *The Edge*, with DJs Humble and Fred, and described what Anne-Marie said she felt during childbirth. She told me it was like rolling down a car window a few inches and then trying to crawl out. They laughed but I realized it was exactly how I'd sum up my first year as a broadcaster.

CHAPTER 12

A Second Chance

I was able to crawl over the finish line my rookie season on television—barely. I made a promise to myself that I'd iron out the kinks in the off-season. However, unbeknownst to me, Scott had decided to make changes to his hockey program by firing me, although he hadn't said anything yet. Less than a week after my first TV season ended, I was sitting in the waiting room of a dealership while my car was in for maintenance. I picked up the *Globe and Mail* and read in Bill Houston's "Truth and Rumours" column that I was getting fired from Sportsnet. The first thing I did was switch my deluxe oil change to the basic one. Then I called Scott Moore.

Scott arranged to meet me at his office a few days later to voice his concerns about my year. When we met up, I asked him if I was being fired like the article stated. Scott said no, he wasn't going to fire me, but he was going to take me off the live component of our program until he saw an improvement. My segments would now be taped. I was more than okay with that. In fact, it gave me a sense of relief. That should have been how we did it during my first year, but as they say, hindsight is a beautiful thing. I thanked Scott and then ran out of his office before he could change his mind.

Years later, when Scott was working for CBC on *Hockey Night in Canada*, I asked him about the Bill Houston article. It was then that he finally admitted I had absolutely been fired at that point. So why did he change his mind? Scott told me that he'd mentioned the possibility of firing me to a few people, who in turn leaked it to Bill, whom Scott wasn't particularly fond of. While Scott was frustrated with my first year, he disliked Bill so much that he decided not to fire me just to prove that Bill had bad intel. Wow, my job was actually saved out of spite. Instead of firing me, Scott took me off live TV for the second season.

It wasn't just me who had been unsure of things in those days. It turns out Darren Dreger went in to see Scott after the first season, wondering if he was going to be fired or reassigned. It's his belief that there were some people on-air and off-air at Sportsnet that most definitely did not have faith in him and me working in tandem, and they didn't like the panel in general. The feeling was that we were too green. But, as Dreger says, everyone at Sportsnet at that time was essentially as green as grass because it was all so new.

Sportsnet created a segment for me called "Two Minutes in the Box." For two minutes I had a blank canvas to fill with basically anything I wanted. I loved it. It really helped me collect my thoughts and get truly creative with current hockey news. I'd read off a teleprompter and the staff would take cash bets on how many times it would take to record it. Early on, it took as many as fifteen attempts for me to get it right. Bob Torrens said it was painful to produce the segment because it would take so damn long. He called it "Two Hours in the Box." At the beginning there was so much editing that Torrens said the actual film looked like Edward Scissorhands had attacked it. I genuinely felt bad for the producers. They were so patient, but they were also laughing. It wasn't all bad for them—because of all the betting going on, someone always went home with cash.

The truth is, after I practiced enough, I felt like things were starting to come together for me. Like in hockey, with enough practice doing the segment became more natural. The taped segments eventually worked so well they ended up putting me back on live TV, about half-way through the season. I should have sent Bill Houston a Christmas card every year after that for saving my job. Bill and I actually had a good laugh over it years later. Scott said the decision to keep me on Sportsnet was more about him being stubborn than me being good. Somehow it worked out well for both of us.

A year and a half after the birth of Zachary, we celebrated the birth of our second son, Theo. Anne-Marie's labour went from twenty-seven hours with Zachary to just four with Theo. Things were getting easier. The pressure I had felt in my first year as a broadcaster subsided. By this time, I started to better understand the journalistic aspect of the sports world.

Like TSN, we were one national station across the country, except we were made up of four regional stations: Sportsnet East, Sportsnet Pacific, Sportsnet Ontario, and Sportsnet West. TSN took the blueprint of ESPN as one main channel, while we were modelled more after Fox Sports.

In the late 1990s and early 2000s, TSN's Bob McKenzie was one of the few credible TV hockey analysts with constant inside information. He owned the market space on anything new to learn about in the NHL. The only way to really break news was through a network of hockey contacts and he had a pretty full Rolodex.

After my first full season I realized I had also heard rumblings about some of the same information that Bob and TSN were reporting, through many of the hockey people I still remained close to. During my first year I never pushed those connections or used the information they provided me like I should have. But later on it became abundantly clear to me that if Sportsnet (or I) was to be taken seriously, we had to compete for many of those story lines. I was still somewhere between a player and analyst at this point. I was nervous about asking for information without breaking the trust of former colleagues who had confided in me about trades or deals. I had to learn to break stories while protecting sources and the trust people had in me that nothing would come back to them. Once I understood this, my role as a broadcaster completely changed. If I could provide just a little to Sportsnet of what Bob McKenzie was doing for TSN, we had a chance to make a name for ourselves in the sports broadcasting business.

Right around this time Eric Lindros was in a dispute with Bobby Clarke and the Philadelphia Flyers. When the twenty-seven-year-old league MVP uttered the words "I'd really like to play in Toronto," all hell broke loose in our mega media hockey market.

While Lindros waited for the trade to happen in the summer of 2001, he stayed in Toronto and trained. Like so many other journalists, I was at the arena trying to cover the story, except Eric asked me to go on the ice with him to help do drills. Eric and I are six years apart in age, so we never played each other in Junior Hockey. The first time I met him was at the Seneca College Hockey School run by former NHL referee Vern Buffey. What a ton of fun we had at this school. Adam Graves, Brad May, Jim Paek, Brian Wilks, Craig Woodcroft, Steve Spott, Glen Featherstone, Brett Kelleher, Ted Dent, Mark Haarmann, Marc Laniel, Troy Binnie, and yes, the occasional cameo appearance of a sixteen-year-old phenom named Eric Lindros. The summers always ended with everyone coming over for a big Greek barbecue at my parents' house.

So Eric knew me a little and asked me to help him out on the ice while he waited for trade news. I can still see the look on the faces of my producers when I came back to the studio with a promise for an exclusive one-on-one interview that he had offered me. It was no small feat for our fledgling cable network to start getting exclusives. My value at Sportsnet started to rise.

My first big NHL trade scoop was that August when I reported that Eric Lindros had been traded from Philadelphia to the New York Rangers. According to Scott Moore, that story really cemented the fact that I could be a news breaker and that Sportsnet could compete.

Looking back on my career, Scott later said, "Most players go into the analysis role and don't try to use their contacts to break news. You make sure you protect your sources. I don't know where Nick figured that out—I don't know if he talked to guys about making sure about how to be a good journalist and I'm not going to overstate that he became a hard-core journalist—but he knew how to deal with source management. I think most guys, if not all of them, that have ever dealt with him felt they could trust him and he would never burn them as sources."

Others began to see the difference, too. "Players would tell him things that they probably wouldn't tell other people because of his background of being a player," Bob Torrens said. "Bob McKenzie was always going to be the Godfather, but Nick and Dreger together were just pit bulls. And man, when they got a sniff of something, those two just went at it from every direction. I've got a lot of respect for what Nick and Dreger did."

At that time I was the only one that could come close to breaking news like Bob McKenzie. It soon got to the point that I was breaking as many trades as he was, sometimes more. Of course, the competitive side of me felt great that I had struck a nerve over at TSN. A hockey news market that they once dominated was now being fought hard for. This is really when the Sportsnet vs. TSN rivalry came alive and my stock at Sportsnet soared.

As an aside, when Bob McKenzie was working as the editor of the *Hockey News* in the eighties, he would often go to a restaurant, which was around the corner from where the paper was printed. That restaurant, Peter's, was owned by my father. Maybe I filled his water glass one day.

Early in the 2001–2002 season, we broadcast a national game between Toronto and Buffalo. What made this game day memorable for me was that I had a source tell me Dave Manson had been traded from Toronto to Dallas for Jyrki Lumme. The producers in the studio were supportive of my story and green-lighted it on the pregame show. But because the trade wasn't announced yet, Leafs Assistant GM Bill Watters publically denied it. Because of that, naturally many doubted the validity of the story. In fact, the Leafs went out of their way to make Dave Manson skate the pregame warm-up just to throw the dogs off the scent. However, Manson did not play that game. Many of my superiors who heard my story on the 6 p.m. show watched Manson warm up in a Maple Leaf uniform. Even Jim Hughson and Craig Simpson, who called the game for us that night, refused to touch the story. Needless to say, there wasn't a lot of support. I knew my sources were strong and I knew, at least up until that point, that Manson was going to be traded.

Sure enough, it happened just like I said. Now, was I worried that I'd made a mistake? I suppose the answer could be yes, but I knew I had the story right. My concern was that one of the teams had changed their mind and called off the trade. There is always the danger in breaking news that last-minute changes to plans can occur, and it happens on rare occasions, but it can't spook you if you want longevity in this line of work. As Doug MacLean often told Sportsnet, "I can't tell if it will happen, I can only tell you what I'm hearing."

It was always best to be the one announcing a trade on live TV, but if we didn't have that luck, we had to get it out on the newswire. Years ago it was a turtle race. We had no Twitter back then. Things were so much different in terms of how the news was disseminated through the Internet. I'd run the story to the assignment desk, and they'd type it up and then clip and paste it to our website. At times it would take ten to fifteen minutes after submitting it before we would see it posted. I'd literally stare at TSN's web page praying nothing popped up regarding the same story. It was like watching daytime soaps and hearing the words "Like sand through the hourglass, so are the Days of our Lives." But when the story popped up first on Sportsnet, it was like a Game 7 win; the studio would erupt in celebration. Then the Canadian Press wire would pick it up and give us total ownership. For us, watching a major NHL story with a tagline "Sportsnet has learned" or "Sportsnet is saying" was like watching your child take his first steps. For those of us who were told Sportsnet wouldn't last two years, it was a big deal! The more tags we had, the more credit came our way.

When it comes to breaking news, it's an interesting dynamic, to say the least. It's not for everybody. A lot of former players who think they want to do it don't really understand it or they find out they don't have the stomach for it. Being an NHL insider is not something I ever set out to become. I didn't graduate with a journalism degree. What the heck did I know about it? In hockey I went from a goal scorer to a tough role-player, and I had to make it up as I went along. In a perfect world I would have preferred not to have been an NHL insider, but there was a huge need for it. Sportsnet needed to gain some credibility in a market that had been owned by TSN. It was all about finding different ways to contribute to your team.

I remember one incident in particular when I really stressed this point in front of my colleagues, including our producer Jeff MacDonald. The national package for playoff games then belonged to *HNIC* and TSN. Even though we didn't cover the actual games, Sportsnet would still have all of the analysts cover the playoff games with both pre- and postgame shows in studio. At this point in the playoffs we are all tired and a little cranky. We often talk about how worn down players are by the postseason, but it's just as true for lots of people working in the hockey world. After the first game, it's not uncommon for some broadcasters and journalists to do the math to figure out how early they could get home. The good news was the days were getting longer and the weather was reminding us that summer was right around the corner. So Jeff and producer Matt Marstrom decided to go out for a walk and grab themselves a Häagen-Dazs ice cream bar. They returned and sat down with us to watch the start of the conference final while eating their ice cream right in front of us.

I asked Jeff, "Where did you get the ice cream?"

He said, "I just ran across the street to get it."

Now my blood starts to boil. "You didn't think to ask any one of us if we wanted an ice cream?"

Before I even gave him a chance to answer, my "team first" mentality kicked into full gear. Now, to be fair, it's been a long-ass season and we were all tired.

I unleashed on Jeff (effectively my boss). "What kind of guy goes out to a store and buys one ice cream for himself and doesn't bother to ask anyone else if they'd like one? You call yourself a team player?"

I really started getting worked up and was tearing him from top to bottom on what a selfish act he'd just done, and how Sportsnet was in big trouble if all we did was think of ourselves. For some reason that one thing was the tipping point for me.

The other guys could not believe how hard I went at him. The crazy part was he just sat there, smirking, not saying a word to me, which infuriated me even more. Then he calmly left the room and grabbed a plastic bag and proceeded to dump fifteen Häagen-Dazs bars on the board room table, laughing his ass off. I paused for a few seconds, rightfully feeling like the biggest jerk. All I could think to say was, "I'm sorry but I really like ice cream."

Early on I had to decide how far I wanted to go for breaking stories. When Félix Potvin was having issues with the Toronto Maple Leafs, he stayed home in Quebec awaiting a trade. Sportsnet asked me to jump on a plane and stake out in front of his house in hopes of grabbing an interview with him as he was coming outside. I said, "You want me to sit in a car outside his house and coldcock him when he comes outside? I'm not going to do that. I'll make a phone call and see if maybe he wants to sit down with me, but I refuse to sit in a car and surprise him."

If I was to be successful in helping Sportsnet, and also keep my dignity with the hockey people that liked and respected me, I had to find different ways of getting information. I needed to attract bees with honey. I never got the interview with Potvin because I didn't want to do it the way Sportsnet had asked. Coming out of the NHL, I had a lot of league friends I could lean on. It didn't work out for me in that instance, but it was the right call.

Breaking news can sometimes mean bargaining with sources. You help me, I'll help you. For some people there was a price to pay for giving up information and they weren't shy to let you know it. One source I had loved baseball tickets when the Orioles came to town, so it didn't hurt us when Rogers bought the Blue Jays in 2000 and provided me with tickets. A favour could also come in the form of promoting people publicly when high-profile jobs were available. There's always a list of names of possible replacements after a prominent firing, so you add one or two to help someone advance. It might sound a tad shady, but that's how breaking news can work on some occasions.

And breaking news can lead to awkward moments. In 2001 I announced at the trade deadline that Craig Conroy had been traded from St. Louis to Calgary for Cory Stillman. Problem was, I called Craig about it before the Blues had told him. He thought I was calling to ask his opinion on an earlier trade that sent Keith Tkachuk from the Phoenix Coyotes.

Many years later, we did a promo for Trade Deadline Day and had a few players say they found out they'd been traded from watching Sportsnet. There was one Trade Deadline Day when, as Dreger recalls, I was "hitting them out of the park, one after another, and it was like someone turned on a tap." He thought the adrenaline rush for breaking trades must have reminded me of playing hockey. He was right.

I suggested the producers let us use cell phones while we were on-air during Trade Deadline Day. It had never been done before. I kept one on the desk beside me so if someone called about a trade, the audience felt like they were right there with me. It was reality TV at its finest. It got to the point where we were getting information quicker than the GMs could finalize the deals. Then Bob Torrens had a great idea to call me on the air in the middle of a live show if the trades were lagging. He'd tell me to get up and leave the desk right before commercial break. I'd say, "Excuse me, I've got to take this call," and walk away. It looked like we were on the verge of a big scoop and forced viewers to stay with us instead of flipping to TSN during the break. Bob made sure the cameras were still following me while I was working the phones even when I didn't have anything imminent. It was a lot of fun.

CHAPTER 13

Expanding My Role

At the end of the 2003–2004 season, the collective bargaining agreement between the league and the players' association was due to expire. These agreements have to be renegotiated every so many years, and can often be a drawn-out process. There is a lot on the line each time—a lot of money. Leading up to the 2004–2005 season, there had been a lot of talk and speculation about it. The big point this time was going to be the proposed salary cap. And sure enough, as the summer went on, it became clear that the NHL and the players' association were not getting closer to a resolution.

I had been involved with the previous CBA as a player, in 1995, when we had successfully fought against a full salary cap. But it was only a temporary victory. Now the league was intent on not only extending it, but expanding it, too.

As we prepared our broadcasting programs for the 2004–2005 season, the NHL started a lockout with no end in sight. In the Sportsnet hockey department we were all worried about whether we'd have work and whether we'd get paid. And we were also worried about losing the momentum we'd gained in breaking news. We'd been growing, and losing the hockey season could stop us dead. But even without a single game being played, there was plenty of news to discuss. With a thirst for gathering information for viewers, we were busier than ever. The lockout was well covered by both Sportsnet and TSN. It was a huge story. Unlike previous NHL lockouts, this one looked like it might not be resolved and the season would be lost. Fans tuned in regularly hoping for some sign that this might not be the case.

Major League Baseball had lost a postseason because of an impasse between the players and owners (back in 1995, when we negotiated the last NHL CBA), but this was the first time a major-league North American sport had cancelled a whole season due to a dispute. But it felt worse than even that. Hockey is a sport predominantly played by Canadians, and good Canadian boys are not supposed to allow a season to be shut down.

For eighty-six straight seasons, fans had been able to enjoy a Stanley Cup championship. The only year that a Stanley Cup had not been hoisted was in 1919, during a pandemic. The final between the Montreal Canadiens and the Seattle Metropolitans came to an abrupt halt when all but a handful of players became bedridden with high fevers. The Spanish flu would later claim the life of a Canadiens hockey great, Joe Hall (he was just thirty-seven years old), as well as millions of people across the globe. A global health crisis is understandably a justifiable reason to lose a season. It's a lot harder to be patient when the issue is millionaire players fighting with billionaire owners for their slice of the pie.

Even as I was writing this book, another pandemic forced the NHL season to close. There is a lot of support and understanding about social distancing to limit the spread of the COVID-19 coronavirus. Fans were willing to be patient as they waited for more hockey, and for the Stanley Cup to finally be awarded. But it certainly gives us insight into what it must have been like in 1919.

During the work stoppage Sportsnet had daily meetings and wall-to-wall coverage. Every time there was a press conference with the players or Commissioner Gary Bettman, we'd be there. While the league was on indefinite hold, it was the complete opposite for the media. We were on standby because anything could happen at a moment's notice. Instead of providing content based on the games, we had to provide content about the negotiations. It turns out we didn't have to worry about anyone losing their job. There was no thought about cutting back coverage.

Inside information was key, and as a broadcaster, I always loved the challenge of gathering it. The lockout wasn't all that different. How did we find out what was happening? Being able to reach out to both the NHLPA and the league office proved crucial.

It wasn't just news we reported. Our discussions on the labour dispute became pretty heated at times. The different hockey analysts at Sportsnet were really able to use their voices. Although I'd like to think I was fair and objective, I always came from the players' perspective. I can't truly tell you what it's like to manage a team, but I can certainly tell you what it's like to be in the dressing room. I know firsthand how players are affected by strikes and lockouts. I have lived through both and fought alongside other players to preserve as many of our rights as possible.

When Bob Goodenow officially took over for the disgraced Alan Eagleson as the NHLPA executive director in 1992, the PA was a mess. My baptism in the big business of NHL hockey started with one NHLPA meeting led by Alan Eagleson and his right-hand man, Sam Simpson, in St. Louis. It was also a complete eye-opener for me. On the team bus I heard one horror story after another about how evil this man was. Dale Hunter, a seasoned veteran of eight years, told me, "Whatever you do, don't ask the Eagle a question." Why not? Dale said that one time, while he was playing in Quebec, his teammate Wally Weir asked Eagleson a simple question in a team meeting. Eagleson snapped back at him, "Sit down and shut the fuck up, Wally, you're lucky to be in the league." Then Hunts says to me, "If he said that to Wally, what do you think he's gonna say to you?" Safe to say at this first meeting I hid in the corner trying not to be noticed. From the moment Eagleson walked in the door, the vibe felt more like a mob scene in a movie than a hockey players' association gathering. Thankfully redemption came in 1994 for many players who were cheated by this man when he was charged with thirty-four counts of fraud, including racketeering and embezzlement, in a U.S. court. A few years later he again pleaded guilty to fraud and embezzlement in Toronto, and this time his sorry ass was thrown in jail for an inconsequential six months. Many ex-players wondered how many people he might have paid off to get such a lenient sentence.

The players' association was very important for us then. I saw what they could do when I had a dispute with the Rangers over my individual playoff bonuses after winning the Cup. Remember, I had a lot of bonus money in my contract from when I was a Whaler. But the Rangers, to my shock, said they didn't feel obligated to pay, even though my contract made it clear what I was owed. I had to file a grievance through the PA and, while on a road trip with the Rangers, come back to New York in February 1996 to attend arbitration. It was an incredibly awkward position to be in. I was fortunate it went my way in the end, but if it wasn't for the PA fighting for me, who knows. The one thing I do know for sure: if Alan Eagleson had still been running things then, I never would have seen a dime.

It was a relief to be rid of Eagleson, but shortly after Bob Goodenow's arrival we started hearing rumblings about that dreaded term: "salary cap." As early as 1992, Bob did everything he could to educate us about what restrictive salary caps would be like for all players. Despite an already restrictive CBA, owners still had the freedom to pay us whatever they felt we were worth. In the 1994–1995 lockout, after missing a little under half a season, we were able to preserve the CBA without a full cap. Now, ten years later, I was playing a far different role, this time as a broadcaster. With my experience of living through both the NHLPA strike in '92 and the lockout in '94 and '95, it was clear that Sportsnet was going to be counting on me heavily for our coverage.

From a personal standpoint, I was also curious about whether the current players could hold tight and avoid the salary cap the way we did in 1994–1995.

Players back then really only had the information provided by the players' association. But this time mainstream media was to have a huge part and Internet coverage was beginning to play a role for the first time. For me, as a broadcaster, it's important to try to cover how both sides approach the impasse and to present their sides. All things considered, I made a conscious decision to broadcast from a player's point of view. With so many broadcasters around me giving Goliath a voice, I decided to play the role of David; if for no other reason than to create better television content.

However, Gary Bettman and the NHL were much more prepared for the PR game. The NHL was effective at working with the media by highlighting the reasoning behind their demands, much more so than the NHLPA. For the first time, the NHL really used media to sway public opinion regarding the contract negotiations. That to me was a strategic move by Bettman and the owners that really paid off. They targeted key players behind the scenes and convinced them the salary cap was the only way a deal was getting done. Starting with NHLPA president Trevor Linden, one by one other star influencers soon followed and gave up the fight as well. The owners won and crushed the NHLPA. Bob Goodenow resigned shortly after, and the once powerful association has been in catch-up mode ever since.

Despite the passion I showed for the players' position, as a broadcaster I had no skin in the game. But I was curious. When Commissioner Bettman and the owners broke Bob Goodenow's players' association, they changed the course of the hockey business forever. It would have a profound impact, especially on the original six teams. I was often asked on-air at the time, "Is this a good thing for big hockey markets or not?"

No longer would we see the New York Rangers, Toronto Maple Leafs, or Detroit Red Wings grab media attention flexing their financial muscle to outspend the smaller markets. Where would the image of the Bronx Bombers and George Steinbrenner be without press conferences announcing massive deals with Catfish Hunter, Reggie Jackson, Dave Winfield, or Derek Jeter? That type of national attention always lifted the image of the Yankees above most teams before even playing one game. Even when the Yankees aren't winning championships, they're always one signing away from making their fans feel like they can. In 2004 I knew that many of the fans believed the players should agree to a salary cap for no other reason than to keep costs down—savings which, in theory, would then be passed on to the fans. I think fifteen years later we've learned that this is ultimately not how it worked.

Without a salary cap, we were genuinely happy for our teammates' success at maximizing their earnings. I remember learning about Luc Robitaille's six-year $19.2 million extension with the Rangers just after training camp. We had a lot of fun booking our free Upper West Side lunches with him covering the bill for weeks. Luc would say, "Boys, keep working hard, it's the Rangers . . . plenty more cash where that came from." And that's how we all felt. Somehow we could all prosper together. Today, however, a player signing a lucrative contract directly impacts his teammates' ability to do the same. "How does his contract affect mine?" A bigger challenge for teams today may be avoiding jealousy among players. It's become more difficult to utter the words to your teammates, "Plenty more where that came from."

Now, an example of a team that managed to elude the cap crunch was the Pittsburgh Penguins. In 2012, Sidney Crosby decided he wanted to be a Penguin for life, committing his next twelve years with an average annual salary of $8.7 million. Because Crosby agreed to spend the prime of his career with a locked-in AAV (average annual value), his contract aged quickly against the growing salary cap. But that enabled Pittsburgh to go and spend the team payroll more evenly. Not only did it allow Pittsburgh to re-sign all their key players around Sid, but they were able to add a significant high-priced player, Phil Kessel. This helped Sid levy two more Stanley Cups. Sid, regarded as the best player of his era, was never the highest-paid player in the league—in fact, he is not even the highest-paid player on his team. That stat belongs to Evgeni Malkin. It just doesn't seem right to me.

Regarding the original six, the Chicago Blackhawks were an exception. They had success with three Stanley Cups in six years, but many of their young stars, who became the core of that team, hadn't yet signed for big dollars. Ever since, they've had to deal with the salary cap constraints.

Not having any actual games to discuss really changed how we broadcasters did our jobs. We had to think on our feet, without first memorizing what we wanted to say. Ask Darren Dreger and he'll tell you that this was an extra learning curve for me. I always wanted to be well prepared, but this wasn't always possible anymore. We would literally be standing on a sidewalk for hours, waiting for any news to break. We could go live the moment we had fresh CBA information, so between gathering the new info, deciphering it, and going live on-air, we had only a few minutes. It was like nothing I had experienced before in my six years. On top of that we never knew if our producers wanted a two-minute update or a one-hour piece. Some of those updates left me feeling like I'd gone through a meat grinder.

During the lockout, I secured an exclusive interview with Mark Messier, at his home in South Carolina, after he officially retired. It was a huge score for Sportsnet, getting Mark's story from there, which nobody had really done before. Bob Torrens always had a good eye for capturing great moments in interviews. Until the editors start putting the film together, you never really know how a piece will turn out. Bob said he had never met a player who was as "embracing" as Mark. Most of the interview took place while playing eighteen holes of golf in the marshy lowland of South Carolina. Mark demonstrated how to run a zigzag formation in order to outrun an alligator. I don't think I ever played a faster game of golf. It became one of my favourite interviews in my twenty-one-years because it showed a fun, sweet side to Mark, very different from the "death stares" he would show his opponents.

That year was also very important to me for an entirely different reason. Anne-Marie and I were awaiting the arrival of our third child. Anastasia was born on May 12 and our family was complete. Sportsnet was always good about family matters, not only for me but for everyone involved in the production of their shows. Anne-Marie received big gift baskets and sweet notes, and so would the other wives upon the birth of a child. Sportsnet even sent things at the end of the season thanking them for all their support. I appreciated Sportsnet's gestures, of course, but you don't realize what a truly thoughtful thing something is until it stops.

We bought an old farmhouse in Toronto that had a rare huge backyard. We decided this was the year to build an outdoor hockey rink. Since I was a kid, it had always been a dream of mine to have a backyard rink. While I wanted my kids to enjoy our rink, I also built it for myself. We have great memories of the time we spent out there.

We also had great neighbours. One night I was on location covering an All-Star Game when Mike Bolton, one of the Hockey Hall of Fame's Stanley Cup handlers, asked me if I was interested in taking the Cup to my home for a few hours. I asked Mike if he was sure I was allowed to have the Cup there. He replied, "Membership has its privileges."

Anne-Marie called a few neighbours and the next thing we know there is a lineup at our front door, people with cameras in hand. I got a chance to skate with the Stanley Cup above my head one more time and the neighbourhood kids ate gummy bears out of the Cup. It was an amazing moment: grassroots hockey with the most prestigious trophy in the world. In a weird way, it helped me better understand what winning the Cup meant. It's true when they say you can't really absorb a moment or capture what it means when you are in the middle of it. I had the chance to celebrate winning the Cup again, this time in a calmer environment, with my children and friends.

We were making great strides as a network battling TSN and with my contract coming to a close it should have been a good time to negotiate a shiny new one. The problem was it happened to be the most tumultuous period I ever experienced at Sportsnet. It was like a revolving door of good people leaving, starting with Scott Moore the year before. For reasons unknown to any of us, our hockey department was also breaking up. It was a total shock after beating TSN in the Trade Deadline ratings for the first time ever. Scott Morrison and Jeff MacDonald, who were key guys on our Sportsnet news floor, were suddenly on their way out the door, and Darren Dreger was rightfully upset about how it all went down.

Because Dreger's contract was expiring, he also contemplated jumping ship. So I was left to negotiate with Rick Briggs-Jude, Sportsnet's new vice president of production. I made a decision back in 1998 that with all my lockout and contract experiences, I was going to negotiate my own broadcasting contracts. It had gone well and smoothly with Scott Moore, so I figured I'd try it with Rick. Unfortunately, dealing with Briggs-Jude turned into a disaster and the thought of spending 10 percent of my salary on an agent didn't seem so far-fetched. Rick was not interested in showing me any love at all and played hard-ass the whole time. After I declined his first offer in early July (which would have been a pay cut), he had me meet him a week later at Bayview Village mall for lunch and reengaged with the contract negotiations. He gave me a piece of paper with a new contract offer on it. He'd added small incentive bonuses tied to improved ratings. I told him I knew nothing about how ratings worked and refused to have those in my deal. He made it abundantly clear that it wasn't going to get much better. I told him, with all due respect, "This is going nowhere," and left before finishing lunch. I informed Sportsnet I wasn't coming back and I wasn't going to deal with Briggs-Jude either.

Coincidentally, that same week Madison Square Garden contacted me because John Davidson was leaving his post as analyst for New York Rangers games and they were interested in me possibly replacing him. I was told they loved the synergy between my involvement in the 1994 Cup run and my present reputation as an insider analyst. Within days of my telling my wife we might be heading back to New York, they flew me down to talk. When I landed and jumped into a cab, I got two calls on my cell phone I could never have predicted.

The first was a call from Darren Dreger, telling me he was through with Sportsnet. He told me a press release was coming soon to announce that he was going to TSN, not in a hosting role but as an NHL insider. I was not overly surprised to hear that he was leaving Sportsnet, but I was disappointed that he couldn't tell me sooner. I knew Darren was not a big fan of the latest moves at Sportsnet because he was not scared to sound his displeasure. We talked a bit and I ended our call, telling Darren, "You have to do what you think is right for you and your family; nothing really matters after that." After that call I truly felt like a man on an island. While things looked really bleak, and despite the huge loss of my eight-year partner in crime, I still had enough people at Sportsnet that I liked and respected to hold out hope for a future at Sportsnet.

Darren never regretted the decision to go from Sportsnet to TSN. There were a number of good reasons. But he regrets that he didn't tell me sooner because of the close relationship we had. We weren't just colleagues, we were great friends. We had kids around the same age and hung out together away from work. It was a tremendous loss for both me and Sportsnet.

The Greek astronomer Ptolemy wrote that the gods cause shooting stars. In this case, the hockey gods. Within one minute of ending Dreger's call a second call came from Paul Godfrey, president and CEO of the Toronto Blue Jays. The Blue Jays, along with Sportsnet, were owned by Rogers. Godfrey said he had heard I was in New York to talk to MSG and he wanted to make it crystal clear that Sportsnet wanted me back. Now, I had never met Paul, let alone talked to him about my situation, but Rogers wanted to find out what was happening with me in New York and got Paul to do it. The moment I said hello, Paul was more straightforward and genuine with me than anyone else I had dealt with the previous few weeks. He was great and totally up-front. He told me Sportsnet had asked him to make calls into MSG because he had various contacts there. They wanted him to find out where MSG stood with me. I was quite taken aback that the president of the Blue Jays had called on behalf of Sportsnet. Paul told me the "Rogers family" wanted me back.

In many ways, Paul Godfrey was the reason I stayed at Sportsnet. He assured me the company didn't want me to go anywhere and they were going to look after me and do the right thing. He made me promise not to commit to or sign with MSG until I'd given Sportsnet one last crack. Because I was so touched by his call, I assured him I wouldn't make any decisions without hearing from Sportsnet one more time. While I was very interested in MSG, my heart was still with the network that gave me my first chance. I returned to Toronto and restarted the negotiations.

Sportsnet removed Rick Briggs-Jude and in came Sportsnet's head of content and production, David Akande. In one phone call that didn't last longer than ten minutes, we closed a new four-year deal that nearly doubled my salary. It was around this time that I hired attorney Gord Kirke, a sports and entertainment lawyer with a great reputation in the industry. I enjoyed negotiating my own contracts but I knew I needed help with the finer details. Anne-Marie often called him the "Velvet Hammer."

With that, the pressure was on for me to give them what they were paying for. I needed to go out and break trades, get inside information, and get interviews. This time I didn't have Scott Morrison or Darren Dreger to lean on. Sportsnet had brought in good people, like Pierre LeBrun and Ray Ferraro, for a short stint, but never offered them full-time jobs. So much at this time was resting on my shoulders. I broke my fair share of trades and secured exclusives with Messier, Gretzky, Lemieux, and Lindros those next few years. Despite the pressure of not having Darren Dreger or Scott Morrison to work with, I was somehow able to come through for Sportsnet.

This was also right around the time Sportsnet hired Bill Watters as well. I enjoyed working on-air with Bill. He was my first agent with Rick Curran before I switched to Harry Francis. We had known each other over the years, including when he was part of Toronto's management and I was a player.

Bill understood the game from a management perspective. Years later, when Doug MacLean joined Sportsnet, he could talk about similar issues since he'd been in hockey as a coach, GM, and president. The player-versus-management perspective sparked some of the great on-air battles Bill and I had.

Bill was almost always on the management side, but on one rare occasion he attacked Leafs co-owner Larry Tanenbaum for how poorly he dealt with his GM, John Ferguson Jr. He called Larry "unethical and unprofessional." And in another odd twist, this may have been the only time in twenty years on-air that I stood up and defended an NHL owner. We were broadcasting our pregame show live at the Air Canada Centre and I'm sure people sitting in the lower bowl gold seats could hear us arguing. Bill yelled at me, "You might get a job with the Leafs if you keep it up, Nick!" I yelled back, "Well, you lost yours, Bill!" Despite Bill and I sometimes having heavy debates, I assure you it was never truly bitter between us. On rare nights we might have taken it a bit too far, but whether it was Bill Watters, Mike Keenan, or Doug MacLean, no one ever took things personally. It was ultimately about bringing the viewers and the listeners into a real opinionated conversation in which we weren't going to walk on eggshells. While the tone of our conversation may have made other people uncomfortable, there was something authentic about it. For the viewers the response on the Internet was off the charts. Hockey bloggers were calling it "must-see TV." If Bill or Doug called me a fourth-line slug or a bench warmer, I never took it personally. It was an unfiltered look at the world of hockey.

When it came to Bill and me, Bob Torrens said he had never seen two guys with such polar-opposite opinions at each other's throats when the camera was on. Once the show ended, though, whatever friction there was between us just went away. We'd leave the set, have a nice conversation, and I'd drive Bill home.

Once you find the perfect topic, and people with opposing views on it, an on-air debate almost becomes a choreographed event—it just flows so well. This type of behaviour was no different than two teammates fighting in practice during a battle drill. Pride and ego don't allow you to lose an inch, so you're okay to watch things escalate. After, these things are almost always forgotten right away (until someone reminds you).

I always prided myself on being able to "read" a dressing room, knowing the strengths and weaknesses of teammates. Broadcasting was just a new kind of team. Sportsnet had made a real investment in me and I felt it was important to help a guy like Bill bring out some of the passion and fire I knew he had.

There was an overall style shift at Sportsnet, from a serious, suit and tie look to something more casual. If you watch the TV industry today, Akande wasn't that far off with his concept; it was just too early for broadcasters to dress in jeans and open-neck shirts. It became a very casual setting, with us sitting around on a couch. The "crotch shot," as we referred to it back then, was now on full display in front of millions. The normal producer instruction we'd hear through our earpieces went from "camera two" to "close your legs, close your legs!" Some viewers liked the concept and some people really struggled with it.

I had been breaking a lot of trades, but now at TSN Darren was starting to get inside information along with Bob McKenzie. Needless to say I started to feel the pressure of being outmanned. And the new format didn't make things easier. David Akande had a different attitude towards covering hockey from a news point of view. The shift in presentation really impacted our trade-deadline shows, particularly coming off a ratings win over TSN the year before. David wanted to continue the casual feel into the trade deadline, so he changed the show into a "pizza party." He wanted a fun, casual environment, and boy did he get it.

To reveal some of the news on Trade Deadline Day, we used the model of the game show *Deal or No Deal*. We had the Hanson Brothers, from the famous hockey film *Slap Shot*, in their uniforms playing bubble hockey. And a blogger called "Eklund" was hired to reveal whatever inside information he wanted. They had asked the rest of us not to worry about breaking trades; we were just to sit around and have fun because the show was not intended to be serious. They felt the fans wanted to be entertained. Meanwhile, TSN continued to break trades in the traditional format.

Eklund's shtick back then was to go on-air but to conceal his identity. During our trade-deadline show, like the banker in *Deal or No Deal*, Eklund was not to be revealed when he relayed trades. He had an Internet following at the time that made him into a sort of cult figure.

Designer jeans, sport coats, sitting on a couch, and an anonymous blogger. This was Sportsnet's attempt to go "hip."

Eklund was actually Dwayne Klessel of HockeyBuzz.com. He was effective as one of the first "bloggers" who broke into the hockey news field. HockeyBuzz.com was key during the 2004 lockout. Klessel was first to use the Internet as an alternative to television and radio. Again, we were a bit ahead of our time, but there is no question that our pizza-party trade-deadline show set us back, at least when it came to our credibility. We had worked really hard to build it up at that point, but we were basically in catch-up mode after that.

When Darren went to TSN and Scott Morrison left Sportsnet, the role of breaking news fell squarely on me. I no longer had allies to help chase down news. Before that time, everyone at Sportsnet had the attitude that they were in it to win it—to beat TSN every day. When the decision was initially made to do away with the news-breaking trade-deadline shows and adopt a new format, everyone on the hockey broadcast side felt our reputation took a hit.

When Bob Torrens produced the *Deal or No Deal* format, he asked me, "How in the hell will we get by for twelve hours without breaking news?" He referred to it as "the *Gong Show* Trade Deadline." The day after the show he was devastated when he read the reviews in the newspapers.

In 2008, I went to Stockholm to interview Mats Sundin at his home, just after he announced he was leaving the Leafs. He was contemplating his next move, to either sign with Vancouver or retire. It was a big deal for Sportsnet and another example of how the locker-room relationships I'd had with players during my hockey-playing years carried over to my broadcasting career.

Like many great leaders, Mats had the uncanny ability to make everyone around him feel like they were integral to the team. When I first came to the Leafs, I had never met Mats before, but I remembered chirping him when he first broke into the league as a skinny teenager with the Quebec Nordiques. I remember playing against Quebec in the early nineties and watching their first pick overall flying all over the ice. I never considered myself a big talker, but I started on Mats and his complexion. It wasn't uncommon for teenage hockey players to have their share of acne, and I was no exception at age nineteen, but for some reason I started mouthing off to Mats. Not a great introduction with the future Hall of Famer. When we met in the Leafs dressing room, Mats reminded me that I called him "Pizza Face" and "Connect the Dots" during that game. Then, to let me know there were no hard feelings, he broke into his infectious laughter and we instantly became friends.

Bob Torrens and I got two days with Mats at his house. Within hours of our arrival Bob and I were invited to a big dinner party at a five-star restaurant. It was set up by Mats, of course. Even during our Stanley Cup celebration I'd never seen bottles of 6L Champagne. My first night in Stockholm was a memorable one.

We shot part of the interview in a sauna, near a dock, and we cranked up the heat. After, Bob suggested I jump into the Baltic Sea as a "bumper," a term that means a tease, for the upcoming interview. Even though the temperature was about twelve degrees Celsius, I did it. I had a high-pitched voice for a week.

It took me a while to feel comfortable interviewing former teammates. They were buddies who I had battled alongside on the ice many times. We hung out together. You're not supposed to critique them or ask them tough questions. It doesn't feel right. One time I was covering a regional Leaf game on Sportsnet and Wade Belak took a couple of bad penalties, which I mentioned during the intermission. When we went to commercial break, my cell phone rang.

"What are you shitting all over Wade Belak for?" I hear a voice on the other end say.

"Excuse me," I replied. "Tie, is that you?"

"Yeah, it's me, why are you shitting all over Wade Belak?" Tie Domi repeated.

"Tie, he took some bad penalties," I said. "Should you really be calling me from the trainers' room right now?"

"Yeah, I should," he answered.

I said, "Happy to discuss this later, but focus on the third period, okay?"

"You better start saying some nice things about him," Tie said, and hung up.

That, in a nutshell, was Tie Domi. His job was to forever protect his teammates on and off the ice, and that's exactly what he was doing in this case—that and watching our intermissions.

Whenever you get questioned like this, your first thought is, *Was I too critical?* Afterwards, I asked my producer to replay for me what I'd said, and I felt it was fair. Even so, I suddenly felt like the bad guy when it came to old teammates. If I had been traded to another team, my former teammates would have fully understood that my job was to help my new team at any cost. But as a broadcaster, it was harder for players to understand why I didn't just say flattering things all the time. The hardest part of my job was to be honest even if it impacted ex-teammates. At times that could really test friendships.

There were other times when I found myself in uncomfortable situations. Later in the year, I received a call from a woman (I will not name) who wanted me to be a voting panelist for the Gemini Awards, Canada's version of the American Emmy Awards. In 2013 they changed the name to the Canadian Screen Awards. Geminis were given by the Academy of Canadian Cinema & Television to recognize the achievements in the Canadian television industry, including sportscasting.

I was honoured they had asked me. She told me that I, along with a panel, would be voting in an entertainment category. We'd all be shown sample tapes of each nominee so we could make our choice on a secret ballot. Sounded simple enough. What is important to understand is that back then individuals and shows were submitted for nominations by their production company or a show's producer. Sportsnet, to my knowledge, didn't care much about participating, whereas TSN and CBC loved it. It gave them a chance to promote their talent and their networks.

The day I went in to vote I found a few surprises. First, I was voting for a candidate in the sportscasting category, not entertainment. The second surprise was that I was being asked to vote on a category in which TSN had submitted Pierre McGuire. The third surprise was that I saw Steve Simmons, a sports columnist with Sun Media and TSN, chairing the voting committee. It was Steve's responsibility to collect all the votes and deliver them back. My first thought after quickly assessing the situation was there wasn't a snowball's chance in hell I was voting for Pierre McGuire for a Gemini. Remember, I happily hated TSN back then. I asked Steve if I could have a word with him in private and I voiced my concern. I said, "Steve, you don't find it a strange and huge conflict, having both you and me involved in this process for the sportscasting category?" To Steve's credit he totally saw my point of view and understood my reluctance. I thanked him and left without voting.

The next day I received a call from the voting committee asking why I hadn't voted. I explained that I had a problem voting for a rival whom I competed against every day. I said, "It's not fair to me and it's certainly not fair to Pierre McGuire." The woman I spoke to asked me to set aside personal feelings and just vote. I responded, "Ah, no I can't." She then told me they knew the voting system wasn't perfect but that's the way it had to be. I sensed her getting pretty irritated with my attitude. She went on to say it was too late for them to replace me and they still needed my vote quickly or the whole category would have to be scrapped. She didn't even care who I picked, "just put an X somewhere."

She now had clearly put the onus on me to save the category and it really bothered me. I finished our conversation with no promises that I would vote. They had the Gemini voting card couriered to my house with explicit instructions to vote and courier it back immediately. The envelope sat on my desk for two days. I told Anne-Marie I wasn't going to vote because it was wrong. She told me, "Just pick someone and send it back." So instead of voting for or against Pierre, I had my four-year-old daughter vote instead. I said, "Annie, see these boxes? Put an X in one of them, whatever box you like, and don't tell Daddy which one." I then stuffed the ballot into the envelope and sent it back. If Pierre ended up winning that year, it may very well have been my four-year-old daughter who helped edge him over Terry Leibel from CBC Sports.

The hockey world offered plenty of news to discuss, not just trades. In September 2009 I had the opportunity to interview a polarizing figure, former NHL player Mike Danton. Some in the media described Danton's story as "one of the most bizarre cases the sporting world has ever witnessed." He had just been released from prison, and served almost five and a half years (of a seven-and-a-half-year sentence) for pleading guilty to conspiracy to commit murder. In 2004, while playing for the St. Louis Blues, Danton was arrested two days after his team's elimination from the playoffs. A few months later he pleaded guilty to the charge of attempting to hire a hit man. At the time it was not known whether he had plotted to kill his father, Steve Jefferson, or his agent, David Frost, who had become like a surrogate father.

I don't know what possessed me to chase this story down, but I had to get it first. I just knew it would take our network to another level. I also knew it wasn't just a hockey story; it was a national human-interest story that mainstream media was covering, too.

I never thought of myself as a big interviewer, but I figured with so much attention on this story, I had to try. I figured finding Mike was not so different from tracking down trade info—just start working the phones. Instead of calling GMs, scouts, and agents, I called correctional facilities, parole officers, and lawyers.

I finally tracked Danton down and learned that he was being released from the Kingston Penitentiary. We initially had a phone conversation that only lasted a few minutes. He admitted to me that he didn't know me well, but trusted my reputation for being fair, so he agreed to let me help him tell his side of the story. I made it clear that I had to be free to ask him anything I felt was necessary for the credibility of the story. To my surprise he replied, "I have no problem with that at all, you can ask me anything you want, I just want the truth out." Even though he sounded sincere and very approachable, I remember ending the conversation and wondering if I had just spoken to a man capable of plotting a murder. What had I signed up for? There were still many hoops to jump through, including determining his official release date and his getting the green light from his parole board to speak to the media.

Up until this point I hadn't mentioned the potential interview with executive producer Mike English or Bob Torrens because I didn't want to overpromise. After I secured the interview six weeks later, Sportsnet turned it into a multipart series to gather more viewers. They called it *The Untold Story* and it drew about two hundred to three hundred thousand viewers each night. That was equivalent to some of our ratings for a National Hockey League game in our early days. Danton had a horrible reputation coming out of prison based on CBC's *The Fifth Estate*, which had been on top of the story from the beginning, but had not been able to interview him.

The public perception going into the Sportsnet interview was that Danton was as guilty as sin and not credible. There weren't a lot of people who believed his "someone was trying to kill me" defence.

Getting an exclusive Mike Danton sit-down over *The Fifth Estate*'s Bob McKeown, whom I considered the best storyteller in the business, was a huge coup for Sportsnet. I went into the interview with no preconceptions. I wanted viewers to draw their own conclusions after watching.

Mike Danton was shockingly candid that day. Mike English, our executive producer, publicly praised my ability to get Mike to open up as much as he did. He was a twenty-nine-year-old with a lot on his mind. I can say with certainty, twelve years of playing professional hockey did not prepare me for asking someone about why they tried to have their father killed. We talked about abandonment, mental and physical abuse, depression, and manipulation. The interview really hit home for me when Mike spoke of shredding a towel in his cell and making a noose. Looking back, it was the most compelling piece of work I had done up to that point.

Every major media outlet had given the Mike Danton story the attention it deserved, and an interview of this magnitude was naturally critiqued heavily. Steve Simmons wrote for Sun Media that I was a "hockey player turned excellent commentator." For me, having a veteran journalist like Steve Simmons write that review was probably the highest compliment I had received since I started broadcasting.

I only wish we could have shown more of the interview. I asked hard and to-the-point questions that didn't make the cut. Things got tricky when Sportsnet lawyers got final approval with what went to air. In the final version, many of the harder aspects of the interview were removed.

I revisited Danton's life later, when Sportsnet covered his first few years after prison, which was a compelling story in itself. In January 2010 he enrolled at St. Mary's University and joined the men's hockey team shortly thereafter. I remember flying to Halifax and sitting down to interview athletic director Steve Sarty and head coach Trevor Stienburg and thinking how incredible they were to give Danton a chance when no other team would touch him with a ten-foot pole. The team went on to win the national championship that season, the first time in the school's history. Danton was named an Academic All-Canadian with a grade-point average of over 3.7. He held the same grade-point average the next season and then headed overseas to resume his playing career. A few years after that, Danton saved his teammate's life when he began choking while on the ice. He used the first-aid training he had received in prison.

CHAPTER 14

More Big Changes

In 2010, Sportsnet and TSN combined to broadcast the Olympics, which took place in Vancouver and Whistler, B.C. Radio host Bob McCown jokingly called the union of the two networks the "Unholy Alliance." It was like Coke and Pepsi joining together. Bob McKenzie and James Duthie from TSN and Darren Pang and I from Sportsnet were side by side for three weeks. Daren Millard also hosted along with the great Dave Hodge. It was a little awkward at first, but by this point I didn't mind taking a mental break from the network rivalry to cover the legendary event together.

Bob McKenzie and I were always friendly, and still are, though people might have thought we hated each other because of the rivalry. His son Shawn joined Sportsnet in 2015 and we became friends also. But at this time, the public perception of how Sportsnet and TSN felt about each other was well documented. Before the Olympic panelists were announced, all the Sportsnet broadcasters were asking the same questions. How many analysts would TSN send to the Olympics compared to us? Who had better assignments? Whose face would get better prime-time coverage?

We didn't have to wait long to get our answers. When I arrived in Vancouver, I was told that Bob, Darren Pang, and I would work together as the main hockey panel on every game played. James Duthie would host all of the Canada games with help from Daren Millard and Dave Hodge. Chris Cuthbert of TSN would be the lead announcer for the games. While Bob, Darren Pang, and I were ecstatic about being the faces of Canadian Olympic hockey for the next two weeks, it didn't sit well with other hockey broadcasters. Because Darren Dreger made the decision to go to TSN in 2006, it likely cost him a role in covering hockey at the Olympics. I wish I could have worked again with him there.

The production was well done. They built the set with a studio desk for our hockey panel just above the Zamboni entrance at GM Place, which was renamed Canada Hockey Place. We were six rows up from the ice level and never had to move from that location. At the end of each period, a button was pushed and hydraulics pushed a floor out and a desk popped up. We were told it cost over $100,000 to build. When we finished our intermission segments, the desk would collapse to the floor and be pulled back underneath the seats as if it never existed. For our set to be in that location with a perfect view of the ice was a sports broad- caster's dream come true. We did three games a day: noon, four o'clock, and evening. By the end we were exhausted. My wife and kids came, but I barely saw them.

As broadcasters, we had very little time to get emotionally involved in the patriotic sentiments of the Canadians who attended. Our focus was to prepare and broadcast like any game. We would get the highlight clips, analyze the teams, collect our thoughts and ideas before each game, and try to be clear and concise. It was by far the biggest fishbowl I had ever been in. We just covered the games, then ate and went to sleep. The next day we did it all over again. It was the XXI Olympic Winter Games, hosted by our own country, but to us it felt more like *Groundhog Day*, covering thirty hockey games in twelve days.

We were right in the middle of the games leading up to the final, yet were so busy that I had a tough time feeling the same excitement and emotion as the rest of the country. But on the morning of the final, when we walked from the hotel through the Olympic Village, the energy was palpable. The final game was billed as "the hottest ticket ever in the history of Canadian sport." Scalpers were charging as much as $100,000 for four seats in the same section Bob, Darren, and I had sat in every single minute of every game.

Canada now had a chance to collectively wrap a big bow around the Vancouver Olympics. Our big focus for the gold medal games was giving Canadians as much insight into Team Canada as we were able. Fans were anxious. Immediately, we knew how devastating a loss would feel. Canada already had thirteen gold medals in these Olympics, but on this February night it felt as if hockey was the only gold anyone cared about. Anything but a win would deflate the historic three weeks for Canada.

During the big game it looked as though Canada had a sure win until Zach Parise scored for Team USA, tying the game with twenty-four seconds left in the third period. What should have been the greatest postgame celebration in Canadian history turned into another game intermission show—our sixty-fifth intermission show in twelve days. What's one more?

Anytime a team scores late in a game to send it into OT there is a natural feeling of momentum, but on the air as a panel, we didn't buy into it. We still gave Canada the edge on-air, but privately we spoke of trying to leave the building if the team lost. I told the guys I've seen Vancouver up close after an emotional win, during the '94 Final—I could only imagine what might happen after an emotional loss. Thankfully we didn't have to find out. Seven minutes and thirty-nine seconds into overtime a special moment played out for all of Canada. We could hear Sidney Crosby yell, "Iggy!" His voice was clear and loud. A split second later, Jarome Iginla made the pass, Crosby then beat Brian Rafalski to the net, and buried the puck. History was made. Chris Cuthbert called it "the Golden Goal"—a name that has stuck. It was a historic win, which completed our coverage, the thirtieth game covered in less than two weeks. We broadcasters were elated and utterly exhausted.

Hours later we saw the excitement unfold in the crowds and the impromptu parades, with car horns honking, and we began to understand and feel it ourselves. The normally twenty-minute walk back to the hotel took two hours. We later heard about the ratings numbers, that it was the most-watched event in Canadian history. The game averaged more than 16 million viewers and peaked at 22 million when Sid scored the goal—that's about 70 percent of the Canadian population. More than 26 million watched some part of the game.

It's really an overwhelming feeling being part of the highest-rated show in Canadian history. At the same time, I was just happy to go home and get some sleep. But it was a memorable experience, with the two networks working together. We stayed in the same hotel and hung out together. There was no tension and everyone got along well. I also had a chance to experience firsthand Dave Hodge's wicked sense of humour. As a kid growing up I had watched him host *Hockey Night in Canada,* so it was a big thrill for me to work with him and share a few beers after a game. With the games over, we returned to our jobs and the competition between the two networks started all over again.

Rogers Communications changed dramatically in September 2010, when Keith Pelley, who was president of Canada's Olympic broadcast media consortium, was hired as president of Rogers Media. In December, Rogers announced that my first boss, Scott Moore, who was executive director of CBC Sports and general manager of CBC Revenue Group, had been appointed president of broadcasting for Rogers Media. On his first day on the job, he did a PowerPoint presentation to the entire Sportsnet staff. The first slide said sports was about winning and the second slide said Sportsnet would be the number-one sports media brand in Canada within five years.

Scott unleashed an incredible amount of power in the sports department. We felt we were now in the game, so to speak, to win. Strategies were developed. Scott had hired me when I literally had no broadcast experience and stuck with me when I struggled early in my career. I saw what he could do and knew his ability to empower people. I was glad he was back, and overnight everyone at the network felt a new boost of confidence.

In late January 2011 Wayne Gretzky celebrated his fiftieth birthday. Sportsnet got word CBC was going to do something on *Hockey Night in Canada* to mark the moment. I was in Utah skiing with my family and Bob Torrens called me to see if I could get Wayne to do an interview. In our schedule, we had *Hockey Central* on for one hour right before CBC's *Hockey Night in Canada*. In asking me, Bob put me in a very tough situation. Asking me to leave my family to work in the middle of our vacation was not ideal. To put it mildly, Anne-Marie wasn't happy about Sportsnet's ask, but understood part of our agreement was to go above and beyond the call of duty when we could. Spouses often feel the stress of taking a backseat to a very demanding industry.

The first time I got to know Wayne on a more personal level was in 1993, at Jerry Bruckheimer's celebrity hockey tournament in Las Vegas. Somehow, I got invited to it. Rick Tocchet, Kevin Stevens, and Wayne were all there hanging out when I checked in and Wayne called me over in the lobby. I was like, "Oh my God, I didn't even know Wayne knew me." I had just finished my best season in Hartford with 17 goals, but safe to say, it was the 325 penalty minutes Wayne identified me with more. The one thing about Wayne is he knows everything that is going on around the league—players, stats, you name it, Wayne knew it. He said, "Come and sit with us, Nick. I can never have enough muscle around me." In an instant it was as if I had been one of Wayne's team-mates. That's how warm he is. He also made a point to ask me if I had plans that night. He invited me to join him and others at a popular spot. That's the type of guy he has always been around me. Every time I've reached out to him for a request, I don't think he has ever said no. For this interview I made some calls and Wayne was amazingly gracious to set up an exclusive in Las Vegas. I arranged to get there from Salt Lake City while Bob Torrens hired a cameraman and joined us.

In typical Gretzky fashion, he was great from the moment I spoke with him. You will never find a more accommodating superstar on this planet. The Palazzo Resort Hotel where Wayne was staying wasn't very helpful and we got bounced around multiple locations, delaying his interview time. Usually these types of delays scare the hell out of you be-cause there's a chance of losing the guest due to overlapping schedules. Not with Wayne. He and Darren Blake, who represented Wayne at the time, were willing to push back their next scheduled appearance to make sure I didn't leave empty-handed. My sit-down with him was a happy look back at the greatest career in NHL history. (I returned to Salt Lake City five hours later.)

Not long after that, in late February 2011, I found myself in hot water. I distinctly remember being on my way back from a Leafs morn-ing skate when I received a text from a source having a good laugh at my expense. "I thought you and Dregs were buddies? Why is his last text picking holes in your story?" I had reported that Toronto was on the verge of trading Bryan McCabe to the Florida Panthers. Darren Dreger then reported that according to his Florida sources the deal was not close. I was so mad at Dregs and TSN I couldn't even see straight. I thought I was texting a direct reply, but instead replied on Twitter: "I'm confident it will get done. Those fuckers at TSN try to discredit me all the time. As always thanks for . . ." I tweeted it to the entire hockey world. Twitter was still fairly new to me at the time and I realized instantly I'd made a huge mistake with the pings I received. But you can't put the toothpaste back in the tube. My insult to TSN spread like a California fire. Bob McKenzie then tweeted out, "@RealKyper, you probably thought that was a direct message, Kipper. LOL." I tweeted that I must have been thinking out loud. Then Dreger jumped on board. "Thinking? Hmmm."

I was so upset at what I had done that my first call went to my wife in a full panic. "Anne-Marie, I think I tweeted my career away by dropping an F-bomb to sixty thousand people on Twitter."

"You what?" was her reply in disbelief. She then calmly told me to take three deep breaths and write back something humourous to downplay my first tweet. She said, "No matter what they say about you on Twitter, it can't be any worse than what they're saying about Charlie Sheen. Blame it on him." At the time, Charlie Sheen was a hot mess, tweeting all sorts of nonsense and making the news every day. So I tweeted, "I passed my BlackBerry to Charlie Sheen for one minute and look what happened!" Excellent advice from my wife as bloggers soon were calling it "tweet of the year." One wrote, "Oh, Kyper, I've disliked you for so many years but gotta say . . . the mistake and the subsequent response has gained you some brownie points in my books."

Regardless, Twitter had a field day with me. Bob, Darren, and the group at TSN had a bit of a laugh over it, but Darren later told me something that I really appreciate. He regretted his reply, adding that at least my tweet was an honest mistake. He was more embarrassed that he provoked it in the first place. But really, the mistake wasn't his, it was mine. And who could blame him for getting in a good jab.

Bob Torrens told me that even though my Twitter response was meant to be a text, everyone at Sportsnet loved it and felt the same way I did about getting debunked. He understood that my competitive juices were exposed in the Twitter message and I wasn't alone. I was happy to hear it was a galvanizing moment at Sportsnet and everyone rallied around me. In hockey, this was the equivalent of taking a hit to make a play. The saving grace in all of this was that the trade happened later that day; it just couldn't be publicly announced till well after the Leafs paid a bonus clause. Information I needed to exclude in the effort to protect a source.

I broke over fifty trades in my career. I never really loved that part of the job, chasing the sources down. I did, however, love the accolades that came with it. The credibility it gave us, pissing off TSN—that was fun. But as far as actually calling sources up and begging for information? Find me one insider who says it's fun to do. As the only full-time insider in the Sportsnet hockey department, with no one to lean on, I assure you it wasn't especially fun. Trying to get people to share classified information isn't easy. Good people have gotten fired over leaking news. It's a big deal because as a broadcaster you can literally put someone's livelihood on the line. Unfortunately, with social media and the instant gratification hockey fans demand, people aren't very sensitive to how risky that kind of news is. Fans have become accustomed to finding out about a trade as fast as those involved in it. It can be easy to justify it all, that players get paid millions of dollars doing something they love and it is just part of the business. But it's still people's lives. That was never lost on me.

I was traded a few times in my career, but I never had to go through a trade with a wife, or pulling kids out of school to relocate them. Trades are a big part of the business and players understand that. But it uproots their lives at a moment's notice and the effect of that can't be underestimated.

A few weeks after that Twitter fiasco, Sportsnet decided to do a new segment called "Crisis on Ice?" There are always hot-button topics in hockey. It could be a slew of knee injuries and people start reacting, "What should we do about the shin pads and all the tripping?" In this case, the topic was concussions and Sportsnet was looking for something more in-depth to sink their teeth into. The network did not want to shy away from more controversial discussions. Concussions and head shots had become a big focus that year around the league, and we were seeing more discussions on the role that violence played in hockey.

Sportsnet didn't have a national package or a huge relationship with the NHL, so the network wanted to create something to grab attention. Originally, the segment was titled "Crisis on Ice" without the question mark, which was never going to sit well with NHL Commissioner Gary Bettman or the league office, so it was changed. The question mark would leave things open for discussion. But Sportsnet still wanted to create some drama, so the producers decided that for the first episode we would focus on the fight that ended my career.

Mike English and Bob Torrens wanted to build the show around my MSG fight with Ryan VandenBussche, but they didn't want to pressure me if it was too personal. I felt that if that's what *they* felt they needed to build a good show, then I would support it.

Ryan VandenBussche, who I fought that night, initially thought it would be awkward to do a sit-down interview with me. Although we had met in passing after my retirement, he and I had actually never spoken about the fight. But I knew Ryan was a good guy and it was important to get his version of our story in our show. In the end, he rationalized that some people might want to know our thoughts before and after the altercation, and he agreed to do it. If anything, I hoped this first "Crisis on Ice?" would help to humanize what the more physical hockey players have to go through.

It was decided we would film in front of a live audience. The segment was shot at Citytv, a station owned by Sportsnet. Bob McCown, who worked as the host of the Fan 590 *Prime Time Sports*, was chosen to moderate. Also joining the main panel were retired players Denis Potvin and Brad May, and former NHL executive and fellow Sportsnet broadcaster Doug MacLean.

The day of the show was the first time Ryan and I spoke about the fight. When we sat down I asked him to talk about his mind-set that day at MSG. I wanted to know how he felt going into the fight and what he'd felt he needed to accomplish.

It was strange to have the person who effectively ended my career sitting beside me and hearing his recollection of the last minute of it. The first thing I noticed was he appeared to me much more sensitive about the optics of the fight than I expected. Because I didn't know anything about his off-ice demeanour, this caught me off guard. I quickly realized he might have been nervous because we were talking about a disturbing event he was a part of, so my broadcasting instincts took over and I began trying to get him to relax—"let's talk as if you and I were sitting down having a beer," I told him. (It just happened to be in front of an audience.)

Ryan knew that nobody would really understand the culture of fighting unless they were a fighter. It's a tough thing to explain. Ryan spoke about going into battle—whether it is on the ice or in the octagon: you're going to war and you've got to have that determination.

Ryan explained in the interview how he was mentally and physically affected in the immediate moments after the fight. "You never ever want to end a guy's career, especially in that [way]," he said. "I'll never forget that feeling of going to the penalty box, looking back, and seeing what I saw. And I'm going to be quite honest with you, it made me sick to my stomach.

"After that, I didn't know how to react. When I was in the penalty box after that incident, [fighting] actually scared me. I didn't have that before. When I was young and anxious, I'd look forward to it sometimes, but after that incident I was like, 'That could've been me on that ice like that.' You had to have a certain mentality when you're on the ice and you're going to do battle with guys twice your size. Nick's not a big guy either, and seeing something like that, that it could happen to me . . . It's a weird mentality. It's almost sadistic to say, but you have to want to get that guy down. Was I happy that I knocked Nick down on the ice? Yes, I was, but I wasn't happy that I ended his career, by no means."

For fighters in the game, this isn't surprising. Unless late hits or cheap shots are involved, we all have immense respect for one another, before, during, and after a fight. The level of respect I had for Ryan went even higher when I learned about his addiction to painkillers, which stemmed from the pain he suffered after many concussions. It would be hard to find anyone who plays the game at a high level who doesn't share Ryan's sentiment. But it was important for fans to hear it—this part of the culture that isn't always obvious. When you see two guys trying to knock each other's heads off out there, it's easy to think they truly despise each other. I guess sometimes they do, but even then, there's respect. The truth is we all had more in common with each other than we had even with some of our own teammates. The willingness to do something most would not attempt. All because we loved the game that much. Even though, in the moment, you're trying to make the guy hurt, no one wants to see someone injured. It's intense, no question about it. And it's important, for the players involved, and their teams. In "Crisis on Ice?" I talked about my mentality going into the fight and why I didn't want linesman Pat Dapuzzo to break it up.

"I was at the end of my career. That was a fight that was much different than anything I experienced the ten years before because that was one of the fights that I needed. For the first time, I felt that I had to win. Not even tie, because I was fighting for a roster spot, and I knew that. I had to basically knock this guy out myself to keep my job. That's when Ryan got his left hand free and brought my shoulder pads in towards him and got me. Ultimately, we knew what we had to do coming out of training camp to keep a job and we were both willing to do it."

Bob McCown asked me if I ever received or wanted an apology from Ryan. I answered without hesitation. "If he apologized, I'd probably try to kick his ass all over again because there's no way that anyone should have to apologize for doing their job. That's not something I ever looked for from Ryan VandenBussche."

I've always felt that way. Later, Bob Torrens said during the filming it seemed like a huge emotional weight had been lifted for both Ryan and me. Bob was a hundred percent right. My way of dealing with the way my career ended was to shrug it off like any other lost fight and forget about it. From a practical point of view, I didn't want or need an apology from Ryan, but from an emotional one, I didn't mind seeing how bad he felt. I didn't mind hearing what adverse effect it had on him after. Hearing it actually humanized his left hook. So here I am going into this show with a broadcaster's mentality, wondering how we could make compelling TV, and leaving like I got real closure, for the first time in fourteen years, to a pretty traumatic experience in my life. Remember, Ryan and I had never discussed any of this before. We both belonged to the same group, and lived by the same code. But he must have wondered, all those years, if I harboured some secret hatred for him. It felt good to let him know, out loud, that was never the case.

I was surprised when Ryan said how bad he felt after our fight while he sat in the penalty box. I never had regrets when I fought another hockey player, although I had never come close to thinking I had possibly killed someone. In my era fighting was a big part of the game. I knew the risks and therefore never held a grudge against Ryan. I've hated guys enough to visualize delivering that type of knockout punch, but certainly can't imagine how it would feel to see them motionless and bleeding, like I was. You can't be successful in that role if there isn't a part of you that accepts that type of savage brutality. You can't go into a fight without being willing to hurt someone. After the show a new thought crossed my mind—what if I had died that night? What kind of feeling would that have left Ryan to live with the rest of his life? Not a question that would have ever entered my mind prior to the show.

To have any chance at being good in that role, to sustain any longevity, you must have a willingness to become a little mental; that, and have a short enough fuse to react at the right place, at the right time, for your team.

Away from the rink it's easy to say you would never want to see anyone permanently hurt or, God forbid, paralyzed or killed, but in the heat of battle you don't feel the same way. I've knocked guys down in a fight but have never been in the position that Ryan was in: watching someone completely motionless and seeing blood seep out of his head, wondering if maybe you had just killed him. I don't know what that feels like; however, I found Ryan to be much more emotional than I had anticipated. It was nice to see and certainly unexpected for no other reason than it showed some humility about how we both earned a living.

Any talk of fighting inevitably leads to a conversation on concussions as well, and we were asked about that. Ryan said he had probably suffered more than a dozen in his career. He played his first game in the NHL in the 1996–1997 season, and went on to play 310 games, with 10 goals, 10 assists, and 702 penalty minutes. He ended his career with the New Mexico Scorpions in the Central Hockey League. Despite all that, officially, he has no concussion history with the NHL because none was ever recorded.

"But that's nobody's fault but my own," he said. "It wasn't the trainers' fault. It wasn't the league's fault or the caoches' fault. It was my fault because I chose not to express it to anybody."

He said that in his 1996–1997 season with the Rangers, he suffered three concussions in a four-week span. After a fight with Stu Grimson of the Hartford Whalers, he didn't show any signs of injury to Coach Colin Campbell, the staff, or any of the players, even though he was dazed by the bout. Stu wasn't known as the "Grim Reaper" for nothing.

"I get to the penalty box and I couldn't even read the scoreboard," he continued. "I get to the bench and Colin Campbell said, 'Get off the ice. Take a rest in the dressing room.' I refused to go to the dressing room because I didn't want anyone to think I was hurt."

We've all been there, hiding injuries. We've all done it. I made a bad call not getting ahead of an injury during my time in Hartford. I was in a stretch of playing the best hockey in my pro career, scoring 8 points in 12 games. Then, instead of letting the scoring energy ride itself out the next game at home, I make a bad decision to pick a first-period fight with Ken Baumgartner of the Maple Leafs. Worse, the fight came off an offensive zone face-off where ice time is usually reserved for your top-scoring forwards. Instead of looking for my sixth goal in this hot stretch, I decided to play tough guy in front of my childhood buddies. Thirty-five seconds later I feel a sharp pain in my abdomen. A lot of guys were going down with groin and abdominal injuries at this point and I did not want my overprotective trainer, Bud Gouveia, to include me on a growing list. The thought of giving up my spot on the roster sickened me more than the sharp pain. So I kept my mouth shut. This ended up being an even worse decision than fighting Baumgartner. Two weeks later my season shut down with a major tear in my abdomen that cost me the last nine games of the season. Keeping my mouth shut also cost me a chance to join the rare list of NHLers with 20 goals and 300 PIMs in a season. I believe concealing injuries is still happening in today's game, just not at the same rate as in past generations. Education about long-term health implications and the need to document injuries for future insurance benefits have changed many players' attitudes. But insecurity is a universal part of our genetic makeup and it will always lead us to make some bad decisions to play hockey when we shouldn't.

I've since spoken to Ryan at many NHL alumni events. Talking with him on "Crisis on Ice?" brought me complete closure about the end of my hockey career—closure that until that moment, I hadn't realized I was even missing.

CHAPTER 15

New Challenges

On NHL free agency day in 2012, Nashville defenceman Ryan Suter was drawing interest from various teams. One of my sources sent me a text with the words "Ryan Suter to Detroit." I wanted to confirm the trade with someone else as well, but I trusted the source enough to throw it out that Ryan may have agreed to terms with Detroit. A big part of what insiders do is tweet the speculation we hear. Within half an hour Suter signed with Minnesota. Not surprisingly, I heard about it on social media. I got back to my source and said, "Why did you tell me Ryan Suter to Detroit?"

He said, "I didn't tell you Ryan Suter to Detroit. I texted you 'Ryan Suter to Detroit?' I was asking you if you'd heard the same."

I said, "Asking me? You didn't put a question mark on that text to me."

"I didn't?"

"NO!"

"Oh, I'm sorry. I meant to put a question mark."

Moral of this story is, punctuation counts. Lesson learned.

Around that same time, we knew in all likelihood there might be a lockout during the 2012 hockey season, and Sportsnet approached me with an interesting proposition. Jennifer Neziol, Sportsnet's director of communications, proposed that I run in the New York City Marathon.

Because we had just secured the national broadcasting rights to the marathon, they would guarantee an automatic entry for someone who wanted to participate. Otherwise, you either have to qualify because you participated in a previous marathon or get in through a lottery system. My first instinct was, "Hell, no. I don't run marathons." We used to do a two-mile run in training camp in Philadelphia and the coaches wanted us to complete it in under twelve minutes. I would spend the whole summer at a track and it was like death trying to run a six-minute mile. Needless to say, I am not built like a runner and I just absolutely hated it. The late Brad McCrimmon didn't have a runner's body either, but he managed to run two miles in just over ten minutes. It was baffling to me. We all loved "Beast" because he played like one but had the body of a bowling pin. If I found two miles at a quick pace torture, how would I ever manage 26.2 miles?

For whatever reason, turning down the chance to run in the marathon kept nagging me. After being out of the game for fifteen years, could I find the discipline to do it? I was forty-six years old, and the older I got the harder it would be; there would never be an opportunity like this and certainly it was a challenge like none I'd ever had before. So a few days later I asked Jennifer if the opportunity was still there. As a marathon runner herself, she was thrilled that I would even attempt it.

I had a few months to get ready. Sportsnet hired a full-time trainer, Jackie Kissel, out of the running gym Absolute Endurance, who was incredibly patient with me. She literally taught me how to run. I had physical therapy at my disposal and everything else I needed. I also went to see my good friend Gary Roberts, a retired NHL pro who has become renowned in the sports world for nutrition and training. He took me grocery shopping and taught me what foods to buy that I needed to fuel my run. I also had Sportsnet take out an insurance policy in the event I hurt myself, or worse, dropped dead on Anne-Marie and the kids. I left nothing to chance.

Doug MacLean, whom I recruited for Sportsnet in 2010 as a broadcaster, told me Oprah ran the Chicago Marathon in four hours and thirty minutes, so that was my time to beat. That became the big ongoing joke. Could I beat Oprah Winfrey?

Sportsnet was following my training leading up to the marathon as a docuseries, part of the behind-the-scenes story. It was in the agreement I made with them. The New York angle was special to me because some of my teammates from the 1994 Stanley Cup—Mark Messier, Mike Richter, Adam Graves—had run in it and told me it was an incredible experience.

I was excited and ready and then Hurricane Sandy devastated the East Coast, causing billions of dollars in damages throughout New York. Many called for cancelling the marathon, but it was still set to go. As NY mayor Michael Bloomberg reasoned, it was the sort of event that could help galvanize the city and bring in much-needed revenue.

Anne-Marie and the kids flew down with me. Always supportive, she had points in the five boroughs marked out to stand at to help cheer me on. Once we arrived in NY we saw firsthand the destruction, and suddenly I felt like I was right in the middle of the controversy about cancellation. I was now waffling on the idea of participating. Mere days before, we had heard they were still pulling bodies out of rubble in Staten Island, which is where the marathon starts. There was public outrage over even thinking of using police officers to "man" the race instead of searching for survivors. I, of course, absolutely no longer wanted to run. On Friday, before the Sunday race, the marathon was rightfully cancelled—the first time in its forty-two-year history. New York City had been pulverized by Mother Nature. The hurricane had killed at least forty-eight people, many were still missing, and thousands had been displaced. Bloomberg was highly criticized both for suggesting we run and for not cancelling sooner.

We were still in New York and now felt an overwhelming need to do something positive. On Sunday, our producer, Jennifer Neziol, my two sons, and I rented an SUV, bought supplies, and delivered them to shelters around Staten Island all day. Sportsnet was kind enough to contribute thousands of dollars toward helping the victims.

Although it was disappointing not to run, when we looked at how people had been impacted by the storm, in the blink of an eye the race became irrelevant. For me the training was about the process of making the commitment at age forty-six. It brought back memories of the discipline that it took to train every day. Not just physically, but mentally and emotionally. I didn't get to run (and try to beat Oprah's time), but it didn't matter. Once we were handing out the supplies to people, everything was put into perspective. And the conveners promised all the would-be 2012 New York City Marathon runners a guaranteed entry in 2013.

That summer of 2012, before the marathon, had been a frustrating time. The hockey community had a work stoppage staring us in the face—the second in less than eight years. The difference was that in 2004, the players and owners were fighting over the entire pie. This time around, in 2012, it was really about the crumbs. As far as I was concerned, the financial war was already over; the owners got the vast majority of what they wanted eight years earlier. The main issue was the percentage of revenue being shared. The league wanted the players to lower their revenue shares from 57 percent to 49 percent. Although many analysts thought it would be another full year of no hockey, I knew that after the players gave up a whole year and lost the fight in 2004, they wouldn't have the stomach to do the same thing again in order to save a few percentage points. In my opinion, a resolution would be reached sooner than it was in 2004.

Sportsnet again spared no expense in covering the NHL updates. We covered any news, every day, as the two sides inched closer to a deal. In January 2013 my lockout broadcasting team looked much different than it looked in 2004. Daren Millard, John Shannon (who was doing some hockey coverage for Sportsnet), and I would now front all news from NYC. We stayed a few blocks away from the NHL offices in order to get closer to the CBA meetings. On the Friday of the impending settlement we got word that both sides had bunkered down in a last-ditch attempt to resolve their issues. The players were staying at the Sofitel hotel, mere blocks from the NHL head office, and both sides started to bounce from block to block in small groups. I put a call in to a trusted source and he assured me a settlement was imminent, and if one was made, it would happen very late into the night. Perfect. I had a small window to take in the $75 million Broadway production of *Spider-Man: Turn off the Dark*. I never would have gambled like this back in 2004, but now, as a seasoned lockout veteran, I liked my chances. I asked my new CBA partner in crime, Daren Millard, to come with me. I assured him nothing of significance would happen until after we saw Spider-Man leaping from wall to ceiling. Daren was a little apprehensive at first, but I convinced him to go and that he had to trust my "spidey senses." When we sat down and spotted Elliotte Friedman five rows behind us, we felt a little better about our decision to take in a play.

Right after the show we raced to the NHL offices, where Bruce Garrioch of the *Ottawa Sun* assured us we had missed absolutely nothing. With no comfortable place to sit, we literally had to stand on the sidewalk outside the NHL offices on Sixth Avenue. It was also fifteen degrees Celsius below zero. We would have tried to stay warm in the bank ATM vestibule, but the crew from TSN had already claimed that spot.

We stood outside for so long that the NYPD asked us not to loiter. We had to find ways to stay warm, so we kept moving. Daren, John Shannon, and I found a broken broom handle and bought a ball from a pharmacy. At 1 a.m., with little to no traffic, we started to play stickball in the middle of Sixth Avenue. It was like a scene out of a Bad News Bears movie. All was good until I hit Millard's curve ball into a late-night garbage truck that was passing by and we lost the ball forever. Game over. Other than during the two NHL outdoor games in Alberta, I don't remember ever being colder than that night.

Finally, after 2 a.m., with negotiations still going, the NHL showed mercy and invited all the media up to their warm cafeteria. I fell asleep on a couch only to be awakened by my BlackBerry with the news we had been waiting for. The deal was done. At 3 a.m. nobody really cared who got to tweet the news first; we were all just glad the wait was over. The league and the NHLPA scheduled a 5:30 a.m. press conference at the players' association's hotel. It had been a sixteen-hour session, but hockey fans got their season back. The lockout ended and the season started later that January.

For the second time in history the league played a shortened season for the Stanley Cup. I hadn't been a big fan of playing a half season in 1995 and I certainly didn't like covering it in 2013. A full 82-game season is a big part of a championship story. Cramming 70 games into 145 days to award the Cup never felt fulfilling to me.

However, there was some excitement as the Leafs somehow managed to lose in one of the most memorable Game 7 meltdowns in playoff history. In Boston, with the Leafs up 4–1 and less than ten minutes to go, we watched fans leave the building, including Bruins owner Jeremy Jacobs. Sitting comfortably in the press box, I received an e-mail telling me my next assignment would be to keep following the Leafs instead of my usual work this time of year, covering the Memorial Cup. I started to trumpet to anyone who was listening, "I'm getting my dream playoff matchup next round: Toronto versus the Rangers." My last two former teams. Easy travel, old friends, great restaurants—perfect. I specifically waited for the ten-minute mark of the third period to feel comfortable enough to book my flight and hotel. What happened in the next nine minutes of the hockey game was truly extraordinary. Three goals, from Nathan Horton, Milan Lucic, and Patrice Bergeron, left the press box stunned. Boston went on to win in overtime, with Bergeron scoring again. My next two weeks still included Broadway, but it was a much different-looking Broadway in Saskatoon, covering the Memorial Cup, than in Manhattan.

After a shortened 48-game season, Chicago and Philly played in the Stanley Cup Final. Chicago won their second Cup in three years.

That summer I began training for the marathon again. Not running in 2012 definitely left me feeling like I had unfinished business. This time Sportsnet was not filming a documentary, but because I had already trained once, I knew what to do. Less than three weeks before the race, as I was tempering back on one of my training runs, I felt a sharp pain in my calf, like I had been stabbed by a knife. I fell down hard on the sidewalk. Anne-Marie, who had been biking beside me, knew something was seriously wrong.

I had an ultrasound and it revealed an eleven-centimetre tear. I couldn't believe that I was so close to running in the New York City Marathon and again, for the second year in a row, circumstances beyond my control were going to take it away. I was told at Mount Sinai Hospital that my injury would require as much as six weeks to heal. If I wanted any chance to still run in the marathon, I knew of one guy that could help me. Sports guru Dr. Tony Galea had worked with some of the most prominent athletes in the world. While other doctors may have pioneered the process, Galea was one of the first in sports medicine to use platelet-rich plasma (PRP) therapy as a way to treat his patients' injuries with a concentration of the patients' own blood. I was desperate to save my run; if Dr. Galea was good enough for athletes like Tiger Woods and A-Rod, he was worth taking a chance on.

Watching the process was fascinating. He drew my blood, spun it in a centrifuge, removed the platelets from the red blood cells, and then buried the platelets deep into my calf with a six-inch needle. It had done wonders for other people and I prayed it would save my marathon.

True to his reputation, I made incredible progress in the nineteen days leading up to the run—enough progress to go to NY and at least try. Although I made great strides in healing the tear, I was far from pain-free. I didn't feel confident I could last one mile, let alone 26.2, but at least I had a chance.

One of the benefits of participating in the New York City Marathon as a "celebrity" was having added security. The vast majority of runners have to wake up around 4:30 a.m. to catch the last ferry to Staten Island, where the race begins. This means some runners need to wait up to six and a half hours before beginning their run. Typically, added security for us meant a bus would drop off our smaller group directly in front of the tent at the start location, meaning we could get a few extra hours of sleep. However, this was not like any of the other New York Marathons.

The senseless Boston Marathon bombing in April 2013, only a few months before, had shocked the world. It left three people dead and over two hundred people injured. Refusing to cancel the marathon for a second year in a row, New York City would do everything in its power to protect the city and preserve the tradition. As runners, we had to go through scanners at the start. Counterterrorism officers were everywhere. There were huge delays in starting the race, but no one questioned the need for them. The city did a great job with bomb-sniffing dogs and scuba divers scanning the bridges. Needless to say, the thought of a bomb or some other senseless terrorist act still weighed on the runners and fans everywhere. Yet fifty thousand people ran and over a million showed up to cheer us on. New Yorkers cannot be intimidated.

Once we got through security, lining up at the start was thrilling. It felt like being in a Stanley Cup parade all over again, but this time I was part of the crowd. We lined up on the Verrazano Bridge, heard the air horn, and the race began.

The first mile in, I didn't think I was going to last long, let alone the entire race. My calf could sustain the pounding, but it felt like someone was snapping a rubber band deep into my calf every step I took. Even with PRP it felt as if my next stride would tear the muscle all over again. I said to myself, *So be it, I'll run until that happens.* Thankfully, it never did. My pace was steady at nine minutes a mile, and I forced the thought of my calf out of my mind.

Hurt or not, it was the hardest thing I have ever done in my life. My mentality from when I played pro hockey kicked in. I had to accept the pain that I was feeling and hope it didn't get worse. I felt that if it stayed the way it was at the start of the race, I could manage it for four and a half hours.

People who have run the marathon had told me there is nothing like seeing New York through the eyes of a marathon runner. You hit all five boroughs and from the moment you start on the bridge from Staten Island and finish in Central Park, it's a twenty-six-mile nonstop parade of people cheering you on; the rush of the crowd never lets up. It was the second time in my life I got to experience traffic-free streets in downtown New York.

Although it had been almost twenty years, some people recognized me from my time with the Rangers. They would scream "Ninety-Four!" As I have said before, there is nothing like Ranger fans, and by the time I reached the end of the race, I needed all the encouragement I could get. Once I made it to Central Park, I still had the last few miles to go. At this stage I felt like my calf was numb, but the rest of my body was about to seize up. I think I could have walked faster than I was running. I watched a man in a Batman suit skip right past me. Then another guy nonchalantly whisked by, barely out of breath, dribbling basketballs, one in each hand. If I'd had the strength, I would have booted that guy and his "balls" right into the Hudson. Once I saw the finish line, I knew I could do it; people were yelling, and it was the last push I needed. When it was all over, I felt numb from sheer exhaustion. A few hours later I did find enough strength to send out one tweet for my pal Doug MacLean: "Overwhelmed by all the support. Finished in 4:43. I didn't beat Oprah, Mac. My wife says I would have if I didn't stop three times for directions."

There is physical pain after running a marathon and it takes a few weeks to recover, but I loved and appreciated the mental challenge. I don't think I'd say no to another one, but what was clear to me in the recovery was that a 210-pound man isn't really supposed to run in that sort of thing. It's really for people who are lighter on their feet, who run like gazelles and don't stop. The winner of the 2013 New York City Marathon was Geoffrey Mutai of Kenya, who ran it in 2:08.24. He is 5'6" and weighs 119 pounds. I think my right leg weighs more than 119 pounds.

Anne-Marie looked for me for two hours. I had collected my belongings and security kept trying to move everyone out of the park as quickly as they could. All the phone lines were down. There was no cell service at all, which was really strange. That part was a little chaotic. In the back of my mind I knew that the terrorist threat wasn't over just because some of us had finished. I gave up trying to reach Anne-Marie and started walking all the way back to the hotel. The sidewalks were packed and it took almost two hours because so many streets were still closed off. We later found out that the counterterrorism task force had jammed the phone lines until all the runners had completed the marathon, in case there was some sort of remote device. They left nothing to chance.

A couple months later, I participated as a celebrity coach in the fourth annual Scotiabank Greater Toronto Hockey League Prospects Game. It brings together for one game forty of the top Minor Midget prospects in the GTHL, my minor hockey league growing up. The celebrity coaches are there just as figureheads, to have some fun and lend support. There are two actual coaches from the GTHL changing the lines and it's a very prestigious thing. I'd participated the year before against Wendel Clark. I suggested getting Doug MacLean for this tournament so we could have some fun—and it *was* fun, even though I lost to him. From a business perspective, what's better than spending time with a player such as Mitch Marner when he was sixteen years old? You got a chance to see firsthand how great these players were at that age and how much they have progressed in such a short time.

Now, I've mentioned Doug MacLean before, my onetime Washington coach, who left the Columbus Blue Jackets after the 2007–2008 season as president and GM. In 2007 I had told Sportsnet the moment I heard Doug was leaving Columbus that they should hire him. He had incredible insight with a distinct sense of humour, and who else could you find that had twenty-plus years as an NHL coach and executive? I told the producers, "Go get this guy."

Doug began with Sportsnet on the local afternoon radio show called *The Game Plan* with basketball analyst Jack Armstrong. Jack was as popular with us at Sportsnet as he is presently with TSN and Raptors fans. Seemed like an odd combination for the Fan to connect Doug and Jack because the only double dribbling Doug knew about was when he spilled his wine. Regardless, the show worked because of their mutual respect and a strong friendship that remains intact today. I also did a great Jack Armstrong impression for Doug that always cracked him up before his show started. Like any New Yorker, the key is to subtly drop the R sound endings. With Jack, it's "How awww yaaa . . . How awww yaaa?" Doug was subsequently moved to a daily show at 1 p.m. and then he joined me and Daren Millard on *Hockey Central at Noon* in 2012. We instantly hit it off. It helped that I knew Doug's sense of humour, which was key. I always tried to work off of my cohosts, whether it was Mike Keenan, Bill Watters, or Doug MacLean, and utilize the fact that we had different points of view. Mine was the players' perspective and theirs was management's. I never looked at them as adversaries, but as part of the more complete picture when it came to hockey analysis.

Doug and I soon started working together on both radio and TV broadcasts with Daren Millard as the host. At times our opinions were in two different hemispheres, but I always found that made good television. This was never more evident than during the 2012 lockout because it was so emotional for the fans. People were either pro-player or pro-owner, but there was also a large group of fans that didn't really know where they stood. I believe our ratings really began to grow at this point because we gave a balanced perspective, not only for hockey fans but also for people who were intrigued by this dog-eat-dog fight between millionaires and billionaires.

Doug and I challenged each other and it got personal a few times. He would give me a few digs then I would knock his coaching record, his inability to find a good goalie—whatever I could find to pick at him with, I would. He'd tell the listeners on-air how I wasn't exactly a Hall of Famer. But our relationship was so deep that the knocks were fairly superficial. Except one time during the lockout.

During one segment, when we were discussing the negotiations, Doug said, "Nobody gives a crap about the bottom four hundred players in the NHL, they only care about the top three hundred." It bothered me so much. I was one of those "bottom four hundred" guys and clearly he was looking straight at me. So I responded, "Maybe that's why you never won in Columbus, because you crapped all over your third- and fourth-line players." Oops. Doug was pissed. It was like watching Yosemite Sam from Looney Tunes when his face completely changes colour in rage and the size of his head triples. Doug came back, "Maybe that's why you got kicked out and only had an eight-year career." He finished me off with, "Don't start throwing darts when you don't know what you're talkin' about."

Now, as far as the bottom-four-hundred comment was concerned, he wasn't necessarily wrong about how replaceable they could be, but I took it personally. He dragged me and every third- and fourth-line player down with that comment. This isn't baseball. It's not soccer, where your stars get to play in 90 percent of the action. You need your depth guys in hockey if you are ever going to win a championship. It was the only time in ten years I can say I honestly got mad at him. Adrian Dater, who spent twenty-five years at the *Denver Post*, wrote an article about the exchange. "Tempers heated up on the radio today but in my mind in a most entertaining way." He went on to say that parts of our show might have been our shtick, but that the passion was very real. There was no shtick, I assure you, but Adrian was bang on with his assessment that the disagreements and the passion were real. I don't want to come across like I'm not human and words could never hurt, but with Doug it was different. I always knew he had my back.

I believe that *Hockey Central at Noon* catapulted Doug, Daren, and me to another level. Daren Millard would often throw to the commercial break with the tag line "*HC at Noon*, where the players hang out" and he wasn't far off on that. Pat Kane of the Chicago Blackhawks, who I really didn't know well, told me he raced into the dressing room after team practice to go watch our show. In fact, Kane loved our show so much that when he made a guest appearance, I convinced him to dress up as a maintenance man who'd come to fix a ceiling panel that had fallen on us earlier in the year. I had a hard hat, vest, gloves, and a power drill waiting for him upon his arrival. Gord Stellick was also on-air that day and didn't even recognize Kane until he came down the ladder. It was a priceless *HC at Noon* moment that helped make that show such a hit. We had league players constantly coming up to us and asking, "Do you and Doug hate each other? You guys make me laugh." Coaches, GMs, scouts—they all loved that show. Doug and I had great chemistry and Daren Millard was at his best when he balanced us out. The year of the lockout our noon ratings actually went up.

The problem, though, was the lack of revenue in radio. Outside of morning and drive-home slots, there isn't much money to be made. We worked with some seasoned producers such as Dave Cadeau and Ryan Fabro for short stints, but most often we'd get young producers with little experience. Another issue was that the Sportsnet hockey department didn't run the radio show and it therefore wasn't a priority for them. The Fan 590 produced it and really wanted us focusing on the Toronto market. They didn't like it when we didn't give local listeners enough Leafs. When the show started to simulcast on national TV, we got a lot of grief across the country for being too pro-Leafs. We couldn't win. It was frustrating for Doug, Daren, and me. At this point we understood where a twelve-noon radio show stood in the pecking order.

If there was one benefit of not having our show constantly monitored, it was the freedom to do and say whatever the heck we wanted. Doug was notorious for mentioning a condo development in PEI he was investing in or his Mercedes-Benz from a Burlington dealership he was running ads for. We love Mac but he was the worst for cutting off a great hockey conversation just to wish little Billy from Kensington good luck in the fortieth annual PEI Spud minor-hockey tournament. Daren and I would look at each other and say, "What the heck was that?" Mac would answer as if we were the only two people listening, "I didn't want to forget." That genuine talk drove some people nuts, but others appreciated its authenticity. Not to be outdone by Doug's self-promoting, I got involved with a water company called GP8, so naturally I would bring cases to the set and time it perfectly. When the camera was on me, I'd take a sip of my "soluble oxygenated water." Hey, I made sure no one at Sportsnet was going to die of dehydration on my watch. Yes, at times we were shameless.

We also had a great opportunity with Halloween, making it a big tradition on our show. I went to the boys and said, wouldn't it be fun to do our radio show in Halloween costumes? They weren't crazy about the idea but soon warmed up to it. The ace in the hole for us was Debra Berman. Deb joined Sportsnet in the fall of 2008 as our national stylist. She had access to some of the best costumes in the country. Daren Millard suggested the rock group Kiss for our inaugural Halloween celebration. In the years that followed there were costumes from *Duck Dynasty, Star Wars, Game of Thrones,* and even *The Wizard of Oz* with David Amber playing the part of the Scarecrow. The response was always amazing thanks to Deb Berman and makeup artists Corrine Berlin and Hilary Whitebread

When TSN launched their all-sports radio station in 2011, it was as if they were playing the part of Sportsnet back in October 1998. They couldn't get any respect at all and it was ironic in our sports-radio world—a total role reversal from what we experienced in 1998. They stood with no radio-sports credibility, and so gave sports listeners no real reason to switch to them. Despite having credible seasoned hockey names on the air, such as Bob McKenzie, Darren Dreger, and Ray Ferraro, TSN would not even register a score on the ratings board for many of their programs. Looking back now, we are lucky TSN radio gave us a good eight-year head start before gaining traction in the ratings. Their strong personalities in Jeff O'Neill, Bryan Hayes, and Jamie McLennan finally found the recipe for radio success: chemistry.

I used to have fun filming behind-the-scenes segments for Sportsnet, with an old-school handheld video camera that the producers jokingly called the Kyper Cam. I took it on the road for All-Star Games or Stanley Cup Final to pick up everything and anything that was going on behind the scenes—things I found interesting or amusing. The producers thought it was so hilarious the way I grabbed anything I could and put it on air. I liked doing it, but it was also hard work, constantly looking for opportunities to film. It wasn't like today, when you have a camera phone you put in your jacket. The camcorder was pretty big and awkward to hold. We did this long before smartphones captured these types of interactions, which put us a little ahead of our time. I was like a fly on the wall and tried to give the viewer a glimpse of the way the players behaved with each other. Now we take for granted the easy access we have in filming private moments.

Because rules and regulations were so lax back then, I could take my camera anywhere. I once used the Kyper Cam while travelling through Dallas. While we were going through airport security, I literally filmed Gord Stellick getting TSA strip-searched. I could barely hold the camera still enough to film it, I was laughing so hard. I thought there was no chance Sportsnet would air the tape, but they showed Stellick buckling his pants back up so that they could show it on national TV. Like many others who I've worked with, Stellick has an amazing sense of humour. Good luck trying to capture that type of footage today at an airport.

CHAPTER 16

The Biggest Deal

On November 26, 2013, Canadian broadcasting history was made when Rogers announced it had entered into a twelve-year, $5.2 billion contract with the NHL, becoming the exclusive national rights holder. The deal would begin in 2014 and the package included the Stanley Cup playoffs and Stanley Cup Final. Rogers would also have exclusive rights to events, such as All-Star Games and NHL drafts. I had heard rumblings that we were in play to pick up some national games, but had no idea Rogers was in the running to secure the whole enchilada. It was common knowledge at Bell and Rogers that CBC was way over their head financially in trying to secure the same package they had always had the rights to.

Bell, which owned TSN, was the lead horse in this race up until Rogers buckled the floor from right underneath them. The dollars were staggering, numbers that were closer to American TV-network deals. We later heard that George Cope, the chief executive officer of Bell Canada, made a special trip to the NHL board of governors' meetings in an effort to reopen negotiations for TSN. I saw Rogers Media president Keith Pelley pacing outside the meeting room. I told him, "Relax, it's not your $5.2 billion you just spent." He didn't even crack a smile. Bad timing, I guess. Little did I know that Cope was on the other side of the door. I would have been nervous, too. Gary Bettman presented Cope's plea to all the governors. They unanimously agreed that the Rogers deal was a very good one and Bettman recommended they stick with it. Gary had given his word to Sportsnet. And once he makes up his mind, it's set.

Many hockey fans were shocked to learn that CBC had lost their crown jewel after providing consistent programming throughout the country for fifty-five years. For most of us in the business, though, that was a foregone conclusion. What we didn't see coming was that the knockout punch also hit TSN. There wasn't a single rumour that Rogers had the wherewithal to do it. All the talk had centred on TSN. I thought it was fitting that TSN's Bob McKenzie, and not me, broke the news regarding the historic deal. For the first time in our existence we had the stage to ourselves. The only thing I tweeted that day was the famous line from *Jaws*: "We're going to need a bigger boat." And boy, did we ever.

"This is a deal that we think is transformational," Gary Bettman said. "Nobody has ever done a deal quite like this in terms of its structure, its length, and its magnitude. It's focused on delivering NHL hockey to the most passionate hockey fans in the world on a countrywide basis in a way that we think will give the greatest connectivity to the game."

Nadir Mohamed, president and chief executive officer of Rogers Communications, called it a game breaker.

"Today's deal builds on an incredible sports legacy and solidifies our position as Canada's number-one sports destination," he added. "Sports content is a pillar for Rogers and NHL hockey is the holy grail. Two years ago I said I wanted Sportsnet to be the number-one sports brand in Canada. Today, we're positioned to do that."

The deal would allow the CBC to broadcast *Hockey Night in Canada* for at least the next four years, but Rogers controlled the production and execution, including editorial content and on-air talent. Rogers would also earn all the revenue from the broadcasts. The fact that Rogers got CBC to do all that for next to nothing was incredible. Especially when you consider that Sportsnet didn't have a national platform to support *Hockey Night in Canada.*

There were some big changes on the horizon. At the launch of the deal at Sportsnet's headquarters, it was announced that George Stroumboulopoulos was coming on board. George began in the business as a VJ with MuchMusic and then began to host his own talk show, *George Stroumboulopoulos Tonight,* which ran from 2005 to 2014. The feeling was he could take his brand into *Hockey Night in Canada* and bring along a lot of those fans, maybe more female viewers and music fans. Even though George would be the new host, many *HNIC* faces were the same. Ron and Don would continue to do *Coach's Corner* in the first intermission. Elliotte Friedman and Kelly Hrudey also remained. A press conference followed introducing George to the media as the new host. I didn't know at that point that I'd be on *Hockey Night in Canada.* I just hoped that call would come.

The summer before Sportsnet secured the national package, I had negotiated a new eight-year deal. I joked to Scott Moore that I wanted a twelve-year contract (and was initially offered something between four and six years). I had been with the company fifteen years—right from the beginning—and had done everything Sportsnet asked me to do: radio, TV spots, and public appearances. Scott Moore also considered me a good corporate public relations ambassador. He wanted to see some of that loyalty rewarded with a long-term commitment. According to him, by that time I had become one of the top news breakers in the NHL and he felt I'd gained respect since my humble beginnings in the industry.

Scott agreed to a long-term deal, which was unusual as far as hockey analyst contracts generally go. He offered me a substantial increase in salary, too, which is almost unheard of. However, he warned me that if he gave me what I asked for, I would never have a reason to complain about my salary ever again (when you negotiate your own salary you get a reputation for never being happy). He would work me on as many shows as Sportsnet needed, within reason. I agreed without hesitation and ran out of his office before he could change his mind.

My contract with Sportsnet was for Monday to Friday; I made it a point that this new contract explicitly didn't include weekends. At various points over the years we ran a program called *Hockey Central* on Saturdays that led into CBC's *Hockey Night in Canada.* Although it got me home by 7:30 p.m., it never gave Anne-Marie and the kids any chance for our family to have quality weekends. So when I signed my deal, having weekends off was a win for my family. That was very important to me, but something else ended up being very significant as well. I added a footnote in the deal that if Sportsnet ever landed the NHL national rights, I could reopen the agreement and ask for more money.

Scott called me later, after Sportsnet secured the national rights to tell me he wanted me on *Hockey Night in Canada.* We convened to discuss renegotiating the deal. We met for breakfast at the Park Hyatt hotel and I put forward a new financial number in return for my giving up my weekends. Scott paused, then he asked me to justify my ask.

It was one of those moments that is hard to describe. It's one thing to feel I deserved to be recognized; it's another thing to have to advocate for myself and, more importantly, to articulate what my years had meant to the success of the network. How do you explain your worth without looking cocky or arrogant, without overselling your contributions? We had taken Sportsnet from an "idea" to slaying Goliath in less than fifteen years. It was, and is, one of the things I am most proud to have been a part of. Whatever I said must have hit home. He paused again, and then said, "Okay."

We shook hands on the contract terms, and when Scott saw it was emotional for me, he got teary-eyed as well. People were looking at us like, "What in the hell is going on?" It was a moment I'll never forget.

I always enjoyed interviewing Gary Bettman. With my reputation for always advocating for the players, Gary and I were known on occasion to knock heads. It was fun having the most powerful hockey man on-air. Whether we were discussing the players' perspective in a lockout or the likelihood of the Phoenix Coyotes relocating, we often spoke from different viewpoints.

On one particular day in April 2011, everything was pointing to Phoenix moving. Doug and I were all over the story. We were convinced that Phoenix was going to Winnipeg. Even Wayne Gretzky came on our show as a guest that day and said, "Things are not looking good for the Coyotes." That turned the story into a media frenzy, and all the Winnipeg fans clung on to this particular theory.

I'll admit that my producers coaxed me to try to stir up some on-air emotion when Commissioner Bettman came on our show. So when he showed up on *Hockey Central at Noon* as a guest the same day Gretzky did, I hammered a few pointed questions. He accused us of not knowing "anything." But Doug and I relentlessly pushed the Phoenix angle and we tried his patience. Eventually, he said, "I understand why you want to cover the story, but enough already!" Although some on the Internet were calling it "great radio," I'm sure Bettman felt otherwise.

Gary had always loved the Phoenix market for hockey. So naturally he came onto our show and flat-out denied that the team was moving; and rightfully so. We felt everything we'd said about Phoenix moving was likely true up to that point, but none of us in the media could have factored in the stubborn resilience of the city council of Glendale. Gary, of course, knew something that we didn't. Local politicians were willing to use Glendale taxpayer money to keep the team afloat. That city had been home to the Coyotes and had taken substantial losses, in the millions of dollars, and were still willing to find ways to bail out the sinking ship. It was unthinkable that the Atlanta Thrashers would be the one to move their franchise north before the floundering Phoenix Coyotes would. But that is exactly what happened.

Doug and I ran with our version of Phoenix moving to Winnipeg. It ran like wildfire, especially in Winnipeg, where fans were dying to bring their Jets back. Behind the scenes, Bettman had indeed promised Winnipeg a team; he just didn't disclose what franchise it would come from. It's clear now that the NHL could have ultimately saved itself a major headache for the next decade if they had chosen the Coyotes for Winnipeg. Say what you want about Gary Bettman, but he was loyal to certain markets. Edmonton, Winnipeg, Ottawa, Buffalo, Phoenix, Florida, and Carolina; he's had every conceivable reason to relocate any one of these teams at certain times, and yet he's chosen not to.

Bettman has certainly made it harder for players to drop their gloves, but he hasn't bent to the pressure to completely remove fighting from the game in his over twenty-five years as commissioner. He never succumbed to the public or media scrutiny on that hot-button topic either. Instead, he simply chooses to listen to the players who actually play the game, who, for now, want fighting to remain. And take a look at his NHL office staff. Although his office hasn't grown in sheer volume, like the NBA or MLB offices, those that got in early have been with him for the vast majority of his tenure.

At the 2014 NHL All-Star Game, Bettman and I had an interesting discussion about Rogers taking over the national package. This was before our first season under the new broadcasting deal. After his state-of-the-union address, he said, "Listen, we've got this partnership now and we're just going to have to figure out a way to get along a little better."

I told him I'd always prided myself on being a good team player, and I'd have no problem with that. We shook hands. I really wanted to make it work for Scott Moore and the entire Sportsnet team. I wanted Gary Bettman to respect me, but like any other dressing room there is a fine line where you want the respect of your veterans but also don't want to suck up to them.

I had a good relationship with most of the people in the league office—I worked hard at it—but there was not a chance they agreed with everything I said about all their decisions. I tried my best to get the facts straight before forming my opinions, and I trust that they respected that. Now, with the new broadcasting deal, it was my job to maintain a good professional relationship with Gary's hockey department: Colin Campbell, Mike Murphy, Kris King, Kay Whitmore, Rod Pasma, George Parros, and Damian Echevarrieta from player safety. They were the day-to-day operational guys with whom I had worked well before. But now it was even more important that I reach out to the league for their perspective, to make sure their voice was also heard.

We had two national shows as part of the contract, on Wednesdays and Saturdays, and they had me on both. The first game broadcast was Leafs vs. Canadiens, on a Wednesday night. I had never seen so many people on the floor of our opening show; it was wall-to-wall Rogers executives, corporate sponsors, producers, and directors while we tried to rehearse. All of them were looking like they had just become new parents. I've never seen so many unrecognizable suits patting themselves on the back.

It was easy to spot some other differences, too. We had the latest technology. Sportsnet spent hundreds of thousands on the newest tech gadgets. We had a digital puck wall that was supposed to push new hockey analytics. It never did much for our shows, though. After they officially stopped using it, I started hanging my coat on it before my radio shows—the most expensive coat hook in history.

Our stage set was second to none, or so we thought. We also had a digital floor that with one push of a button could look like ice and create a regulation face-off circle. The studio was big enough to demonstrate key on-ice scenarios. We had nets and used hockey sticks on set to reenact plays, but all that slowly dissipated. Little did we know that four years later the only constant in our shows would be a giant monitor screen behind four chairs and a desk.

Three days later came my first Saturday night on *HNIC*. I never thought I'd be able to replicate the nervous excitement I had right before my first NHL game, but this day did that. While Wednesday felt "Sportsnet," Saturday felt to me all *Hockey Night in Canada*. Besides the obvious difference of Ron's and Don's presence, it had a far different tone. Saturday felt more traditional because it was. Senior management was smart enough to not tinker with the overall feel; Brian Spear, Heather Jenken, and Kathy Broderick were all longtime seasoned *HNIC* producers who protected the blueprint of what made that show so special. Compared to the bells and whistles from Wednesday's extravaganza, Saturdays had a completely different vibe.

Some of my earliest memories are of watching *Hockey Night in Canada*—listening to the theme song, and then watching smooth-skating Dave Keon, Jim McKenny, and Eddie "Clear the Track" Shack. Saturday was the only day in the week when the country slowed down, gathered around a TV set, and waited for puck drop. My Saturdays now as a broadcaster felt the same way. The day slowed down and I prepared for the big night ahead. Never did I imagine that I would be on the other side of the television set, sitting at a desk, talking to millions.

On a typical Saturday during the year, a variety of producers and on-air talent would meet up for the morning skate, if the Leafs were in town. It was usually around 10:30 a.m. It wasn't mandatory for us to attend skates, but I found it was great prep for the night. It was all about interacting with the Leafs, the visiting team, and the other members of the media. It was like standing around the water cooler. It often provided a wealth of knowledge from players, coaches, and reporters who shared their insights. Saturdays became a routine for Elliotte Friedman and me. Right after the skate, we would go straight to Sunset Grill for lunch.

I always felt that Kelly Hrudey, Elliotte Friedman, Strombo, and I had a good rapport. I had known them over the years when our paths crossed in broadcasting, but I didn't know them well until I began working on *HNIC*. I thought our first few months weren't like we'd been shot out of a cannon, but they were solid. It was a big transition for everyone. A mix of Sportsnet and CBC staff had to learn how to work with one another. George and I were new to the show and had to learn the ropes. Kelly and Elliotte already had years of Saturday experience under their belts and we looked to them to help us find the right chemistry on set. It was certainly our goal. But after a few months some comments on social media showed a relentless inability to accept change. While we all took our fair share of criticism, the fans seemed to respond especially negatively to George Stroumboulopoulos taking over for Ron MacLean.

I felt bad about how things went for George. He is a fantastic broadcaster, a great interviewer, and a generous and truly likeable guy. He had earned his image as a pro at the CBC with his award-winning interviews. But in my opinion George never really stood a chance. It was a strategic move by Rogers to try to capture a new demographic. They felt someone like George would help define the new era. It just didn't happen.

George's style was unlike anything seen before on the show. He also made it clear that he didn't want to conform to the conservative coat-and-tie persona that *HNIC* had always had. It was paramount to George that he be able to preserve and protect his look and his image, and I respected that. He wanted to be himself and wore an earring and a skull ring, which is unfortunately a far cry from what the fans were used to. It just wasn't the right fit.

Even before the first broadcast, the tone was set at the press conference announcing that George was going to be the new host. Ron MacLean is famous for his tongue-in-cheek remarks, but he probably didn't do George a favour when he uttered at the live presser, "Don't screw this up, it's a big show." But there were challenges for George. He had strong music followers that he wasn't ready to trade in for new hockey ones. He also commuted from L.A. a lot during the season, which kept him from most morning skates. He had a lot going on behind the scenes. George may only have been on a few hours one day a week, but there's no question that following the NHL is a seven-days-a-week job.

Other things continued much as they had before with *HNIC*. Don Cherry was as big a presence walking through the studio as he was in front of the camera. Even at eighty years of age, he still had swagger. Anne-Marie Maugeri, a CBC production assistant, would escort Grapes into the CBC studios. Like clockwork his car would drop him off underground at 4:15 p.m. and Maugeri would take his garment bag containing whichever famously flamboyant suit jacket he had chosen for the night.

He always arrived much later than we did and I would make a point of meeting up with him in the hall prior to the main show's production meeting. Sometimes he and I would talk about what happened during the week and other times he'd just walk past me and say, "Hey, Nicky boy!" He was bigger than life. He was treated much like Vito Corleone, the godfather of *HNIC* (stopping short of kissing the pinky ring). After our panel's production meeting, Grapes and Ron would go into their own meeting right at 5 p.m. for *Coach's Corner*. It was a well-oiled machine.

I first met Don when I played for the Hartford Whalers, in 1992. He asked me to do a segment on his *Grapeline* TV show, out of a restaurant called Grapes, one of a chain that he owned at the time. We filmed in front of a live audience. By then his Rock'em Sock'em videos were the rage and any sort of endorsement from Grapes took your hockey profile to another level. He and I got along well. He loved my passion and told me that was the way I always needed to be. At the end of the show he told me, "You're my type of guy." Needless to say, every Canadian player yearned for those five simple words. That's when I started to focus on his career. Whether you liked him or not, he picked a side that he believed in and it made for fantastic television.

Don Cherry filmed *Coach's Corner* live, just behind our main set. Other than Ron, no one got to watch him. The camera was locked in place and we could hear him through the walls, and like anybody else around the country, we waited for it. *Coach's Corner* was the centrepiece of *Hockey Night in Canada* for thirty-eight years.

Unfortunately for many of us on the inside, it was an acrimonious relationship between some in senior management and Ron and Don right from the start. Some executives felt that their time had passed. Not all the decision makers felt that way, so they kept them on. But when it came down to keeping *Coach's Corner*, the compromise was to limit their time on-air. That didn't sit well with Ron and Don at all, and they often voiced their displeasure on-air, which caused more tension on the set.

The producers of *HNIC* were also willing to try to get us away from the "desk." Instead, they had us stand on the video floor for some portions of our segment. We held sticks in our hands, as if we were shooting or lining up for a face-off, on a floor that looked like ice. I actually liked it because it felt like I was a kid in my parents' basement on their linoleum floor. But viewers were averse to it and it seemed to pour gasoline on the social media fire.

Our saving grace that year was five Canadian teams making the playoffs. With Calgary and Vancouver facing off in the first round we were guaranteed a Canadian team in the final eight.

A lot had changed, but for the most part, my responsibilities were the same. Provide in-depth analysis while still hunting for big trades—and the next two seasons I landed doozies. The first one happened on July 1, 2015, during the annual NHL Free Agent Day. Free-agent shows slowly developed into big shows for the networks much like Trade Deadline Day. The show was winding down when I received a text that revealed that the Toronto Maple Leafs had traded high-scoring winger Phil Kessel to the Pittsburgh Penguins. Without giving anyone in the production room or on set a warning, I blurted out the news on-air. I caught everyone completely off guard. With TSN still on-air we must have owned the story a good seven to ten minutes before they even got wind of it. Very seldom did anyone get to announce a trade without hundreds on social media confirming it within seconds. When I said it, Daren Millard, who was hosting that day, ran hard with it, as did Sportsnet. It was a far cry from the Dave Manson/Jyrki Lumme trade I announced in 2001. It was big deal, with various players and draft picks moving. But Kessel was the hot topic. Some thought he had an untradeable contract and it would be hard for the Leafs to move him. But NHL GMs are creative and they find different ways to make trades. I'd been in on the possibility of the Kessel trade almost a week before, during the NHL entry draft, and it was close to happening then. The same source that gave it to me said they couldn't make the deal happen at the draft because of a couple particulars, but I was advised to just be patient. Sure enough, it did happen.

The second season did not get off to a great start with so many Canadian teams struggling. As a panel, we were still working on gaining the trust of the Canadian fans. We felt it was all becoming more regular and Rogers was determined to stay the course. We continued doing segments away from the desks. A unique one was when Christine Simpson brought in basketball great Charles Barkley, who was in town for the 2016 NBA All-Star Game, in February. He really loves Canada. I had met him previously on a couple of occasions when Wayne Gretzky, who is good buddies with Charles, invited him to his Pro-Am golf tournament in Collingwood. Charles loves hockey, too. He once said publicly that the NBA stunk compared to the NHL, and that he was watching hockey instead of basketball. It was one of the few times shooting pucks in the studio was well received. My job this segment was to teach him how to do a wrist shot—at least I attempted to. I had as much luck as he would have had teaching me to dunk a basketball. I think his notorious golf swing is still smoother than his wrist shot. The pucks were rolling all over the studio, anywhere but close to the net. Finally, he managed to put one in. We had a blast with him because he gets the whole TV/entertainment personality thing. The chemistry between him and Shaquille O'Neal is great on TNT. That day with Charles was so smooth and so fun; he put everyone at ease.

It's always fun to interact with players from other sports. Gregg Zaun, Rogers's lead baseball analyst, and I engaged in a friendly competition back in 2008. We filmed a fun segment together. I would shoot ten pucks at him and Gregg, a former MLB catcher, would play goalie and attempt to stop them. Gregg, who played for the Toronto Blue Jays from 2004 to 2008, had become Sportsnet's lead baseball analyst and embraced Canada's culture; he understood what hockey meant to the country. I took him to a game one night and he loved it. He liked Don Cherry and the way he came across as a personality, and started to shape himself into the Don Cherry of baseball in Canada. He would wear outlandish suits on Canada Day—an attention grabber that he loved. People started calling him a Don Cherry wannabe, but it worked for him. Zaunie even started taking skating lessons that year so he could play pickup hockey. We asked Curtis Joseph to the rink to help him out with his goaltender positioning for our TV segment. The funniest part was watching Curtis help him get his jersey over his goalie equipment.

At the filming you could tell he had a tough time holding his balance, but he of course had a great instinct for catching a puck. He would glove everything remotely close to him. Even if he was falling over or moving in a different direction from where the puck was going, he was still going to try to find a way to catch it. Even so, of the ten shots, I scored nine in a row. I scored stick side and five-hole, and I deked him on the left side and right side, but I avoided his glove. So on the tenth shot I decided I was going to give him a chance and shoot to his bread and butter. I shot hard from about twenty-five feet out and he looked like Bernie Parent in his prime. His reaction was priceless. It was as if he'd won another world championship. Even his sidekick, Jamie Campbell, the host of Sportsnet's in-studio baseball coverage, held up a sign that read "Zaunie Nation." A perfect ending to our segment. That whole thing was fun. We were also supposed to do something on the Blue Jays' pitch, but it never came to fruition.

At the end of the season there was a memorable day, June 29. Three big announcements were made. Bob McKenzie told the hockey world about the trade of Taylor Hall for Adam Larsson, I revealed that P. K. Subban was being traded for Shea Weber, and then it was announced that Steven Stamkos had re-signed with Tampa for an eight-year deal. All that in just twenty-three minutes. I was in Muskoka that day, north of Toronto, with terrible cell service. I had to stand on a cliff waving my phone around to send the news. That was my other doozie.

We had some good times, but when all the Canadian teams missed the Stanley Cup playoffs in 2016—the first time since 1970—it was the perfect storm. It was no secret that viewership and playoff revenue hinged on the success of Canadian teams. That year Sportsnet decided not to send our *HNIC* panel to cover the Cup Final on location. If we thought the morale was down in the hockey department with no Canadian teams in the playoffs, not going to the final was even more devastating. Big changes were coming.

Rogers felt after two seasons into the national deal it was a good time to replace George with Ron MacLean. Scott Moore and Keith Pelley envisioned that George would bring a different type of energy and fan to the game, but for whatever reason it just didn't happen the way everybody had hoped. Subsequently, Gord Cutler was no longer running the hockey department and Rob Corte became our new VP of hockey production. I liked Rob and had known him for many years at Sportsnet.

No more than a couple of days into his tenure he promptly pulled El-liotte, Kelly, and me into a meeting and gave us a stern message. "You are having too much fun for my liking. Too many inside jokes. You guys are way too loose." I don't remember being too loose or having so many inside jokes, but it was clear he wanted to let us know that there'd be changes to how we were doing things.

With the switch back to Ron, our show reverted to a simple question-and-answer-style coverage at the desk, and that was it. No bells and whistles. No standing on the floor. No more sticks and nets. It was "Let's broadcast safe." We knew the retreating philosophy was in direct response to Twitter backlash. We were okay with it. We were a team and our reaction was, "Hey, Coach, just tell us what you want." After what we'd been doing, I thought at times we were broadcasting too conserva-tively, but with Ron back, going back to the basics drew less negativity. Mission accomplished.

CHAPTER 17

The New Hockey Night

Ron MacLean is an amazing broadcaster and the transition from George was seamless. I had the seat right next to him on the panel and what I learned early on was to just stay the hell out of his way until he's done. Not because he was difficult—he was just that good. Watching him up front and close on *HNIC* was like watching a maestro working with his orchestra. My job during his opening was to lean back and not screw up the camera's single shot of him.

Some nights I would get caught listening to him, like every other viewer, and I'd have to snap out of it quickly as he directed the next question to me. Ron worked his magic and as a panel we just needed to be ready to follow his queues. There was not a lot of banter between the four of us, something I missed as I preferred having that sort of interaction on air. But that is not what this show was about. After his opening monologue it was up to us to make quick strong points and then move on. He would lead us into our segments with short questions. "Nick: Toronto's power play?" "Kelly: Carey Price's glove hand?" "Elliotte: What's the word in Edmonton?" And off we went. As long as we hit our marks within our time frame, all was good in the *HNIC* universe.

When Rogers began the national package, they had offered Ron a Sunday night *Hometown Hockey* show. It would be filmed from different towns throughout Canada. That meant Ron's Saturdays would now only include a pregame show, a one-minute opening of the show, *Coach's Corner*, and then he would finish his night with the second intermission. Due to a hectic Sunday travel schedule, he'd often leave right before the third period started. Then David Amber would relieve Ron, finishing off the night. Despite the unconventional arrangement among our hosts, I was able to pick up the rhythm and energy of the show. Amber was solid and fun to work with which made the transition each Saturday easier.

I'd heard stories before starting on *HNIC* that certain topics could suddenly be taken away from hockey analysts if Ron and Don made a late decision to use those ideas for *Coach's Corner*. That caused some headaches for the producers on the *HNIC* set prior to Rogers taking over. I can tell you unequivocally that that never happened when I was there. Once we started developing a storyline or topic it stayed with us and at no time did anyone ever say to me, "Sorry, you can't talk about that because we are now saving it for *Coach's Corner*."

After Ron came back to host *HNIC*, everything seemed to be on track. Everyone on the panel got along really well and was respectful to one another, and we accepted our roles happily. However, the show was very different from when George was host—it was a tighter run ship. There were still some challenges, though, including sharing Ron with his Sunday *Hometown Hockey* show. Some Saturday nights, I felt Ron was preoccupied, with good reason. Travel schedule was always a huge concern when it came to the weather. He had to make the flights early the next morning or out that night or risk missing the show. He did few on-air programs during the week, but I can only imagine the prep work he had to do behind the scenes going into that Sunday show. *Hometown Hockey* is not your typical "talk hockey show." This was also about geography, history, and hockey culture. It is Canada's version of *Escape to the Country*. After thirty-five years, Ron could do *Hockey Night in Canada* with his eyes closed, but having to prepare two national shows like that, back-to-back, was challenging even for him.

One year, North Bay was chosen for *Hometown Hockey*, and because it was where I played Junior Hockey, the producers did a story about me and my parents. I picked my parents up with my film crew and we drove the four hours, talking and reminiscing about my years with the North Bay Centennials (now the North Bay Battalion). Stan Butler, the GM and coach of the Battalion, really embraced me because of my long history in North Bay. The *Hometown Hockey* crew did a fantastic job telling my story. A good portion of the feature was in the four-hour car ride up with my mom and dad. Hearing my parents' North Bay experience thirty years later gave me an even deeper appreciation for Junior A parents and what they sacrifice. It also gave me a real inside look at the work that went into that Sunday show; from the producer Deidre Hambly, who was with us every step of the way, to the "roadies" who lugged the gear and stages from town to town. It was a tremendous amount of work. It's really easy to see why small towns love that show. I got to meet up again with former Junior teammates Bill Houlder and Darren Turcotte, who both live in North Bay. An amazing full-circle moment for me.

Much like when I was a player, by the time the playoffs came it was like everything had just been a buildup to that. In the Stanley Cup playoffs, we had to broadcast almost every night for two months straight. As demanding as it was, I got to go home every night to my own bed. I could at least say hello and goodbye to my family in passing. I felt worse for Kelly Hrudey, who had to stay in a hotel on his own starting in April until the Cup was raised. If broadcasting Olympic hockey was a sprint, the Cup is a marathon. Some years we'd count the days and Ron, Kelly, Elliotte, and I would work sixty-four out of sixty-eight, including some late nights with double or even triple overtime periods.

Even so, I enjoyed being front and centre of it. Playoffs are exciting, and in the first couple of rounds the anticipation was awesome. But we were *Hockey Night in Canada* not *Hockey Night in America*; it was hard to be as excited if there were no Canadian teams in the playoffs.

There's a lack of energy when a Canadian team loses a round, or if they don't qualify for the postseason in the first place. That's natural. How excited is Canada with a first-round matchup of Anaheim and Nashville? A hockey purist may like it, but it certainly didn't help the bottom line. That's what happened to us in 2016. For the first time since 1970, there were no Canadian teams in the Stanley Cup playoffs. As Canadian broadcasters and journalists, we aspire to be part of an exciting championship run, like the Toronto Raptors had in 2019. Without that energy, it can be tough to keep viewers engaged.

Playoff morale would return with a vengeance the following season. Whatever we experienced twelve months earlier was a distant memory. Canadian teams came back in force. Toronto made the playoffs for the first time since 2013. Montreal made the playoffs, too. Ottawa almost had the Cinderella story, coming within one goal of going to the Stanley Cup Final. Although there was no Canadian team in the final, we had the draw of Sidney Crosby, and Nashville was a favourite with the country music fans of Canada. *HNIC* was never afraid to pull in celebrities from the music scene, and Scott Oake did a terrific job with that. Shania Twain, Keith Urban, and Nicole Kidman were often featured throughout our shows. Nashville was a fun town to cover a game in.

Our *HNIC* panel was on location once again, covering the Pittsburgh and Nashville final. We went from covering the playoffs from a studio in Toronto to Sportsnet chartering our flights for a crew of over thirty people to make the schedule easier on us. What a difference a year makes. Sportsnet realized the toll it took on us and made amends.

The next year, in November 2018, I was interviewed for a documentary, *Making Coco: The Grant Fuhr Story.* Grant had gone through a lot of challenges in his life, on and off the ice. Director Don Metz, who had worked with the Oilers for forty years, knew Grant really well and wanted to film a documentary about his life.

Metz put together a list of people who should be interviewed, and wanted to speak to me because of the incident in which I collided with him in the 1996 Stanley Cup playoffs. Grant suffered a season-ending knee injury that effectively ended his team's chances for winning the Cup that year.

I did not know Grant Fuhr at all before our incident. After I retired in 1998, we ended up together at a charity golf event in Tahoe, but we never exchanged any words about what had happened between us. I had heard through inner hockey circles how upset he was at me, and I felt it best to leave it alone. A year after that, at the NHL All-Star event, Mark Messier asked if I had ever spoken to Grant about the incident. I told him I hadn't. Mess told me that Grant was a great guy and would never hold any grudges. Mess would know, having played with Grant in Edmonton during the Oilers' dynasty years. Then, in typical Mark Messier fashion, he took complete control of the situation, grabbed me by the arm, and dragged me to where Grant was standing. Over the next few moments it was as if a thousand pounds fell off my shoulders. It was nice to finally clear the air because I had always felt bad. Grant was as gracious as Mark had described him as being and has been that way ever since.

He made reference to the incident in his book, *Grant Fuhr: The Story of a Hockey Legend.* "I was pretty mad at Nick for a while, now we laugh about it when we see each other," he said in the book. "Those things happen in the playoffs. He was just trying to help his team, not hurt me."

I did the interview for the Metz documentary at the home of Mike Wilson, a longtime Toronto Maple Leafs fan, who at the time had an amazing hockey memorabilia collection in his home. It looked like the Hockey Hall of Fame. In the doc I said, "It was first and foremost a hockey play and I was just trying to create some havoc in front of the net. I did it because Chris Pronger was there and he cross-checked me and it's a play I've done a countless number of times. Every time I've done it, goaltenders have gotten up and finished the game and were never, ever hurt. Grant, unfortunately, couldn't finish the series and had major surgery on his knee."

Chris Pronger followed that up, saying, "I remember pushing Kypreos to the right and him somehow diving left. I'm not sure how that happened. It was definitely an unfortunate situation. Thankfully, nobody blamed me because it could have been my fault again." Pronger was not exactly a choirboy in the NHL. He once got suspended eight games for taking his skate and stomping on Canucks forward Ryan Kesler. I always made it a habit to stand in front of the crease facing the goalie. It is a good zone because few players would risk having me fall into their goalie. I dared Pronger to take a good shot at me. At other times other defenceman have pulled me out of the crease. When Pronger cross-checked me, I did nothing to avoid Grant Fuhr. Pronger pushed me into him and I didn't try to move left or right. If he had no concern for his own goalie, why should I? But I certainly had no intention of injuring anyone. I wanted to draw a power play. Which I did. But the price was high.

Metz added that Grant's perspective as a player changed after the incident: "That moment was so important in the documentary because that's when Grant realized he's not Superman, his knee was done."

Grant's comments followed. "We're still friends. It's understandable. In the playoffs, you fall on goalies. Did he mean to hurt me? Not really, but at the same time did he mean to bother and disrupt things? Yeah. But that's part of the game and you understand that. At the time you're bitter. I could say at the time he was my least favourite person. If I hadn't wrecked the knee, I think we definitely had a chance [to win the Stanley Cup]."

I didn't talk to Grant after I spoke for the documentary because I knew I would see him at the Toronto premiere. He and I did a Q&A

with Elliotte Friedman on the stage after it was shown. I was honoured to do it. I appreciated hearing Grant's story—how he battled throughout his life to become one of the greatest goaltenders in history is inspiring.

Twenty-five years later I still get horrible things said about me on social media—that I ruined St. Louis's chance to win the Stanley Cup that year. Some fans are still upset after all this time. However, I do feel I made peace with many St. Louis fans when I successfully predicted that the Blues would win the 2019 Stanley Cup prior to the season starting. I was the only one to pick them. I am a big Ryan O'Reilly fan. I thought he would be the difference maker who would get them over the top. The first rule of broadcasting is, no cheering in the press box. But twenty years after Grant Fuhr's injury I was internally rooting for the Blues. Although I never made it obvious on camera, I was genuinely happy that St. Louis won.

The incident between Grant and me wasn't a big part of his documentary—more of a strong footnote. But it did explain Grant's thoughts on what happened. Until someone has walked in our shoes, I don't think they can truly understand what we go through and why we make the decisions we do.

We all have some regrets in life and moments we would do anything to change. When I think about what-ifs, there are some big ones: Mike Ware's high stick that knocked out five of my teeth; the fight I had with Jamie Huscroft, after which I had to have major reconstructive knee surgery; breaking my leg in a fight with Matthew Barnaby; breaking Brent Ashton's jaw; my career-ending knockout from Ryan VandenBussche; and hurting Grant Fuhr. There are times when I wonder how things would be different if those events hadn't happened. Although I don't regret the way I played, I regret the way some things turned out. Would it have changed my life, or theirs? It's like the movie *Sliding Doors*. Turn one direction off a subway platform and your life unfolds one way. Turn the other and the picture changes.

CHAPTER 18

Changing Media

In early October 2018 Scott Moore resigned from his position at Sportsnet. He had followed Keith Pelley and Nadir Mohamed. Collectively they engineered Rogers's deal with the NHL. Nadir left a few months after the deal was done and Keith left in spring 2015 to run the PGA's European Tour.

In the media release announcing his resignation, Scott said, "We got Sportsnet to number one [among sports networks in Canada], which is what I said I would do when I got in here on the first of December 2010 . . . It's a mature business, it's a successful business, and I feel good about leaving it in the condition it is in."

Although Scott had not been at Sportsnet regularly since the day we launched, he was there at the beginning and had been a big part of its success. Scott was one of the few people, in my twenty years there, that had a real connection not only with me, but with many who worked around him. Keeping good relations was very important to me. There was constant communication and feedback so we always knew where we stood and what to work on. And he valued our opinions. We also knew that he fought for us. It was disheartening when he left because everyone at Sportsnet liked him and liked working for him; there aren't many of those sorts of bosses around. He would later end up partnering with basketball great LeBron James in a company called Uninterrupted, a multimedia platform for athletes.

I understood why he felt it was time to move on. Our sports media world was changing, the market was changing, and how we could tell stories was changing; Rogers needed to make changes, too. Scott's vision and the direction mainstream media was heading in didn't align anymore. It was clear to me at this point that personal connection was still vital to Scott in the way he conducted his business.

Enter Rick Brace. When Scott resigned, a search for the next president was quickly under way and Brace, a former TSN president, took over in the interim. I knew of him as the head of the rival network that we had battled hard against during our rise. He had the reputation on our floor of being cold and impersonal. He lived up to that reputation. You couldn't find a more polar opposite from Scott Moore. While one wanted to motivate and influence, the other didn't even introduce himself. No pep talks. No reassuring e-mails to touch base on how things were going after changes. No anything. He never ventured near the hockey department. Many on our floor questioned why he never formally addressed us. But once we saw the constant changes around us, it wasn't hard to understand why.

Some in the media claimed that Scott was the fall guy because Rogers paid so much for the NHL rights and lost a lot when it didn't translate into revenue. I don't buy that for one second. One big issue we had in the first half of the national package was the lack of Canadian team playoff success. In the absence of Canadian teams qualifying for the playoffs, or getting beyond the first round, Sportsnet suffered. Most poignant was the lack of success from the Toronto Maple Leafs.

CBC's version of *HNIC* was always accused of being too pro-Toronto. From a broadcasting standpoint it was, and that didn't change when we took over. It drives non-Leafs fans nuts, especially in western

Canada, and with good reason. Everyone that works under that roof knows the vast majority of their bread is spread with Toronto advertising butter. And so the Leafs absorbed a great deal of our airtime. That didn't lend itself to equal airtime coverage. Simply put, Rogers needed all the Canadian teams to be successful, but especially the Toronto Maple Leafs.

No one can stop the evolution of sports TV and radio. You can't put the genie back in the bottle. Bigger than a few Canadian teams missing the playoffs is how the world is changing in the way we receive news and watch sports. Conventional TV and conventional media have taken a major turn.

Historically, major advertisers have had only a few options for where they could put their dollars: newspapers, TV, and radio. Now there are countless options in the digital world. Consumers were limited on where they got their information. In the past athletes needed TSN, Sportsnet, and *HNIC* to get their voices and image out to the fans. Today, players have much more control and many more options over their image. Advertising dollars are starting to follow them more than ever.

Larger companies take a longer time to implement changes; they have so much invested in their strategies and more red tape keeping them from making changes quickly. Smaller companies are more flexible and able to capture the dynamic digital market more easily. Blockbuster Video is a great example. They were massive and no one thought that they could fail. But they were destroyed because they didn't change with the times. Netflix came in and became bigger with none of the brick-and-mortar costs that Blockbuster had.

PalmPilot, one of the first smartphones, had a peak valuation of $55 billion in 2000. Within a decade they were finished. The music industry is another example. Does anyone remember MP3s? CD sales disappeared overnight and the music industry suffered for twenty years. It wasn't Capitol Records or Universal that found the solution. It was a small startup in Stockholm that started Spotify.

Not changing with the times has become a real threat to mainstream television. It will be interesting to see what Sportsnet and TSN look like ten years from now.

In February 2019, I travelled to New York for the twenty-fifth anniversary of the Rangers' Stanley Cup win. It was a great moment for all of us and it was total first class by the Rangers. Team owner James Dolan hosted every player and their families. He flew people from all over the world as a thank-you for what the win still means to the city.

As a group we also got a chance to address the current players prior to their game with the Winnipeg Jets. Rangers head coach David Quinn was adamant that his young players see and hear firsthand how a New York City championship could change their lives. What I noticed specifically was how fixated the players were when we spoke to them before the game, especially when it came to Mark Messier, who has legendary status at Madison Square Garden. The players also came out of the dressing room and sat on the bench to watch our lengthy ceremony before their game. David Quinn told me as I was leaving the dressing room that our visit was more important than any pregame talk he could have given them. They had all the season-ticket holders dating back to '94 on the ice, wearing Rangers jerseys and forming an honour guard as each one of us was paraded onto the ice.

The stories were flying at the reunion. There were so many conversations going that it was hard to keep up. Iron Mike Keenan was there, one of the toughest coaches most of us had ever had. On this particular weekend, though, he was anything but Iron. Mike was fun, polite, warm, and couldn't have been more engaging. The big joke was, "Who in the hell is this guy and what did he do with Mike?" Even his stories had changed; many seemed to include a far more gentle version of his coaching past. Brian Leetch kept repeating, "I don't quite remember it that way!"

It was amazing to see everybody and reminisce, with one notable exception. Our teammate Alexander Karpovtsev lost his life, along with the rest of the Lokomotiv Russian hockey team, on a charter flight on September 7, 2011. He was an assistant coach with the Kontinental Hockey League team. His wife, Janna, and daughter Stacy were there at the Rangers reunion. When we took team photos, Stacy represented Karpovtsev and wore his jersey. It was an important moment for all of us to remember him.

After the 2018–2019 NHL season, Sportsnet continued to reshape and change directions. Budgets were stretching throughout network television. I was not overly happy with how the previous year and a half had felt, especially when I looked back at the work that I used to do. Even when we didn't have the national package, it felt more creative and fun than what I was doing in 2019. I'd go in, sit at a desk, speak about hockey, and then leave. The next game would feel the same way to me. Wash. Rinse. Repeat. It felt like I'd lost direction for the first time in twenty years. I had one more year left on my contract and there had been zero talk about any extension. That had never happened to me in my twenty years at Sportsnet. I was the longest-surviving hockey talent left there, from that first day in October 1998, and it was time to read the tea leaves.

Our industry was not spending the money it used to and that was clear to everyone. After you help build something up for twenty years you don't necessarily want to give up on it. But there were nights I would come home from work and stay up for hours, so frustrated with the lack of direction I felt. Change will always happen, but this was something more than that. I would look at Anne-Marie and say, "I just don't know how much longer I can do this."

I had to dig pretty deep to better understand why I was less happy and fulfilled now, at the pinnacle of my career, than I was when I began. I discovered that I liked the climb. Tell me I can't do something and it gives me a mark to reach. I like being the underdog. Helping to build something from nothing gave my work more meaning.

Rogers changed direction because they had to. And I can't even pretend to know how to run a multibillion-dollar company. But what I do know is if you don't feel inspired by what you do anymore, it's time to move on. Coming to that conclusion empowered me. But at the same time, the sad reality was I would be leaving the first and only job I had ever interviewed for.

After extensive talks throughout the summer of 2019, Sportsnet and I agreed that my run there was over. I sent out a heartfelt Twitter message in late August.

> After much consideration, Sportsnet and I have decided to part ways. I am proud to have been part of our growth since we launched in October of 1998 and thankful they took a chance on me so long ago. I am truly grateful to have had twenty-one years of a post playing career. From covering Sid's golden goal in Vancouver to a Saturday night seat on *Hockey Night in Canada*, I could not have asked for more.

> Most of all, I would like to offer a sincere thank you to the hockey fans. Simply put, hockey is nothing without you. I've felt your passion since day one.

> My family and I are excited for the projects and adventures that will occupy the next phase of our lives. Until we meet again . . . Kyper.

Sportsnet's press release immediately followed:

Nick was one of the first hockey analysts to join Sportsnet and has been an integral part of Sportsnet's hockey coverage for more than 20 years. Over that time, he established himself as one of the most trusted and respected in Canadian sports broadcasting. He is a true professional and his commitment, dedication and passion for the game helped Sportsnet grow into the leader it is today.

From the entire Sportsnet team, we wish Nick all the best and sincerely thank him for his contributions as he moves on to his next chapter.

Along with my departure, Doug MacLean and John Shannon also announced they would not return. When Sportsnet and I parted ways, it was amicable, and there were and are no hard feelings on either side. I am forever grateful for the day that Sportsnet gave a guy in a T-shirt a shot.

It seems poignant that at the funeral for Ted Rogers, who started Rogers Telecommunications, his son said about his father, "He loved to be the David up against a Goliath. He loved to be the scrappy underdog."

I think Ted would have been proud of Sportsnet's climb. I am immensely proud to have been a part of it.

EPILOGUE

For forty-seven years, since the age of seven, hockey has been a pivotal part of my life. The people whom I've met through this sport, who inspired me not only in my career, but in my life, too, were a gift I could never have imagined as a young boy.

I have always been attracted to people who try to connect and make a difference in the lives of those around them. Although I don't know if I was always successful, I have tried my best to emulate certain qualities of the people I respect most. People who invested in me. The patience of Bobby Clarke, who waited for me to develop as a player; Bob Goodenow and Ian Pulver, for teaching us how to advocate for ourselves as players; Paul Holmgren, who inspired me to offer more of myself; Messier's ability to read a dressing room; Glenn Healy's ability to stay true to his principles and beliefs no matter what; Tie Domi's protective instincts; Doug MacLean's sense of humour, which includes laughing at himself. The list could go on.

The months after I left, things became tumultuous. Don Cherry, a hockey icon, was fired with cause after using words on-air that Sportsnet considered derogatory. The ironclad bond between two Canadian icons—Ron and Don—was broken. The Leafs coach, Mike Babcock, was fired. Toronto fans were becoming impatient after over fifty years with no Stanley Cup in sight. Racism and physical abuse were at the forefront in hockey like never before. An NHL investigation followed

Flames coach Bill Peters, costing him his job. It was a tough time to be a hockey broadcaster.

Then the unthinkable: another hockey work stoppage. This time it had nothing to do with owners and players. COVID-19 paralyzed the world with inexplicable horror. Over a century after the Spanish flu, the world was brought to its knees once again with a pandemic. While so much of our lives is up in the air, the one takeaway has to be finding humanity and connecting to other people.

Who knows what the future brings? Perhaps I will turn into that Greek papou, spinning a spit of lamb at the side of the house, embarrassing my grandchildren. I might be that old guy dancing around with a white napkin in my hand, leading the line like Zorba the Greek, just to really push the kids over the edge.

Inside, however, I will somehow always be that eight-year-old boy outside Maple Leaf Gardens, where the ground was shaking from the roar of the fans inside, holding my father's hand. I did not know it then, of course, but that moment would shape the rest of my life. Years that I would not trade for anything. The rest is up for grabs.

ACKNOWLEDGMENTS

Nick Kypreos

In writing this book, I've had the chance to revisit many memories. When you retire, you do look back, but there's nothing like the experience of writing it all down to make you realize just how much you have to be thankful for.

So many people have helped me develop as a person and a professional. People who encouraged me and taught me it's not how many times you fall, but how many times you get back up. To all my mentors, teachers, and teammates who believed in me, a heartfelt thank-you. You made me laugh, you made me cry, and you made me stronger. In particular, Ian McPherson, Andy Thornley, Bert Templeton, John Paddock, Brian Burke, Paul Holmgren, Colin Campbell, and Mike Keenan, too (in his more positive moments). Early in my career Bobby Clarke, Tim Kerr, Don Nachbaur, Kevin McCarthy, David Fenyves, Dale Hunter, Rod Langway, Alan May, Steve Leach, and Mike Liut gave tremendous support and showed me how to be a pro.

To the whole Rangers organization, including Barry Watkins, John Rosasco, Darren Blake, and the entire PR department, thank you for getting me out there to represent our team and our championship to the great fans of New York. To Mark Messier, Brian Leetch, and Mike Richter, thank you for letting me experience New York City with you—best coattails I've ever ridden. To Glenn Healy, my chess partner, thank you for teaching me to only worry about the things I *can* control. Thank you to Adam Graves, the consummate gentleman. And to all my Rangers teammates, we continue to walk together.

Thanks to Cliff Fletcher and Neil Smith for the chance to fulfill my childhood dream of putting on the great Maple Leafs sweater. I had amazing teammates who remain great friends: Doug Gilmour, Mats Sundin, Tie Domi, Wendel Clark, Kirk Muller, and Fredrik Modin, just to name a few. It was an honour to play with you all in my hometown and retire a Toronto Maple Leaf.

Thank you to the excellent trainers I've had over the years: Chris May, Dan "Beaker" Stuck, Stan Wong, Bud Gouveia, Dave Smith, Jim Ramsay, Chris Broadhurst, and Brent Smith. And a special shout-out to the doctors who kept me healthy and playing too, Dr. John Greg and Dr. James Kelly. Thanks also to the great equipment managers who never kept things dull: Craig "Woody" Leydig, Doug Shearer, Skip Cunningham, Mike Folga, Brian Papineau, and my personal goaltender/trainer, Scott McKay.

I was lucky to have two great careers in my life. I'm not sure if my second one would have started without Glenn Adamo from the NHL office, who saw something in me. Thank you "Humble" Howard Glassman and Fred Patterson for having me on their popular radio show on 102.1 The Edge. They helped me a lot in finding my on air sense of humour. Thank you Scott Moore, Doug Beeforth, David Akande, and Sportsnet for giving a shot to a guy who showed up to his first "real" job interview wearing a T-shirt and flip-flops. I've worked with some real pros in the broadcasting world and benefited greatly from their experience and knowledge: Steve Lansky, Gord Cutler, Peter Schmiedchen, Bob Torrens, Darren Dreger, Daren Millard, Christine Simpson, Kevin Quinn, Scott Morrison, Scott Woodgate, Paul Graham, Pat Grier, Matt Marstrom, Paul Bromby, Matt Green, Andrew Hopkins, Michelle Jones, Jennifer Neziol, George Stroumboulopoulos, Ron MacLean, Kelly

Hrudey, Elliotte Friedman, Don Cherry, David Amber, Rob Corte, Ed Hall, Mitch Kerzner, and everyone else over an amazing twenty-year career. Thank you also to Brian Spear, Sherali Najak, and Kathy Broderick for making Saturday night extra special. To Corinne Berlin, Hilary Whitebread, and Lianne Cousvis, I would have looked hideous on TV without you. And on camera, it's all about the style—that responsibility belonged to Debra Berman and Jessica Chambers, and I couldn't be more grateful. And thank you Bob McKenzie, James Duthie, and all you f*ers at TSN for always pushing me hard.

I have a lot of great memories from my years at Sportsnet. I will always be grateful to Mark Messier, Wayne Gretzky, Mario Lemieux, Mats Sundin, and Eric Lindros for granting me exclusive interviews when they didn't have to.

And a special thank-you to Doug MacLean, who has been my coach, my broadcasting colleague, and most importantly a great friend. We had some good battles together on the air and it's only fitting that you wrote the introduction to this book.

To Bob Goodenow, Ian Pulver, Jonathan Weatherdon, Devon Smith, and the entire staff at the NHLPA, thanks for being there for me. And to the NHL head office, Gary Bettman, Bill Daly, and Gary Meagher, thanks for taking my calls; and thank you Colin Campbell, Mike Murphy, Damian Echevarrieta, Kris King, Kay Whitmore, and Rod Plasma for keeping me in the loop.

Thank you to my representatives and agents over the years for always looking out for me. Harry Francis did a lot of heavy lifting on my behalf. And Gord Kirke, "the velvet hammer," is a fantastic sports and entertainment lawyer who made sure my contracts were air tight. Thank you Voula Michaelidis for helping me transition from Sportsnet to the next phase of my life. I am excited for what comes next.

Perry Lefko, I wasn't sure people would be interested in my story; thank you for convincing me otherwise. You helped me shape the book and provided invaluable research. And you introduced me to the publishing world, something I never dreamed I'd be a part of. At our first meeting with Simon & Schuster Canada, I didn't know what to expect. But president and publisher Kevin Hanson and senior editor Justin Stoller saw the potential in my story right away and ran with it. To the whole team at S&S Canada, thank you for your support and hard work.

To my big Greek family: my mom and dad, Dorothy and George, and my big sisters, Stelle and Tess, who I constantly looked up to, I am eternally grateful for the love and support you've always given me over the years. A special thank-you to my cousin George Kypreos, who was like a brother to me growing up. To my aunts and uncles, nieces and nephews, cousins, and in-laws Glen Flack, George Pappas, Mark and Laurie Jenkins, Jim and Melody Schroeder, and my mother- and father-in-law, Annette and Ray Jenkins (who trusted me over twenty years ago), thanks to all for not expecting free tickets. And thank you to friends who have had a lifelong impact on me, including Joey Grech, Jeff Guilbert, Neil Mason, and Jim "Elvis" Mandala.

Most of all, I am nothing without Anne-Marie, Zachary, Theo, and Anastasia. Anne-Marie, you helped me find the right words to express myself as we put so many moments of our life together down on the page. You're a fantastic writer and I can't wait to read your story soon. You and the kids inspire me every day. Words can't describe what you all mean to me. You simply make me better. I love you.

Perry Lefko

There are many people to thank for helping me with this book. First and foremost, I want to thank Nick for opening up his heart and his mind when I first approached him with the idea. We'd known each for some time and had talked about doing a book before, but this just seemed like the right time because he was ending his broadcast career to move on to another phase of his life. I enjoyed hearing Nick tell stories about his life, in particular growing up as a Greek Canadian. He exudes such pride talking about it. I think we should break some plates celebrating this book. Opa!

I enjoyed meeting and talking to his parents, George and Dorothy, both of whom immigrated from Greece to Canada seeking a better life. They bestowed Nick so much, including the greatest laugh I have ever heard.

I also want to thank Nick's wife, Anne-Marie, or AM as she is known. She is a writer too and helped immensely with this project. When her first book is published, I'll buy it and ask her to autograph it.

I'd also like to thank Simon & Schuster Canada publisher Kevin Hanson and senior editor Justin Stoller. I'd always wanted to do a book with Kevin, who is really sharp and has done exceptionally well with sports books. I had done a book with Justin when he was with a different company, and he had just joined Simon & Schuster when I called. He embraced the idea right away. I think it was serendipity.

Various people helped me with the book, either through interviews, research, or providing me with contacts, and I'd like to acknowledge their participation: Jim Mandala, Brian Wilks, Tim Green, Herb Morrell, Craig Campbell, Bob Clarke, Neil Smith, Eddie Olczyk, Mike Hartman, Darren Dreger, Daren Millard, Bob McKenzie, Doug MacLean, Ryan VandenBussche, Jorey Middlestadt, Tom Harrington, and Bob Torrens. Norris McDonald, who has become a good friend and mentor, helped with some ideas for this book. If I have left anybody's name out, it was not by design.

Thanks to Ed Sousa and Jay Perez of Classic Bowl in Mississauga for their technical support. Don't know what I'd do without these guys. Like me, Ed is a Blackberry guy, and when the Bberry ship goes down, we will both be on it.

Thanks also to Michael Hunter of Moosehead Breweries for the generous liquid support.

ACKNOWLEDGMENTS

Thanks to Clive Renteria-Farrington and Andrew Mann for writing the song "The Promise." These guys totally rock.

I want to especially thank the people who have always supported me: My parents, Lou and Myrna Lefko; my brother, Elliott, my sister, Robyn, (who is my guiding light), and my in-laws, Don and Louise Lloyd. Charles (Donald) Lloyd passed away during the writing of this book. He touched my life and so many others with his class, dignity, care, generosity, and words. We spent some great times together and I will cherish those memories. I've dedicated this book to him.

And lastly, but always first in my heart, my wife, Jane, and our two amazing kids, Ben and Shayna. They have been through the highs and lows of my life and career, but have always believed in me, my dreams, my love of words and storytelling. I am blessed and lucky to have them.

INDEX

INDEX

INDEX

INDEX

INDEX